William Macpherson

Materials for a history of the church and priory of Monymusk

William Macpherson

Materials for a history of the church and priory of Monymusk

ISBN/EAN: 9783337161767

Printed in Europe, USA, Canada, Australia, Japan

Cover: Foto ©Lupo / pixelio.de

More available books at **www.hansebooks.com**

MATERIALS FOR A HISTORY

OF THE

Church and Priory

OF

Monymusk

ABERDEEN:
PRINTED AT THE ADELPHI PRESS
BY TAYLOR & HENDERSON
MD CCC XCV

ILLUSTRATIONS, &c.

FRONTISPIECE.

The Monymusk Reliquary—front and end views.

TITLE PAGE.

"The Common Seal of the Monastery of Monymusk," with what is probably a view of the Priory Buildings.

Map showing the Ancient Monasteries—Facing Page 40.

THE MONYMUSK CELTIC CROSS—Page 85.

'MONYMUSK' STRATHSPEY—Facing Page 285.

CONTENTS.

CHAPTER I.
Tradition as to Early Origin.—The Brecbannoch   1

CHAPTER II.
Columba and the Celtic Church 6

CHAPTER III.
The Keledei or Culdees in Scotland 30

CHAPTER IV.
Malcolm III. and Queen Margaret 60

CHAPTER V.
The Building of the Church and Priory 68

CHAPTER VI.
The Endowments of the Priory and the Change from Culdees to Canons Regular, as recognised by Pope Innocent IV. 1078 to 1245. (The Chartulary of Monymusk) 87

CHAPTER VII.
Records from 1268 to 1500.—Writs regarding the Brecbannoch.—'The Monymusks' 131

CHAPTER VIII.
Records from 1500 to the Reformation in 1560.—The Decadence of the Old Order.—The Spoliation of the Lands.—Feu-duties from the Estate 155

CHAPTER IX.
The Strife between the Forbeses and the Gordons.—The Fiction of Archangel Leslie 220

CHAPTER X.
Ministers since the Reformation.—Sir William Forbes and the Covenant.—The Family of Urry of Pitfichie.—The Poll-book of 1696.—The Forbes Family.—The Grant Family.—The Episcopal Clergymen.—The Schoolmasters of the Parish 234

INTRODUCTORY NOTE.

THESE materials were gathered together without the slightest thought of their ever being printed. They are the result of a desire to tell what could be learned about the Priory that was for long the central point in our district, but whose existence was becoming almost forgotten among us. As no ruins of it even have been preserved, the Culdees have no separate visible memorial among us, and the school-children have been playing on the ground they so long trod without knowing that persons bearing such a name ever lived and worshipped in our parish, and although the Church bears evidence to every one of its antiquity, few among us know much about its history. The writer thought it might make a little variety if he delivered a few lectures on the subject on Sunday evenings during last winter. He intended simply to bind the lectures together afterwards, and put them among the parish records, to be looked at by any one who might care for such matters at any future time. But the parishioners were unwilling to let the information be lost sight of again, after being gathered from books, many of which are inaccessible to most of them, and without his knowing it, they formed a committee, and desired to have the lectures printed for subscribers. He felt that he could not refuse agreeing to this, although he did not realise how much care would have to be expended on them before they could be issued. He regrets exceedingly that the work has not been done by some one with a natural aptitude for such research, but he has tried to let the records tell their own story. It is often most difficult for an inexperienced person to translate the Mediæval Latin in which they are written, and all he can say is, that he hopes that, with the help that has been so kindly given him, the sense and general drift have been reached. It would have been much easier to compress many of the records, but as they may never again be translated, he hopes readers will not become impatient over any tedious amplifying, but may remember what a far-distant age they bring before us. He has never sought to express opinions of his own, but has been anxious to learn the facts from those who are best entitled to be heard on the various matters that are touched upon. Such a wide range of history is brought before us, that he can hardly hope to have avoided mistakes, but as he has not wished to support any preconceived ideas, he trusts the truthfulness of the statements may be relied on. He thanks the parishioners and other subscribers for their kindness, and trusts that in reading this little book, they will recollect that its purpose is simply to illustrate the history of our secluded locality. The books from which the information is drawn are of so special a class that he is grateful for the use of the volumes of the Spalding Club in the library of Monymusk House, and of a large number of books from King's College Library. Several friends have been most kind in lending other books, and in affording invaluable assistance. He acknowledges the liberality of the Council of the Society of Antiquaries of Scotland in giving, without any fee, the use of the two electros of the Monymusk Reliquary, the prints of which he thinks subscribers will be very pleased to have, and as the parishioners wished the lecture on the Culdees in Scotland to be retained entire, he has added, by permission of the Society for Promoting Christian Knowledge, a map showing the ancient monasteries referred to in the lecture.

WM. M. MACPHERSON.

MONYMUSK MANSE,
BY ABERDEEN, September, 1895.

IN the foot-notes works have frequently to be referred to under contracted titles. Among them may be mentioned the following :—

Dr. Joseph Anderson, Scotland in Early Christian Times (Rhind Lectures).
The Duke of Argyll, Iona (reprinted from 'Good Words' of 1869.)
Rev. Dr. Campbell, Balmerino and its Abbey (in Fifeshire).
Rev. Dr. Davidson, Inverurie and the Earldom of the Garioch.
Bishop Dowden of Edinburgh, The Celtic Church in Scotland.
St. Giles' Lectures on the Scottish Church, 1st Series, 1881.
Mr. Cosmo Innes, Scotland in the Middle Ages.
Mr. Cosmo Innes, Sketches of Early Scottish History.
Mr. Andrew Jervise, Epitaphs and Inscriptions in the N.E. of Scotland, vol. II.
Bishops Lightfoot and Westcott, of Durham, Leaders in the Northern Church.
Count de Montalembert, St. Columba.
Rev. Dr. Reeves, Bishop of Down and Connor, Adamnan's Life of Columba, original edition, Dublin, 1857.
Rev. Dr. Reeves, "On the Culdees," original edition in the Transactions of the Royal Irish Academy, xxiv, 1873, pp. 119-263.
Register of the Priory of St. Andrews (Bannatyne Club).
Dr. Joseph Robertson, Concilia Scotiæ, Statuta Ecc. Scot. (Bannatyne Club).
Dr. Joseph Robertson, Scottish Abbeys and Cathedrals, Quarterly Review, 1849, reprinted 1891.
Rev. Dr. Hew Scott, Fasti Ecc. Scot. part vi. (In Chapter X. it has been thought unnecessary to give the references to this work, as they are so easily found by any one who uses the ' Fasti ').
Principal Shairp, LL.D. of St. Andrews, Sketches in History and Poetry (Queen Margaret, reprinted from 'Good Words,' 1867).
Spalding Club : Collections on the Shires of Aberdeen and Banff.
,, Antiquities of the Shires of Aberdeen and Banff.
,, Registrum Episcopatus Aberdonensis.
Dean Stanley, Lectures on the Church of Scotland.
Rev. W. Stephen, of the Episcopal Church, Dumbarton, History of the Scottish Church, only vol. I. published as yet.
Rev. Dr. Temple, Forgue, Thanage of Fermartyn.
Rev. M. E. C. Walcott, of Chichester Cathedral, Ancient Church of Scotland.

MONYMUSK: ITS CHURCH AND PRIORY.

CHAPTER I.

TRADITION AS TO EARLY ORIGIN.
THE BRECBANNOCH.

MONYMUSK is a Celtic name, probably meaning "moor and river."[1] Dr. Davidson in his work on "The Earldom of the Garioch" says that it was "the first seat of Christianity" and "Celtic civilisation in the Garioch," and that from it as their home, "preachers travelled far and wide over Mar, and their stations became sacred places . . . centuries before there were any parishes in the country."[2] He thus expressed his concurrence in the tradition that has been uniformly received in our district, but it is to be frankly admitted that no positive proof can be looked for in its support. Mr. Cosmo Innes writes of it in a similar manner :—"In the north, Monymusk, a house of the Culdees, was another of those foundations of immemorial antiquity—the institutions of the great preachers of the truth to whom Scotland owes its Christianity." . . . "Next come the Monasteries—not those old families of missionaries, the very beginning of Christianity among us—not Iona, nor Deir, nor Mortlach—not Abernethy (on the Tay), nor old-Melrose, nor old pre-episcopal Brechin, nor the Culdees of St. Serf and Monymusk—none of those primeval Monasteries—of whom all we know is that they did their work in bringing the whole land from paganism

---

[1] Monadh (móna), a moor, heath, mountain. Uisge (ûshge), water.
[2] The Earldom of the Garioch pp. 156, 126, 14, 26.

to Christianity. Of their manner of life and teaching, and the means of their support, we know little or nothing; of their discipline and subordination scarcely enough to found a useless controversy."[1] Mr. Stuart in his preface to the "Book of Deer" speaks of "the history of the Culdees of Monymusk, a house of early but uncertain date . . . placed on the fertile banks of the river Don in Aberdeenshire."[2] Mr. Walcott says, without hesitation, "we should bear in mind that as Melrose . . . Monymusk occupied an older site."[3] Mr. Skene, indeed, in his "Celtic Scotland,"[4] after mentioning King Malcolm's charter, says, "So far we may infer that it was not an ancient Columban foundation." But Dr. Reeves says, "the founder of the Church of Monymusk is said to have been Malcolm Canmore, about the year 1080. . . . The probability, however, is that he was a restorer, not a founder, and that, as in the subsequent case of Deir, he revived a decayed Monastery and enlarged its endowments. At all events Monymusk was affiliated at the above date to the Church of St. Andrews, and partook of its discipline as an institution of Kelidei." He also says that the society of secular priests, thirteen in number, as arranged in 1211, "was probably the representative of an ancient monastic foundation."[5]

On this "probability" we may be content to rest. We have no actual information enabling us to determine at what time or by whom our holy faith was first planted here. After Malcolm III.'s time we have abundance of authentic charters regarding the endowments bestowed on the "Culdee" Monastery, but whether it had been a "Columban" home long before, must be left undetermined. Nor need we wonder that we have nothing local to guide us here, for we must remember

[1] Sketches, pp. 9, 91.
[2] Book of Deer, p. cxviii.
[3] The Ancient Church of Scotland, p. 5.
[4] Celtic Scotland, II. p. 389.
[5] Culdees, pp. 172, 173, 174.

what a far-distant age this brings us in contact with. " During the whole of Columba's life the conquest of Britain by Angles and Jutes and Saxons was being carried on, and it was only finally completed about the period of his death."[1] "In this long lapse of time the English Crown, the English Parliament, the English nation itself, have come into being."[2]

But there remains a most interesting traditional link with Columba in "a very beautiful and very remarkable reliquary"[3] that has been preserved time out of mind in Monymusk House, and that is evidently a small casket for containing some relics of a saint. Dr. Anderson makes an elaborate statement regarding it, and says that as far as he knows it is the only one of its kind and period now existing in Scotland—and that, if it is not the Brecbannoch of St. Columba, it is one of the strangest coincidences that a reliquary answering so closely to it should have been preserved at Monymusk. Dr. Reeves says that the name seems to be formed from *breac beannaighthe*, "maculosum benedictum"—the blessed speckled, or spotted thing. One Breac, that of St. Moedec, is preserved in the museum of the Royal Irish Academy—a small shrine in the form of a box covered with gilt plates. The difficulty lies in the fact that while authentic charters remain with reference to the Brecbannoch of St. Columba, it is mentioned in them simply by name. They naturally assume that since it was in the possession of those who gave over its "custody," there was no need of any description of it being given. Different lines of argument lead to the belief that it was not a banner or standard, but may have been a small shrine for holding relics, probably one or two small bones of Columba, and that its shape, in all likelihood,

[1] Iona, p. 15.
[2] Bishop Lightfoot, Leaders, p. 4.
[3] Dr. J. Anderson, Scotland in Early Christian Times, pp. 240-251.

corresponded to the one preserved at Monymusk. This is a small wooden box hollowed out of the solid, and covered with plates of pale bronze and silver. It was originally jewelled, and is still enamelled, and the tracings of the characteristic Celtic spiral ornaments that were engraved on it, are still visible. At both ends it had a hooked plate with a hinge, and a strap might readily be inserted into the hook to let it be carried on one's breast, but one plate is now lost.

King William the Lion founded the great Abbey of Arbroath in memory of Thomas à Becket, who had been killed a few years before, and among other gifts he bestowed on it between 1204 and 1211 the custody of the Brecbannoch, along with the lands of Forglen that were attached to that office. How King William obtained possession of it is not known, but probably it had been kept in the parish of Forglen by the hereditary tenants of the Church lands.[1] One obligation attached to it, and to holding "the fair barony"[2] pertaining to it, was that its guardian should carry it as often as the Scottish army went into battle. Bernard, abbot of Arbroath, was present at the battle of Bannockburn, and, doubtless, performed the service binding on him by carrying it round Bruce's army, but seven months after the battle, with consent of his abbey, he executed a charter, which is dated 18th January, 1315, making over its custody, along with the lands of Forglen, to "Malcolm of Monimusk," with the provision that he and his heirs should take the place of the abbot in bearing it in the king's army as often as there was need. It remained for three generations in the care of the Monymusk family, until a female becoming the heiress, its custody and the lands were granted in 1388 to her husband, who was of the Fraser family. In 1411 the lands of Forglen were surrendered to the Convent, and about nine years after

[1] Dr. Reeves, Adamnan, p. 332.   [2] Book of Deer, p. cx.

they were conferred on Sir Alexander Irvine of Drum, and in the charters of that family in 1481 and 1483 the service in the army connected with the Brecbannoch is again specially mentioned.

If this casket is really the Brecbannoch,¹ it is singular how it found its way again to Monymusk House, and no one can say at what time it did so. It has been always regarded as a much venerated treasure, and it would be strange indeed if this shrine was carried round Bruce's army to give them courage for their victory.

While we cannot hope to have the uncertainty removed as to whether Monymusk is really a Columban foundation, yet, if it owes its origin to some of Columba's followers, as we are pleased to think such an authority as Dr. Reeves says is "probable," it is a matter of interest to try to reproduce a picture of the life and thoughts of those first Christian teachers that our country had. Chief of all our sources of information is the authentic biography of St. Columba by his kinsman Adamnan, who was born only twenty-seven years after Columba died, and who, becoming ninth abbot of Iona (from 697 to 704), "was the ablest and most accomplished of his successors." In his work, "the oldest existing book known to have been written in Scotland"—"an inestimable literary relic"—he embodies an earlier life by Cumin, the seventh abbot (from 657 to 669), who was near enough in time to have seen Columba.

---

1 The spelling of the word varies—Brecbannoch, Bracbennach, Brachbennoch, Brecbannach.

Chapter II.
COLUMBA AND THE CELTIC CHURCH.*

More than one thousand three hundred years have passed since Columba, "Colum of the Church"—"willing to be a missionary for Christ," as Adamnan tells us, left his native glens in Donegal and crossed to Iona with twelve companions, whose names are recorded, nearly all of them his blood relations, in a frail coracle of wickerwork covered with hides, landing on Whitsunday, 563. He was then in his forty-second year, and through both his father and his mother he was connected with the ruling family of the Dalriad Scots—a lineage that aided him greatly in the work of his life—"being treated on a footing of perfect intimacy and equality by all the princes of Ireland and Caledonia, and exercising a sort of spiritual sway equal or superior to the authority of secular sovereigns."[1] Iona was, as it were, on the border-land between the Northern Picts and the Dalriad Scots, and after a short time being favoured by the chiefs of both races he made it the home from which he and his followers evangelised the Picts who were still heathens, and taught more carefully the Scots who were already Christians, at least in name. His coronation at Iona of his cousin Aedan, the Celtic chief of the Hebrides, as king of the Scots, in 574, is the first authentic coronation in Western Christendom.[2] There is abundant proof that he founded small Churches and planted humble Monasteries in many widely separated parts of our country; so that by his enthusiasm and guidance Christianity

*The writer intended to condense very much this chapter and the next one, as they go far beyond Monymusk itself, but the parish committee desired him not to do so, as they wished to have the information contained in them.

[1] Montalembert, p. 11.   [2] Dean Stanley's Lectures, p. 23.

Columba and the Celtic Church. 7

was established on a firm basis to the north of the Tay and Clyde. The old Churchyard of Kingussie in Badenoch, for instance, still bears testimony to his presence when he crossed the Gynach on his mission in 565 to Bruidh, the king of the Picts, whose hill-fort stood on Craig Phadric, a commanding eminence two miles from Inverness—its outlines visible to this day, though moss-grown, in parts vitrified by the action of fire.[1] Inverness is one hundred and fifty miles from Iona, but he repeatedly travelled as far as that district, if not farther, covering the whole North Highlands with a net-work of mission stations or Monasteries—so many miniature Ionas.[2] Along with Drostan, his devoted nephew, he personally planted the famous Monastery at Deer and the Church at Aberdour about 580. His work can also be traced on the Tay, in memory of which the Cathedral at Dunkeld was afterwards dedicated under his name—some saying that the mission there was founded by himself. Machar, one of his Irish disciples, undertook to preach the Gospel in the northern parts of the Pictish Kingdom, and settled his Christian colony near the mouth of the Don—for its windings there resembled the figure of a bishop's crosier, which was the sign given him—and founded the Church that still bears his name in the Cathedral. Another adventurous band pushed farther into the pagan fastnesses and settled on the Fiddich, where they must have thriven by the benevolence of the people, since, in the beginning of the twelfth century, the Monastery of Mortlach, with a bishop residing within its walls, had connected with it a subordinate Monastery at Cloveth (Clova), and was possessed of five Churches with their territories.[3]

After thirty-four years of labour in our country, Columba died June 9th, 597, in his own little Church, at the service

[1] Principal Shairp, Sketches, p. 18.
[2] Ibid, p. 21.
[3] Mr. Cosmo Innes, Sketches, p. 86.

conducted soon after midnight, and heralding the Lord's Day—
"some three or four weeks after Augustine had landed on the
shores of Kent."[1] He thus occupies, in missionary history, an
entire generation preceding Augustine's arrival. His was "the
noblest missionary career ever accomplished in Britain."[2] "He
was not perfect, but he was a saint, complete not in faultless-
ness but in the unreserved consecration of his whole nature."[3]
He was a principal agent in one of the greatest events the world
has ever seen, the conversion of the Northern Nations, and to
have planted Christianity successfully among the people then in
our land necessitates his having been a man of powerful character and of splendid gifts.[4] "In that bleak, lonely island
under his fostering care a religious house had sprung up, the
nursery of saints and scholars, who were to carry the faith of
Christ and the light of learning far beyond the boundaries of
the British Isles, beyond even the lofty mountain barrier of the
Alps, invading Italy itself with a peaceful invasion . . .
Iona was at this time the focus of intellectual light to Western
Christendom."[5] "The 'family' of Columba reclaimed the
pagans of the farthest Hebrides, and sent their Christian
embassy and established their worship in Iceland, and spread
Christianity in every glen and bay where a congregation was to
be gathered. This is not a matter of inference, but is proved
beyond question. We know that the first Christian Church in
Iceland, which was at Esinberg, was dedicated to St. Columba."[6]
"Another of their discoveries was the Faroë Islands, where the
Norwegians at a later date found traces of the Irish monks—
Celtic books, crosses, and bells."[7]

St. Gall, beside the Lake of Constance in Switzerland, still

---

1 Bishop Lightfoot, Leaders, p. 6.
2 Mr. Stephen, History, p. 81.
3 Bishop Westcott, Leaders, p. 178.
4 Iona. pp. 49, 53.
5 Bishop Lightfoot, Leaders, pp. 41, 42, 47.
6 Mr. Cosmo Innes, Sketches, pp. 1, 2, Middle Ages, p. 101.
7 Montalembert, p. 101.

Columba and the Celtic Church. 9

takes its name from the Celtic missionary who settled there about 614. From manuscripts preserved there we gather what was the appearance of these pilgrim Scots. They travelled in companies and were provided with long walking-sticks and with leathern wallets and water bottles. Their heads were shaved in a different style from other priests, and they were clad in rough garments, yet they were possessed of accomplishments that their clothes strongly belied. They were apt learners of the languages of the countries they traversed, and addressed the people everywhere with all the fervour of their native eloquence.[1]

From Iona the succession of Columba's clergy was believed to be continued by the touching of his relics,[2] and it is easy to suppose that the Brecbannoch may have been made to contain a few fragments of his bones that were preserved, although his remains had to be moved several times. His followers went in thirteens—one being "the head" with the other twelve under him, for they had a great desire to imitate the features of the Apostolic system. When showing this from various examples Dr. Réeves specially mentions "Monymusk, where was a College of twelve Culdees and a Prior."[3] Their homes were "centres of civilisation" to the different districts,[4] but only in one or two small islands where uncemented stone had to be used, can there be found any traces of their buildings, for their Churches, "with three times of prayer by day and three by night,"[5] were of squared timber, of hewn oak, and their dwellings huts of wattles, thatched with reeds.[6] Not till the end of the eighth century did stone buildings begin to be substituted for wooden ones, as a protection against the ravages of the Danes.[7] Wherever they founded a home, they had them-

[1] Dr. J. Anderson, Scotland in Early Christian Times, p. 162; Mr. Skene, Celtic Scotland, II. p. 6.
[2] Dean Stanley, Lectures, p. 6. and "At St. Andrews."
[3] Adamnan, pp. 299-301.
[4] Dr. Davidson, Inverurie, p. 14.
[5] Principal Shairp, Sketches, p. 15.
[6] Dr. Joseph Robertson, Abbeys, p. 15.
[7] Mr. Warren, Liturgy, p. 17.

selves to hew down the oaks and bear them from the woods—
taking those for Iona in boats from the mainland—build the
Church and huts, clear and cultivate the neighbouring wood or
moor for sustenance, and win the confidence of an untaught
heathen people.[1]

In Iona the walls would doubtless be woven together with
climbing plants, specially ivy,[2] and "probably some external
plaster covered the timber and the wattled walls;"[3] while the
little settlement had a high turf embankment encircling it for
defence. "The glory of those early buildings was within."[4]
It has been often said that the monks knew where to fix their
habitations. The favourite situation was on the bank of a river,
and their Churches were probably dedicated under the name of
their original founders or of other native saints.[5] In our own
quarter Lonmay, Daviot, Belhelvie, Monycabo (New Machar),
Birse, and Alvah (near Forglen) were dedicated to St. Columba;
while the sand-covered parish of Forvie in Slains, Forglen, in
which Church the Brecbannoch of Columba was preserved,
and Aboyne were dedicated to St. Adamnan.[6] Dr. Reeves
observes that both in Ireland and in Scotland the dedications to
St. Columba and St. Adamnan keep very close together, while
at Forglen the two saints are in a most singular manner joined
in commemoration. If Monymusk was one of the early
Columban homes, the site was not only beside the river, but
also only á few hundred yards distant from what is still called
"the Druid Field," with its upright stones—such stones being
now regarded as undoubtedly sepulchral monuments. Part of
a large circle also stands on the high ground at Tillyfourie
towards the farm of Whitehill—and another stood on what is

---

[1] Principal Shairp, Sketches, p. 10.
[2] Dean Stanley, Lectures, p. 28; Montalembert, p. 37.
[3] Iona, pp. 90, 91.
[4] Dr. Grub, History, I. p. 51.
[5] Ibid., p. 14.
[6] Dr. Reeves, Adamnan, pp. 296, 462; Book of Deer, p. cxxxv.

now the farm of Nether Coullie, on the north side of the river—one upright stone yet remaining, others having been removed.

Their settlements were marked by severe simplicity, and were little colonies of self-denying, hard-working men, scattered over the country.[1] "The brethren of the community lived each in separate huts or 'cells.'"[2] "The Monastery was not a retreat for solitaries, whose chief object was to work out their own salvation, but the home of those whose purpose was to preach the Gospel among the heathen."[3] They were missionaries, fervent and devout, and monks, strictly monastic, and without doubt celibate. "There is every reason to believe that the brethren were bound by the rules of obedience, chastity, and poverty."[4] "This exclusively monastic constitution of the Church was closely bound up with its missionary character, and was at once the cause of its temporary triumph and of its ultimate decay."[5] Bede says that "priests, deacons, singers, readers, every ecclesiastical order, including the bishop himself, observed the monastic rule." In their system "the continuous round of divine worship, the cultivation of the spirit of devotion, the study of divine truth, the practice of self-discipline were all duly cared for";[6] while their self-denial was not for its own sake, but that they might be better able to spread the Gospel.

Going forth two and two after the example of the Seventy, they radiated over a wide district among the different tribes, preaching in hamlets where no missionary had ever before been seen, and after spending weeks or months in this work, they returned for rest and encouragement and mutual help to their special home, which was like a strong centre from which they

1 Dr. Joseph Robertson, Abbeys, p. 28.
2 Iona, p. 91.
3 Dr. Grub, History I., p. 51.
4 Bishop Dowden, Celtic Church, p. 127.
5 Mr. Warren, Liturgy of Celtic Ch., p. 12.
6 Bishop Dowden, Celtic Church, p. 83.

carried the blessings of religion. Their preaching would be mostly in the open air, and we are told of the power of Columba's voice in reaching great distances as he repeated the Psalms or addressed large numbers of men. Of him it is said, that when absent from his home, he went about always doing good, and the same spirit would pervade those he sent forth.

"There are passages which prove that a married priesthood was not unknown in various parts and at various periods in the history of the Celtic Church."[1] One point of variance in the British Christians from the subsequent Roman model was the marriage of the clergy.[2] St. Patrick, Columba's great predecessor in the Celtic Church, who went from this country to Ireland as a missionary about 432, cannot have been opposed to marriage among his clergy, for he says of himself that he was of "gentle blood," and that his father, who was a deacon and a councillor, was the son of a presbyter, all which he mentions as a mark of his respectability, and in the legend relating how he sought "the materials of a bishop" among his pupils, his words are, "Find for me a man of rank, of good family and good morals, one who has one wife and only one son." But Dr. Reeves says[3] that celibacy was, without doubt, strictly enjoined on the community of Iona, and that though marriage existed among the secular clergy, the practice seems to have been disapproved of by the regulars. Montalembert says[4] that "marriage was absolutely unknown among the regular clergy," and Dr. Grub[5] remarks that "not one instance of a married monk or priest in the early days of Iona has been pointed out." It is even said that Columba would not let a woman land on the island.[6] Mr. Cosmo Innes also says,[7] "They undoubtedly

[1] Mr. Warren, Liturgy, p. 13.
[2] Archdeacon Hardwick, Middle Age, p. 7.
[3] Adamnan, p. 344.
[4] Montalembert, p. 149.
[5] History I., p. 149.
[6] Dr. Reeves, Adamnan, p. 432.
[7] Middle Ages, p. 100.

practised celibacy and enforced penance and the most rigid asceticism. This has always been a great engine for swaying a simple and uninformed people. They associate such self-denial with the absence of all the passions to which they feel themselves most addicted, and soon come to think the preacher who can subdue his human nature, as something raised above humanity."

Mr. Skene, in his "Celtic Scotland," describes generally the paganism of the Northern Picts as a sort of fetichism which peopled the air, the earth, the water, and all the objects of nature with malignant beings, to whose agency its phenomena were attributed, and who were always bent on working evil to men, while persons named Druadh, or sorcerers, exercised great influence among the people, from a belief that they were able through their aid to practise a species of magic or witchcraft which might be used either to benefit those who sought their assistance or to injure those to whom they were opposed. "Savage and bloody rites to propitiate the evil powers were not unknown. It was indeed a religion of darkness and fear"[1]— "chiefs and Druids not lessening but aggravating the evil."[2]

Mr. Skene also points out how admirably the grouping of clergy in lowly monasteries was calculated for spreading the leaven of Christianity among the surrounding heathen.[3] The Church in such circumstances needed not only dissemination, but "strong centres," and "during the whole of the Celtic period this was its dominating characteristic. The Monastery was everywhere the home and seminary of Christian learning, the centre of Christian work, and everywhere, as it were, the military base of operations against the powers of heathendom."[4] We learn of Columba's fearless bravery in presence

[1] Bishop Dowden, Celtic Church, p. 22.
[2] Principal Shairp, Sketches, p. 43.
[3] Celtic Scotland, II., p. 74.
[4] Bishop Dowden, Celtic Church, p. 216.

of King Brude and his Druids, and in the same spirit his followers "penetrated into the wildest regions, entered without fear into the strongholds of chieftains, receiving from them grants of land, and planting settlements within their territories, and by their dignity of character and singleness of purpose making themselves and their faith respected wherever they went."[1] Such was the state of the country that when a leader consented to be baptised he led his people with him to the font. All over the country their little churches sprang up even in most secluded parts. There was a house for a few brethren at Hinba, a little south of Iona, where the ruins of a church only twenty-one feet long, of undressed stones, built without lime, and of two bee-hive-shaped cells still remain, being preserved owing to the island's being uninhabited, and marking the site of this early Christian home. It is a very sacred spot. Adamnan, Columba's kinsman and biographer, tells us that Columba's uncle Ernen presided over Hinba, and that Columba had a cell there for himself when he visited it, and that there met him there four great founders of Irish and Scottish mission churches —Comgall of Bangor and Cainnech of Aghaboe, who had both been his fellow-students at the great Monastery of Clonard on the Boyne, with its reputed three thousand monks, and had gone with him to Inverness on his first visit to Brude, Braidan of Clonfert, and Cormac "the far-famed voyager" who sailed into the Northern seas and established missions in Orkney. All these five heroic men worshipped together in that tiny church at Hinba, Columba being asked by the others to preside at the communion service. So distant is the time that we can know little regarding our first teachers beyond what Adamnan says, but their piety and preaching wrought a great change. Dr. Reeves gives a list of thirty-two Columban foundations among

[1] Dr. J. Anderson, Scotland in Early Christian Times, p. 161.

the Albanic Scots and twenty-one among the Picts of Scotland —together fifty-three—and considers the list confessedly incomplete. Others give the number showing traces of early origin as fifty-three churches and about forty-four Monasteries, including St. Andrews and "Monymusk."[1]

The ordinary dress of the clergy was a garment called a tunic, over which was worn a cloak with a hood of rough texture made of wool of the natural, undyed colour. Priestly garments they had none—the tonsure being the external mark of distinction of the ordained clergy. On festivals, we read of their going into church in a white garment. In cold weather they had a warmer cloak. We read of their puttting on their shoes of hide in the morning and preparing for their different duties, and they seem to have taken them off before sitting down to meals—and of Cainnech's rising and running to the church with but one shoe on to pray for Columba's safety when he felt that a storm had arisen. They slept on beds covered apparently with straw, with a pallet and coverlet, but Columba himself slept on the hard floor or on a bare stone, with a stone for his pillow, "whence he would rise at the dead of night and spend whole hours, besides the stated one, praying alone in the oratory."[2] "What the coverlets were is not recorded, but few probably were required, as they slept in their ordinary clothes, as may be inferred from the promptness with which they responded to the midnight bell."[3]

"Columba never could spend," says Adamnan in his preface, "the space of even one hour without study or prayer or writing or even some manual occupation (*vel etiam alicui operationi*). So incessantly was he engaged night and day in the unwearied exercise of fasting and watching that the burden of

[1] Mr. Walcott, Ancient Ch., p. 230.
[2] Principal Shairp, Sketches, p. 29.
[3] Dr. Reeves, Adamnan, p. 357.

each of these austerities would seem beyond the power of all human endurance. And still in all these he was beloved by all, for a holy joy, ever beaming on his face, revealed the joy and gladness with which the Holy Spirit filled his inmost soul."

Wednesdays and Fridays were observed as fasts, except between Easter and Whitsunday, the forty days after Easter being the season of greatest relaxation in the year. The forty days of Lent were kept, the fast then being prolonged every day, except Sunday, till evening, when a light meal was taken.[1] The special joy of Easter is several times mentioned. Sunday and festival days commenced after the sunset of the previous day.[2] Three times a day at least, but probably oftener, the brethren of Iona met for the worship of God, and the canonical offices were celebrated with the usual alternations of Prayers and Lessons, Psalms and Hymns.[3]

The way in which they shaved their heads as the badge of religious vows—their tonsure—comes afterwards into special prominence. They shaved the "fore-part" of the head, from ear to ear, probably in the form of a crescent, allowing the hair to grow behind, while the monks of Rome shaved the "crown," leaving a circle of hair, which represented our Saviour's Crown of Thorns. Regarding this, Professor Rhys of Oxford says:—
"Some of the customs of the pagans of these islands may be detected in the observances of their Christian descendants; thus among many nations a mild form of mutilation is found to have been the symbol of slavery, and the minimum consisted not unfrequently in cutting off some of the hair of the head. Among the Brythons we find in the Welsh romances called the Mabinogion, a youth who wished to become one of Arthur's Knights, having his hair cut off by the king with his own hand.

---

[1] Dr. Reeves, Adamnan, p. 348.
[2] Ibid., p. 346.
[3] Dr. Grub, History, I., p. 147.

The tonsure usual in Britain and Ireland was the same, and it was merely a druidic survival."[1] Bishop Dowden, however, cannot think that there is the slightest evidence for this supposition.[2]

"The great body of the Columban monks were laymen, and were necessarily much occupied with tillage, the care of flocks and herds, and the varied labour connected with the maintenance of the community."[3] "Such were not required to attend the services during the day, and fatigue would probably demand unbroken sleep at night."[4] Bede remarks that though the monks lived by the labour of their own hands, they gave away to the poor all they did not absolutely need. "In many instances we find lands bestowed on the family or Monastery, but doubtless in the greater number the servants of the Church lived on the voluntary offerings of their flock."[5] "The brethren of tried devotedness were called "seniores," those who were strong for labour "operarii fratres," and those who were under instruction "juniores, alumni, or pueri familiares." They had all things common and personal property was disclaimed;"[6] while hospitality was a leading feature among them.

When a new mission centre was founded, a presbyter, well-grounded in faith and knowledge, was chosen to be its "head" —"pater" or "abbas"—and of his twelve associates the minority are said to have been presbyters, the majority being simply "fratres" or unordained men. It is said that these "fratres" were in general married men, living in separate huts or cottages within the turf-rampart enclosure. We read of the clergy reaping their own corn, grinding their own meal, cooking their own food, making their own variously-sized boats and becoming expert sailors. They were not the regular ministers of an

1 Celtic Britain, pp. 73, 74.
2 Celtic Ch., pp. 241-245.
3 Ibid., p. 201.
4 Dr. Reeves, Adamnan, p. 346.
5 Mr. Cosmo Innes, Sketches, p. 5.
6 Dr. Reeves, Adamnan, pp. 342, 343.

C

organised church, but missionaries whose object was to preach the Gospel and plant the Church of Christ in an almost pagan country. For this purpose they spread themselves over the land, teaching the truth of God, telling of His Commandments, and administering the Sacraments.

In their lowly Monasteries prayer and praise and the reading of the Word formed a large part of their unvarying duties—the "senior" brethren being responsible for the frequent services. "The Bible was their daily study and constant meditation, and it was their business and delight to impart its sacred treasures to all who came to them for instruction."[1] They were unwearied in multiplying copies of the books of the Bible, and carried their manuscripts in leathern satchels which they hung on the walls of their huts. The Psalms were constantly repeated by them, and their love for the Gospels was intense. In 553 Columba, before crossing over to our country, founded Durrow, the largest and most permanent of his Irish Monasteries. Its most interesting relic is a MS. Gospel-book, believed to be of the Columban age—perhaps, as some think, from the pen of Columba himself. "The Book of Kells" in Meath resembles it but exceeds it in the elaborateness of its illuminations. Both are now in the Trinity College Library, Dublin, and are marvellous monuments of the decorative art of the Columban Monasteries of Ireland in the seventh century. An illustration of a page of the "Book of Kells" forms the frontispiece of the first volume of the illustrated edition of Green's History of England, and at page 70 there is an illustration from the Lindisfarne Gospel-book. So beautiful are they and so thoroughly Celtic in their character that we should have greatly erred if we had relied on what we know of their houses, as indications of their culture. "They were men of such acquirements and tastes that

[1] Dr. Grub, History, I., p. 144.

they multiplied their books laboriously, and counted it a virtue to be diligent in doing so; and the skill they thus acquired, enabled them to produce MS. volumes written with a faultless regularity and precision of character, rivalling the best caligraphy of the most literary nations, which they adorned with illuminations of exquisite beauty and intricacy of design."[1]

"The rocks and islets all round Iona swarmed with seals, and their oil, doubtless, supplied the light with which during many long winter evenings Columba pored over his MSS. of the sacred text or performed midnight services before the altar."[2] The annals of an Irish Monastery state, with no doubt an excusable exaggeration, that he wrote no fewer than three hundred copies of the Gospels with his own hand, giving one to each of the churches he planted. The night in which he died, he was engaged in copying the 34th Psalm, his last written words being "'They that seek the Lord shall not want any good thing."

A manuscript of the Celtic Church has been preserved which is of special interest to ourselves. A few MSS. that had belonged to the monks of the Abbey of Deer, somehow found their way after the Reformation to the library of Bishop Moore of Norwich, and in 1715, at his death, to the Cambridge University library—among them a small octavo MS. of eighty-six parchment folios closely written on both sides, now called "The Book of Deer." It is the solitary Liturgical relic of the Celtic Church in our country. It contains a copy of the Gospels in Latin, the first three in fragments, St. John's in full, also the Apostles' Creed in the handwriting of the ninth century, with a portion of a "Communion for the Sick," also in Latin, but having a rubric in the vernacular Celtic in a later hand. Written by a scribe of our own district one thousand years ago,

[1] Dr. J. Anderson, Scotland in Early Christian Times, pp. 165, 166. [2] Iona, pp. 93, 94.

the *facsimiles* supplied by Mr. Stuart give us samples of the writing and illumination practised in our Northern Monasteries at that early date. "It also discloses something of the culture that existed in our remote district nearly ten centuries ago, showing that the clergy of Deer still followed the example of their first founder, and besides being expert caligraphists, having some skill in painting and illumination, were educated men, having a sufficient knowledge of at least one language beside their own to enable them to transcribe it intelligently and use it in the services of the Church."[1] "It furnishes probably the earliest authentic written record of Scotland,"[2] "next in the order of importance and of age to Adamnan's 'Life of Columba,'"[3] "and it is one which in few words throws much light on Celtic polity and social conditions throughout a long series of years."

"The Book of Deer" is of special value in regard to the nature of the Liturgy in use in the Celtic Church, and Mr. Stuart in his preface[4] states that it has been shown that it "belongs to the Ephesine family of Offices, thus establishing the very important and interesting fact of the Gallican origin of the early Celtic Churches of St. Patrick in Ireland and St. Columba in Scotland." Mr. Warren also in his special work, "The Liturgy and Ritual of the Celtic Church," shows at length that its Liturgy was of Gallican—not of Roman—origin, following that of Ireland from which Columba came. It was derived from the East, from Ephesus, the home of St. John, and was quite independent of Rome. St. Patrick, while in Gaul, may have come in contact with Churchmen from the East at Marseilles, which was itself a Greek colony and had

---

[1] Dr. J. Anderson, Scotland in Early Christian Times, pp. 138, 139.
[2] Quarterly Review, Oct., 1894, p. 394.
[3] Mr. Stephen, History, p. 195.
[4] Book of Deer, p. lviii.

Columba and the Celtic Church. 21

continual intercourse with the Levant, and near which at the beginning of the fifth century Cassian established a convent.[1] Even in Kent Augustine was left "at liberty to select a ritual for the English Church from the Gallican and other 'uses,' instead of copying the Roman rules entirely."[2]

Adamnan tells us that Columba wrote a volume containing hymns for the various services of the week. "The Brito-Celtic Church had many hymns."[3] Three Latin hymns "of considerable beauty"[4] are ascribed to Columba, one of which his followers loved so much that they thought it was handed down from Heaven by one of the white-robed. "Even if a strict criticism throws doubts upon the authorship of the Irish poems which are attributed to him, these show at least what he was supposed to feel. And nowhere can we find more vivid images brought together, 'the song of the wonderful birds,' 'the thunder of the crowding waves,' 'the level sparkling strand,' all summoned before the eyes of the singer's heart that he may bless the Lord—that is the end of all—in prayer and praise and meditation and work and almsgiving."[5] He was himself a poet, the friend of poets, and fired with the love of poetry.[6]

"Columba and his followers believed all the articles of the Christian faith as contained in the Holy Scripture and handed down in the Creeds of the Church."[7] "At this time the faith of Christendom was substantially one."[8] The Monastery of Iona was a branch or off-shoot of the great mother Church in Ireland, and there was a most interesting unity in the three Celtic Churches of England, Ireland, and Scotland, as regards

---

1 Principal Shairp, Sketches, p. 26.
2 Archdeacon Hardwick, Middle Age, p. 9.
3 Mr. Moorsom, Companion to Hymns A. & M., p. 185.
4 Dr. Reeves, Adamnan, p. lxxviii.
5 Bishop Westcott, Leaders, p. 182.
6 See Dr. Reeves, Adamnan, pp. 285-289, and 253; Iona, pp. 73, 74, 79. For a translation of the Altus see Bishop Dowden's Celtic Church, pp. 321-328.
7 Dr. Grub, History, I., p. 144.
8 Bishop Dowden, Celtic Church, pp. 217, 218.

religious spirit and doctrine and practice, making them sister-churches in the truest sense, and showing that for several centuries they were independent of the Church of Rome, and free to do their own work and spread the Gospel as made known in the Word of God. Adamnan testifies that "from his boyhood Columba was instructed in the love of Christ," and "that the foundation of his preaching and his great instrument in the conversion of the heathen was the Word of God "—and another records that "he received nought but the doctrine of the Evangelists and Apostles."

In Adamnan's Life of Columba some have thought that there is proof of the Invocation of saints, among his last words, for instance, being, "God, the comforter of the good, will be your helper, and I abiding with Him will intercede for you," but this is the promise of his own invocation of God, "which is quite a different thing."[1]

Never is there a "symptom of the worship of the Virgin."[2] There is not even a trace of the first missionaries having dedicated a Church in the Virgin's name, though Churches that we know were founded by them, as at St. Andrews, came afterwards to receive this dedication. Speaking of St. Cuthbert who died in 687, ninety years after Columba's death, Bishop Lightfoot says, "As we read the 'Life of St. Cuthbert,' by Bede (who died in 735), amidst much credulous superstition, we are struck with the entire absence of that taint of Mariolatry which poisoned the well-springs of a later theology. God in Christ, Christ in God—this is all in all to him."[3]

Columba's labours were all but ended before the writings of Pope Gregory the Great gave the main impetus to the belief that souls could be relieved from purgatorial pains by the

[1] Mr. Stephen, History, p. 107.
[2] Iona, p. 42.
[3] Leaders, p. 84.

Columba and the Celtic Church.

prayers of the faithful, and nowhere in Christendom in the sixth century do we find the formulated doctrine that afterwards came to be known as transubstantiation, a doctrine unknown in all the Church until the ninth century, and then only entertained as a pious opinion by scholars.[1] In the "Book of Deer" there is definite and independent proof that both the Bread and the Wine were given to all communicants. Its "Communion Service for the Sick" expressly says, "The Body with the Blood of the Lord Jesus Christ be health to thee for eternal life and salvation," and then immediately follow the words, " Refreshed with the Body and Blood of Christ, let us ever say to Thee, O Lord, Allelluia, Allelluia." In fact there is no question that down to the twelfth century the Communion was given in this manner.

"The Columbite Church acknowledged no homage to the Pope."[2] "In Columba's Life there is not even an illusion to such an idea as the universal Bishopric of Rome, or to any special authority as seated there."[3] "The truth seems to be that since Ireland had derived her earliest Christianity from Gaul at a time before the Roman system had got matured or begun to claim for itself universal dominion, the naturally free Celtic spirit maintained this independence; Columba carried it out to the full and owned no fealty to Rome ; and when in afterages his descendants confronted the fully Romanised clergy of Saxon England, there were found to be between them differences irreconcilable."[4] "Celtic Christianity grew up a strictly native growth. The influence of Rome for long centuries was practically unfelt. Long after the English Church had submitted to the Roman domination, the Irish Church remained essentially free. This independence Columba brought with him. Iona became

---

1 Bishop Dowden, Celtic Church, pp. 226, 227, 218; Mr. Stephen, History, p. 107.
2 Principal Shairp, Sketches, p. 58.
3 Iona p. 42.
4 Principal Shairp, Sketches, p. 33.

now the light of Christendom. For many generations it was the centre of the great evangelistic movements of the time."[1] "Columba was the chief abbot and was looked upon as the head, the primate of the whole Celtic Church of his time,"[2] and "to him, not to the Bishop of Rome, the Celtic missionaries owed allegiance."[3]

With reference to Episcopacy, Columba being simply a Presbyter, it became the rule that his successors at Iona, should not have a higher dignity. Of the first eleven abbots who succeeded him, nine were of the same family as himself, and only one not of his kindred. "He made the ties of the clan the model of his own order."[4] But "in the service of his own Church he set the example of veneration for the bishop's office and disclaimed all pretensions to equality with one of that rank. Priests' orders were conferred by the bishop, but the previous imposition of the abbot's right hand was required as the bishop's warrant for his interference."[5] "The whole ecclesiastical fabric was constructed on the monastic foundation, a system that for ages placed the episcopate in a subordinate position. The essential officer was the abbot, but the presence of the bishop was an accident."[6] Bede says that in his own day (he died one hundred and thirty-eight years after Columba) "to the Presbyter Abbot of Iona, all the province, even the bishops, contrary to the usual method, were subject, according to the example of their first teacher Columba." The names of several bishops who were consecrated at Iona are given, "which manifestly proves the presence of a bishop in the island."[7] When a presbyter was to be ordained in Tiree, where men were

---

[1] Bishop Lightfoot, Leaders, p. 7.
[2] Dean Stanley, Lectures, p. 22.
[3] Bishop Lightfoot, Leaders, pp. 12, 7; Archdeacon Hardwick, Middle Age, pp. 7, 8; Mr. Warren, Liturgy, p. 29
[4] Bishop Westcott, Leaders, p. 185.
[5] Dr. Reeves, Adamnan, pp. 341, 348.
[6] Dr. Reeves, Culdees, pp. 146, 147.
[7] Dr. Reeves, Adamnan, p. 348.

educated and trained for the ministry as well as at Iona, a bishop was summoned for the purpose. There being no dioceses and no jurisdiction and no endowments in the country, it was easy for any considerable Monastery to possess a bishop for the performance of such offices as were confined to the highest order of the ministry.[1] A presbyter who presided over a Monastery, was the abbot or father of that Monastery; and in cases where a Monastery by missionary labour succeeded in forming congregations of Christian converts in the surrounding country, the spiritual oversight of these congregations was undertaken either by the abbot himself or by some other of the presbyters who was named to the office, thus becoming a bishop. The duty of the bishop thus lay chiefly outside the Monastery, having to do with the congregations beyond its walls, gathered by the labour of the clergy who had it as the head-quarters of their mission.

Dr. Reeves says it is very doubtful whether Columba composed any systematic rule, but he has drawn from Adamnan's Life a statement of the constitution, discipline, and arrangements of his monastic system.[2] "He represents one of the earlier forms of the monastic life which seems to have materially differed from that which it assumed in the great Orders of mediæval times. The first of those great Orders was founded in his day. He was a contemporary of the famed St. Benedict. But rapid as was the spread of the great monastic Order which poured forth its legions from the sunny ridge of Monte Casino, as a centre, more than a century elapsed before they reached the distant shores of Britain. For aught we know Columba, though he survived him more than fifty years, never heard of the Rule of Benedict."[3]

[1] Bishop Dowden, Celtic Church, p. 259.
[2] Dr. Reeves, Adamnan, pp. 339-369.
[3] Iona, pp. 24, 25, 26.

The clergy of Lindisfarne were originally one with those of Iona. Aidan came from Iona in 635, and he, not Augustine, is the true "Apostle of England."[1] The third bishop was Colman, and in his time points of difference emerged that were fraught with great issues, though they were "about matters unimportant in themselves," as the reckoning of Easter which was "a question of convenience rather than of principle," and the matter of the tonsure "in which there could not be a right or a wrong," but was wholly trivial in itself. "The real issue lay behind all these petty disputes. It was the alternative of allegiance to Rome or allegiance to Iona."[2]

As to the reckoning of Easter the British Church was never Quarto-deciman, but always kept the feast on a Sunday, and its "rule was probably the same with that of Rome at the time of the Nicene synod,"[3] but in some years owing to the use of the antiquated cycle, the Sunday varied as much as a month from that observed by the rest of the Western Church.[4] The trial came first in the North of England. The queen of Oswio followed the Roman usage which prevailed in Kent, while the king cherished the memory of Aidan, so that while the queen was fasting on what in her calendar was Palm Sunday, the king was holding his Easter festival with rejoicing. In 665 a synod assembled at Whitby, the Convent of the famous Abbess Hilda, and the king was won over to the Roman side. "But sooner than abandon the traditions and customs of Iona for those of Rome, Colman and his brethren retire altogether from the field, leaving the rich fruits of their labours to others at the very moment when the harvest is full ripe."[5]

Bishop Lightfoot calls the time of Celtic ascendancy in Northumbria "the golden age of saintliness such as England

---

[1] Bishop Lightfoot, Leaders, p. 11.
[2] Ibid, p. 13.
[3] Dr. Grub, History I., pp. 71, 72.
[4] Dr. Reeves, Adamnan, p. 347.
[5] Bishop Lightfoot, Leaders, p. 12.

Columba and the Celtic Church. 27

would never see again,"[1] but "a host of conspiring causes gradually resulted in the spread and ascendancy of Roman modes of thought."[2] Adamnan was Abbot of Iona from 679 to 704, and became a convert to the Roman uses and tried to induce the clergy to adopt them, but without success. "Roman direction was treated as absolutely valueless by them; Roman wishes were disregarded."[3]

The conversion of the Northern Picts by Columba and his disciples seems to have been followed by a century and a half of friendly intercourse between Picts and Scots, and for these one hundred and fifty years the Church of Columba was the national Church of our country. But dark days were falling on the land, and the state of peace was put an end to by the religious revolution effected among the Picts by the Roman missionary Boniface, through whose efforts the Celtic Church was brought into conformity with the Church of Rome. About 710 Nectan, King of the North Picts, conformed to the Roman usages and the clergy in Iona yielded. About seven years after he ordered all the Columban clergy to conform in regard to tonsure and the keeping of Easter, or leave the country. Those who were unwilling to give up the ways that had come from the first Christian teachers in our land, were driven across the hills that divide Perthshire from Inverness and Argyll, and the primacy of Iona came to an end. In the Irish annals this act is spoken of as "Expulsio familæ Iæ trans dorsum Britanniæ a Nectano rege."[4] The struggle was painful but the Columban clergy preferred expulsion to conforming to Nectan's decree, for they were "instinct with zeal and energy." The old Celtic customs and Celtic liturgies were rigidly suppressed and are not heard of after 730.

1 Bishop Lightfoot, Leaders, p. 14.
2 Archdeacon, Hardwick, Middle Age, p. 14.
3 Bishop Lightfoot, Leaders, p. 12.
4 Dr. Reeves, Adamnan, p. 184.

In 736 the Picts conquered Dalriada, which nearly corresponds to Argyll, and for about one hundred years the Scots were ruled by princes of the Pictish race. From 794 onwards the light was trampled out in Iona and the homes that sprang from it by the devastating Norsemen. The Irish records narrate in quick succession " the ravaging of Icolumkill" (794), "the Hebrides laid waste by the Danes" (798), "Icolumkill burnt by the Gentiles" (801, 802), "the family of Y slain by the Gentiles" (806). The wood and wattle-work Cathedral of the island was destroyed in 802, and in 806 sixty-eight of the brethren fell by the sword. The name of "The Martyrs' Bay" commemorates this massacre and another in 825 when the Church was attacked while the Lord's Supper was being administered and the bishop and other clergy were slain by the Danes. Again in 877 it was burned by the Danes, and "when the calamity was overpast"—the Monastery at Iona being plundered and burned no fewer than six times—"and the clergy towards the close of the ninth century and in the tenth century gathered once again to the ruined Churches and Monasteries, they practised no more the old austerity."[1] "That light was put out which had shed religion and civilisation over Britain, and the harassed successors of Columba found uncertain shelter in the Monasteries of Ireland. Then comes a period of thick darkness, and when we again become acquainted with Iona (in the reign of William the Lion) it is the seat of a convent of Cluniac monks of unknown foundation, and the memory of St. Columba and his family is gone."[2]

In 850, Kenneth MacAlpin, who was descended from Aedan, King of Scots, Columba's friend, had built a new Church at Dunkeld, dedicating it under the name of St. Columba, and removed some of his relics to it, making Dunkeld chief in

[1] Principal Shairp, Sketches, pp. 58, 59.   [2] Mr. Cosmo Innes, Middle Ages, pp. 110, 111.

Columba and the Celtic Church. 29

ecclesiastical importance, and probably its bishop, Tuathal, was the "first" who had episcopal jurisdiction. About 903 Dunkeld in its turn was laid waste by the Norsemen, and probably at that time the relics were removed to Scone, the Capital.[1]

Whether we in this Church are worshipping or not on a spot where the first wooden Church in this district was built by some of Columba's followers, the lessons to be drawn from their earnest self-denying lives are our inheritance and may well stir our hearts. "Of these splendid traditions, of this bright example, of these evangelistic triumphs we are the heirs. The simplicity, the self-devotion, the prayerfulness, the burning love of Christ which shone forth in those Celtic missionaries of old, must be our spiritual equipment now."[2]

[1] Dr. Joseph Robertson, Stat. Ecc. Scot., p. xx. [2] Bishop Lightfoot, Leaders, pp. 16, 17.

Chapter III.
THE KELEDEI or CULDEES IN SCOTLAND.*

"OF the four hundred years extending from the days of Cumin and Adamnan, who wrote lives of St. Columba, to the death of Malcolm Canmore, we possess scarcely any of those native contemporary chronicles in which England and Ireland are so rich."[1] "In that long, dark blank there are names of kings and dates of battles, but hardly a vestige of what can be called personal history."[2] "It is a curious fact that our knowledge of the state of Christianity in Scotland before the seventh century is much greater than during the four or five centuries following, which were ages of darkness and confusion."[3] Only when we reach the twelfth century does land come to be held by feudal charter and are gifts to religious houses inscribed in their registers and attested by witnesses.

For one hundred and fifty years Columba and his followers were the evangelists of our country. The clergy who succeeded them differed from them in many ways, and the circumstances of the country became greatly altered. A name that we shall find frequently used in the Latin writs of the Priory of Monymusk in designating the clergy who worshipped in this Church began to be employed, although formerly unknown — the Latin name KELEDEI familiar to us as CULDEES. In these charters, from 1131 onwards, the clergy at Monymusk are called "Keledei," or "Canonici qui Keledei dicuntur," or "Keledei

---

*Before reading this chapter, see particularly the note at the beginning of the previous chapter, neither being essential to our narrative.

[1] Dr. Campbell, St. Giles, pp. 65, 66. [3] Dr. Campbell, Balmerino, p. 13.
[2] Principal Shairp, Sketches, p. 45.

sive Canonici." Then this alternative is dropped, and in subsequent writs they are termed simply "Canonici" till 1245, when the "Keledei" or Culdees vanish from the page of our parish history, and in their stead there appear "The Prior and Convent of Munimusc of the Order of St. Augustine." In these writs we leave behind us all traditional accounts and reach the sphere of authentic history, and as the name is so often used to denote the clergy who lived here and are buried in our Churchyard, it is of special interest to us to gain as comprehensive an idea as we can regarding them. Dr. Reeves, however, the chief authority on this subject, says that "Culdee is the most abused term in Scotic Church history,"[1] and that it "has been the subject of much speculative error and historical mystification.[2]

Who then were the Culdees? It has been fully established that they had nothing directly to do with Columba and his Church. "There was no connection between them and the Columbite Monasteries other than that both were of the Irish type."[3] The primitive Church in our country was not a Culdee institution. "It is certain that for nearly two centuries after the arrival of St. Columba, the Culdees had no known existence in Scotland, nor probably anywhere else."[4] "It is not till after the expulsion of the Columban monks from the kingdom of the Picts in the beginning of the eighth century, that the name of Culdee appears."[5] "No doubt Culdees were found in the tenth and eleventh centuries in Churches and Monasteries which had been founded by Columba and his immediate followers. But though" in these cases "they filled the place of the Columbites, they led another manner of life, and were of another spirit."[6] We must not fall, says Dr. Reeves, "into

[1] Adamnan, p. 368.
[2] Culdees, p. 123.
[3] Smith's Dict. of Ch. Ant.
[4] Mr. Stephen, History, p. 308.
[5] Mr. Skene, Celtic Scotland, II., p. 226.
[6] Principal Shairp, Sketches, p. 58.

the national error of supposing the Culdees to have been a peculiar order who derived their origin from St. Columba; in other words, that they were Columbites, in the same sense that we speak of Benedictines. It is true that, after the lapse of centuries, Culdees were found in Churches which he or his disciples founded; but their name was in no way distinctive, being in the first instance an epithet of asceticism, and afterwards that of irregularity. Among the numerous references to Iona in the Irish Annals there is only one notice of Céli-dé as existing there, and this solitary example is of so late a period as 1164."[1] In the tenth century "almost everywhere," says Dr. Joseph Robertson, "on both banks of the Forth, in Celtic Scotland, in Teutonic England, the old monastic discipline died out, the name of monk disappeared. Many Monasteries were suppressed by lay usurpation; many were swept away by the fire and sword of the heathen Norsemen. Most of those which survived were peopled—the Cathedral and Collegiate Churches were served—by a new order of Canon Clerics or Regular Clergy, who, falling away from the comparatively easy rule which they professed to follow, became loose, worldly, self-indulgent, too often neglecting the offices of religion, not always respecting the duties of morality. The reform or expulsion of these degenerate servants or worshippers of God— 'Servi Dei,' 'Cœlicolæ,' 'Deicolæ,' 'Cultores Dei,' 'Colidei,' 'Culdees,' as they appear to have been called—was the great work to which, with the characteristic impetuosity of reformers St. Dunstan, St. Ethelwold, St. Oswald set themselves in the latter half of the tenth century."[2]

The question of the origin of the Culdees has been much debated and there is still much that is obscure regarding them. They were not an order peculiar to Scotland. The name seems

[1] Culdees, p. 149.   [2] Stat. Ecc. Scot., pp. ccvi.-ccxiv.

to have originated in Ireland. About 790 it was appropriated to a specially ascetic order of monks established by St. Maelruain, abbot and bishop, at Tallaght near Dublin. About twenty-five years before this, canonical rules were formed by the Archbishop of Metz for the clergy of his own town, which became so popular that they were enlarged in order to be applicable to the whole Church, and in them the name of "Deicola" appears, and the canon clerics are spoken of as "servi Dei." "They were an intermediate class between monks and secular priests, adopting to a great extent the discipline, without the vows, of the monastic system and discharging the office of ministers in various Churches. Possibly the institution of Maelruain may have borrowed from or possessed some features in common with the order of Canons, for certain it is that in after ages both the Keledei of Scotland and the Colidei of Ireland exhibited in their discipline the main characteristics of secular canons."[1]

The word Culdee is derived from the Irish Céle-Dé, "a servant of God," "a God-fearing man," being "a Celtic translation of the Latin 'Servus Dei' in its limited and technical sense of a monk."[2] "The devotion and self-denial which characterised monastic life upon its introduction into the Latin Church procured for those who adopted it the special designation of *servi Dei*, which in process of time acquired a technical application, so that *servus Dei* and *Monachus* became convertible terms. To this origin we may safely refer the creation of the Celtic compound Céle-De, which in its employment possessed all the latitude of its model, and in the lapse of ages underwent all the modifications or limitations of meaning which the changes of time and circumstances, or local usage,

[1] Dr. Reeves, Culdees, p. 128. [2] Dr. Joseph Robertson, Stat. Ecc. Scot., p. ccxiii.

D

produced in the class to whom the epithet was applied."[1] "Ceile Dé was the phrase adopted by the Scotic Church as the proper Gaelic rendering of the Latin 'Servus Dei.' In process of time and under the influence perhaps of a false etymology, the phrase was variously written Calledeus, Keledeus, Colideus, finally settling down into Culdee. The meaning of the phrase would seem to have been quite as elastic as the form."[2]

The name is frequently met with in Irish records, details of eight separate Irish Culdee homes being given by Dr. Reeves.[3] "In some instances their head was married and his office hereditary—in others they are distinctly called celibate."[4] The name is found at Armagh as early as 921, and there the ancient title survived even the Reformation, existing as late as 1628.[5] But it was not confined to Ireland and Scotland. The officiating Canons of York Minster in 946 were called "Colidei," and discharged the double duty of divine service and charitable hospitality.[6] Even at Canterbury, in a charter of King Ethelred in 1106, Canon Clerics are called "Cultores Clerici, a singular expression which seems to intimate that the collegiate clergy were even then styled Culdees—Cultores Dei—in the South as well as in the North of England."[7] They were similarly styled at Winchester in 966, and the name also appears on the Continent, in Gaul. "The same indiscriminate use of 'Cleric' and 'Canon' which prevailed at Winchester," says Dr. Joseph Robertson, "prevailed generally elsewhere, as at Rochester, at Durham, on one side of Tweed, at St. Andrews, at MONYMUSK on the other. It was so from the beginning of the Order."[8] About 1190 the Island of

---

[1] Dr. Reeves, Culdees, pp. 119, 120.
[2] Prof. M'Kinnon, Edinburgh University.
[3] Culdees, pp. 125-143.
[4] Smith's Dictionary.
[5] Dr. Reeves, Culdees, pp. 128-137.
[6] Dr. Reeves, Culdees, p. 177.
[7] Dr. J. Robertson, Stat. Ecc. Scot., p. ccxiii.; Dr. Grub, History, I., 229, 230.
[8] Stat. Ecc. Scot., p. ccxiv.

Bardsey, on the Coast of Caernarvon in Wales, is mentioned as inhabited by "most devout monks called Celibates or Culdees. Indeed, "the Welsh word for a hermit, which is 'meudwy,' means 'God's slave,'"[1] which corresponds exactly with the Celtic " Céle De," " God's servant," " Culdee."

" Passing over to Scotland, whither the term had been imported with the language and institutions of the Scotic [Irish] immigrants, we find about the middle of the thirteenth century, certain ecclesiastics entitled *Keledei sive Canonici.* In fact, during the range of time in which the term is of record, we discover the greatest diversity in its application—sometimes borne by hermit, sometimes by conventuals; in one situation implying the condition of celibacy, in another understood of married men ; here denoting regulars, there seculars ; some of the name bound by obligations of poverty, others free to accumulate property; at one period high in honour as implying self-denial, at another regarded with contempt as the designation of the loose and worldly-minded. . . . When at last *Célé Dé* does become a distinctive term, it is only so as contrasting those who clung to the old conventual observances of the country with those who adopted the better organised and more systematic institutions of mediæval introduction, in fact, as denoting an old-fashioned Scotic monk in an age when the prevalence of such surnames as MacNab (son of the Abbot), MacVicar, &c., indicated a condition of clerical society not exactly in accordance with the received notions of ecclesiastical discipline."[2]

Culdees are without doubt found in Scotland about 840, but by some this date is thought too late. Our earliest record of them is in the Register of St. Andrews Priory,[3] which contains

---

[1] Prof. Rhys, Celtic Britain, p. 73.
[2] Dr. Reeves, Culdees, pp. 120, 121.
[3] Register of St. Andrews Priory, pp. 113-118.

memoranda of some early gifts during the Celtic period. One of these states that Brude, son of Dergard, by old tradition the last of the Pictish kings, gave the little island on Lochleven, called St. Serf's, to Almighty God, St. Servanus, and the Culdees, who are spoken of as "Keledei, hermits dwelling there, who serve and shall hereafter serve God in that island." About 950, during the rule of their abbot Ronan, on condition of receiving food and clothing, the Culdees gave over their island to the first Fothad, Bishop of the Scots, at St. Andrews, who was held in high repute all through Scotland and who died in 961.[1] The next writ refers to a gift by the renowned Macbeth, and preserves his father's name, Finlach, and also Lady Macbeth's own name, "Gruoch daughter of Bodhe." In it they are styled "King and Queen of the Scots," and it records a grant of lands near Lochleven still retaining the name of Kyrkness, which they made to these Culdees between 1037 and 1054—the lands being given, it is stated, from feelings of piety and for the benefit of their prayers, and being expressly declared to be free from all lay services. Macbeth also gave them the lands of Bolgyne, and they received the grant of a church—Markinch, Scoonie, and Auchterderran—all three in the neighbourhood of Lochleven—from each of the three bishops who ruled at St. Andrews between 1028 and 1093. "They were a small community, and preserved, even as late as the reign of Malcolm III., who died in 1093, their original character of a hermit society. They were the oldest Culdean establishment in Scotland, and thus exhibited its earliest form."[2] We shall learn by and by with what harshness they were treated by David I.

"It is worthy of observation that in the early Irish notices of the Céli-de the superior is generally styled 'head,' not

[1] See Dr. Reeves, Culdees, pp. 243, 169, 170.   [2] Mr. Skene, Celtic Scotland, II., 388.

'abbot' or 'prior.' This distinction is also observed in some of the Scotch records, where the superior of the Keledei is called *Præpositus* (Provost). There are two instances, however, where he is termed *Abbas*. In Brechin he appears as *Prior*; but the term is qualified at MONYMUSK, *Prior vel Magister*."[1]

"In considering the name of Culdee, there are two things which should be kept in view : (*i.*) that it seems to have been less an authoritative, technical, or proper designation, than a loose popular term, as appears from the way in which it is so often used 'Clericos qui Keledei vulgariter appellantur,' &c.; (*ii.*) that, in Scotland at least, the name is said to have been given by the common people to priests of all kinds, without discrimination."[2]

Of old the Celtic Clergy used often to seek retirement from their brethren for a longer or shorter time. In Iona, for instance, a place at a little distance from the general buildings of the settlement was set apart for seclusion and was called "the Desert." This word gives its name to the parish of Dysart, on the shores of the Firth of Forth, where St. Serf scooped out for himself a cave as a "desert."[3] He is said to have usually spent the forty days of Lent there. "This cave was used as a Church up to nearly the time of the Reformation."[4] Also "close down upon the shore is still the tower of the deserted Church of St. Serf, ivy-mantled and surmounted by a quaint saddle-backed and crow-stepped gable."[5] Probably when the discipline of the Columban clergy, or of those who succeeded them after their expulsion, becamed relaxed, the Culdees owed their origin and their name to a reaction from the lowered tone of the monastic life and an attempt to reach its higher

---

1 Dr. Reeves, Culdees, p. 126.
2 Dr. Joseph Robertson, Stat. Ecc. Scot., p. ccxiv.
3 Dean Stanley, Lectures, p. 25.
4 Sir James Simpson.
5 Fringes of Fife.

perfections.[1] "The busy life of the monastic communities came by some to be regarded as a state less perfect than the life of retired devotion which might be found in a 'desert.'" At first retirement to such a place was only for a time, but afterwards there were those who sought a life-long seclusion in these or in remoter solitudes. Absolute solitude seems to have proved, as time went on, too trying for human nature, and by and by groups of cells were formed, and "anchorites," "hermits," and Céle De (in Scotland "Keledei") were names bestowed upon their occupants."[2] "They were finally brought under the canonical rule along with the secular clergy, retaining, however, to some extent the nomenclature of the Monastery, until at length the name of *Keledeus* or Culdee became almost synonymous with that of secular canon."[3] Some, however, think that in all probability the Ceile De were never solitary hermits, but were "communities from their origin."[4]

Whatever their actual origin, the Culdees were most probably at first severely ascetic, and they seem always to have been small communities. Some of their homes were widely separate, with few bonds, if any, uniting them. We shall find one writ mentioning the Prior of St Andrews and the Prior of Monymusk meeting at St Andrews regarding their respective money-matters, but this is after Monymusk has ceased to be Culdean, and it is to the Augustinian Prior at St. Andrews, not to the still-remaining Culdean Head, that account is given. At St. Andrews and Monymusk at least the Culdean bodies were thirteen in number—the Prior and other twelve priests under his authority. When we first hear of them at Monymusk they are receiving endowments, being thus independent of bodily labour and able to devote themselves to the services in the Church and

[1] See Mr. Stephen, History, p. 310.
[2] Bishop Dowden, Celtic Church, pp. 204, 205.
[3] Mr. Skene, Celtic Scotland, II., p. 277.
[4] Dr. Campbell, Ch. of Scot., Past and Present, Vol. I.

Priory. We shall find that at Monymusk they were excluded from all parochial functions, and as regarded the rights of the Parish Church were placed upon the footing of ordinary parishioners—that they were bound by no vows, and that their peculiarity consisted in their collegiate character and the absence of spiritual cure.[1] This may doubtless go far to account for their decay. How very different from the missionary spirit of Columba and his followers! How strange to think of as many as thirteen Clerics being engaged in constant worship here, by day and night, and yet being hindered from helping to build up the parish and district in piety by labour as well as prayer! Little wonder that we shall find such a quarrel raging for years in their home, that an appeal in regard to it had to be taken to the Pope himself!

"Among the Cotton Manuscripts in the British Museum is preserved a Catalogue of the religious houses of England and Wales, at the end of which is a List of the Scotch Sees and the orders of their respective societies." It is annexed to Silgrave's Chronicle which comes down to 1272, and probably records the state of things anterior to its own date. This List is regarded as the work of Silgrave, and from it, and from charter-sources as to some non-cathedral Monasteries, it is found that no "record-evidence" remains for more than THIRTEEN homes in Scotland where Keledei existed.[2] The notices of even some of these are of the most meagre nature, and all of them, except two of which we have hardly any record at all, were on the East Coast, while none of them were south of the Forth. Although the number is so small, the system is spoken of at a very early time as if it extended over all the country, and the "Celtic" or "Columban" Church is even in our own day often spoken of as the "Culdean" Church. When Turgot,

[1] Dr. Reeves, Culdees, p. 174.   [2] Dr. Reeves, Culdees, pp. 150, 151.

Queen Margaret's friend and chaplain, was elected Bishop of St. Andrews in 1107, it is recorded in the Chronicle of Durham, of which he was Prior,—"In diebus illis jus Keledeorum per totum regnum Scotiæ transivit in Episcopatum St. Andreæ"— "in his days the rights of the Culdees over the whole Kingdom of Scotland passed to the Bishopric of St. Andrews"—"a loose and exaggerated statement; but there can be little doubt that Bishop Turgot checked the Culdees in their alienation of Church property at St. Andrews."[1] This also "evidently points to the completion of a great ecclesiastical revolution, the change from Abbatial to Episcopal jurisdiction."[2] "During his tenure of office, however, Turgot appears to have done nothing to affect the rights of the Culdees."[3]

The chief of their homes was at ST. ANDREWS, one of the earliest Celtic homes of piety in our country, founded, it is thought, by Cainnech (Kenneth), the patron saint of Kilkenny (which is named after him) and a friend of Columba's. He had a hut at St. Andrews, and died in 600. An abbot of the Culdees at St. Andrews is recorded in 944, and "it would seem that its Culdees had the privilege of electing the Primate of all Scotland, who was now a 'bishop,' and not a simple 'presbyter' like Columba, although the nomination itself was probably vested in the king."[4] Many records of the Culdees at St. Andrews remain, and are given by Dr. Reeves. They were thirteen in number—"twelve brethren and a prior, as in Monymusk"—and among them "it is evident that the condition of matrimony was no disqualification for the office of a Keledeus, and such as were married men before their admission were likely to have families, from which in process of time persons would be chosen to fill up vacancies *carnali*

---

[1] Dr. Reeves, Culdees, p. 154.
[2] Mr. Stuart, Book of Deer, p. cxxiii.
[3] Mr. Skene, Celtic Scotland, II., p. 373.
[4] Dr. Grub, History, I. pp. 227, 236.

THE EARLY ECCLESIASTICAL HISTORY OF SCOTLAND.

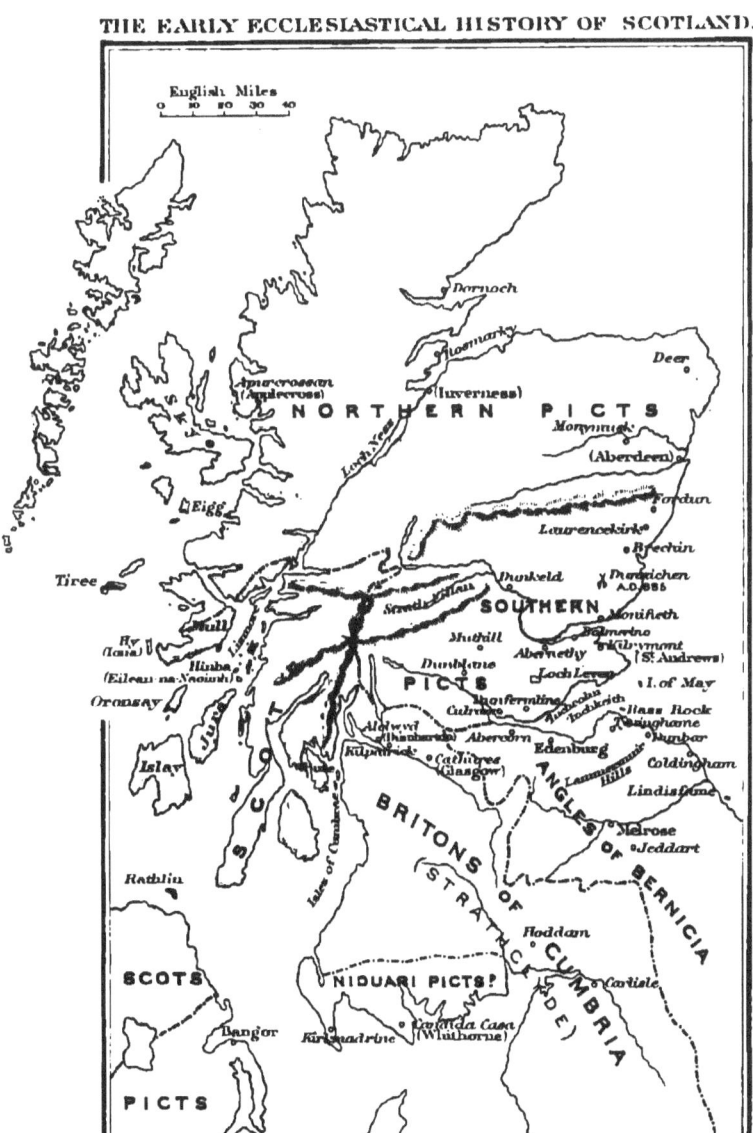

successione, and their wives were excluded only from their official residences which they occupied when on duty." A writ of 1250 shows that the Keledean Church of St. Andrews was dedicated to St. Mary ; — "that of Monymusk also bore the same name."[1] So tenacious was the hold they had on their own separate Church, and so resolute were they against being transformed into Augustinian Canons Regular, that a distinct Priory of this Order was "artfully" planted by Robert, Bishop of St. Andrews, so near them as to be within hearing of their chants, and the little Romanesque Church and tower that have received the name of St. Rule—"still a landmark in St. Andrews"—were built by him between 1127 and 1144 within their own precinct and within a stone-throw of their altar. They got the option of entering the new Monastery as Canons, or of retaining their life interests as they were ; but as they severally died, Canons were to be chosen in their room, and their possessions were to pass to the new Order. Even then they were able to retain their own small Church, and also a voice, along with the rival Canons, in the election of the bishop. When a vacancy occurred in 1297, for instance, the twelve Culdees put forward as a candidate their own Provost, William Comyn, brother of the Earl of Buchan, who was strongly supported by Edward I., but the Pope decided in favour of the choice of the Augustinian Canons, William Lamberton, the friend of Wallace. By and by "the little priestly caste," "the native clergy" began to pine and wither. Yet, notwithstanding all the efforts to dispossess them they continued as late as 1322, but after this the name of Culdees seems to be heard no more, though their little Church continued to be regarded with veneration until the Reformation. After this the Provostry became vested in the Crown, and in 1616 was annexed,

[1] Dr. Reeves, Culdees, pp. 224, 225, 232.

together with the appendant benefices, to the See of St. Andrews.[1]

DUNKELD was another of the earliest Columban mission centres. "Both St. Columba and St. Cuthbert appear in its traditions." It is said to have been refounded with Culdees about 820, and a short time after some of the relics of St. Columba were removed to it for safety, and it was constituted the "mother-church" over the Columban Churches, the supremacy of Iona having passed away. After Kenneth MacAlpine made good his right to the Pictish throne in 843, we read in 864 of the death of Tuathal, who is called "primus" Bishop of Pictland and Abbot of Dunkeld. There seems no reasonable doubt, Dr. Reeves says, that he was the head of the Culdees there. Some writers make "primus" equivalent to "chief"; others hold the meaning to be "first" in point of time; while, as we have said before,[2] it may probably point to his being the first bishop who had episcopal jurisdiction. After this the Church lands were secularised, and the Culdee Monastery had a "Lay-Abbot," whose office was of such rank as to be hereditary in the royal family. Cronan (or Crinan) its lay-abbot was married to Bethoc, daughter of Malcolm II and was the father of "the gracious Duncan." Ethelred, a younger son of Malcolm III and Margaret, who was also Earl of Fife, became its lay-abbot. While the Abthein or Abbacy, together with its lands, descended to him, the inferior ministers retained their corporate and clerical condition as the officiating clergy of the Church. When the Culdees were superseded, and made the Cathedral Chapter by David I (another of Malcolm III's sons) its actual abbot, Cormac,

---

[1] See also Dr. Joseph Robertson, Stat. Ecc. Scot., pp. ccxix.-ccxxvi.; Mr. Skene, Celtic Scotland, II. pp. 356-360; Mr. Stephen, History, p. 319; Principal Shairp, Sketches, pp. 89-91.   [2] p. 29.

became the first bishop about 1127. The two societies of secular clergy and regular canons with the bishop at their head, co-existed for nearly two centuries, and in Silgrave's Catalogue they are both mentioned—"Canons" and "Culdees."[1]

BRECHIN had long been a sacred spot, and its remarkable Round Tower still remains a striking token of its early connection with Irish missionaries, being, "as it were, the gnomon of the original monastic group." It is one hundred and six feet high, "modernised, no doubt, at its apex, but bearing evidence in its general character that it belongs to about the period of Kenneth, son of Malcolm—that is, 970-992." It stands close to the Cathedral built by David I, but it had not been actually joined as a building to any Church. A Culdee community was added to the original Irish foundation, but "the place totally disappears from history till David's reign."[2] The abbacy was secularised, like Dunkeld, and held by a layman, who took the name of "Abbe," and inherited a large share of the Culdee patrimony, and transmitted it to his descendants, who soon lost even the name of abbot.[3] Leod, the lay abbot, signs, as a witness, the Charter of the Abbey of Deer by David I, and the names of his grandson and other descendants are known, all in the twelfth and thirteenth centuries. The prior and his Culdees became the Chapter of the Bishopric, founded by David I about 1145, and successive bishops speak of them with affection as "Keledei nostri,"[4] and even after other clerics were introduced into the Chapter, the Prior was still the President; but in 1248, the last year of Alexander II's reign, the Culdees have disappeared, and we hear only of the Dean and Chapter.[5]

[1] Dr. Reeves, Culdees, pp. 159-161.
[2] Ibid, p. 162
[3] Dr. Joseph Robertson, Chambers' Ency., Dr. Reeves, Culdees, pp. 237, 238.
[4] Mr. Cosmo Innes, Sketches, p. 156.
[5] Mr. Skene, Celtic Scotland II., pp. 400-402.

DUNBLANE is named after the royal St. Blaan, Bishop of Kingarth, in the end of the sixth or early portion of the seventh century. It was an ancient Columban settlement. Silgrave's Catalogue mentions that the religious society of the Church were Keledei, but beyond this notice Dr. Reeves finds no express mention of their existence at Dunblane.[1] There were Culdees at Muthil, situated farther North, "which seems to have grown on the decay of Dunblane." After 1214 Muthil became the seat of the Dean of Dunblane, who had already taken precedence of the Culdee Prior.

ROSEMARKY, near Fortrose, on the north shore of the Moray Firth, was, we may reasonably assume, an Irish foundation, probably belonging in origin to the latter half of the seventh century. It was dedicated, like Mortlach, under the name of Moluoc of Lismore. Of its succeeding history we have not a particle of information until David I revived the see, and made it the Cathedral town of the Bishopric of Ross. Silgrave's Catalogue designates the society as Keledei—that is the representatives of the old secular college.[2]

DORNOCH, in Sutherland, became the seat of the Cathedral of the diocese of Caithness—the most northern diocese on the mainland. It may be regarded as an Irish foundation (dedicated to St. Barr, "St. Fimber of Dornoch") "out of which grew, in course of time, that peculiar development of the ministerial office called Keledean. What the ecclesiastical process was through which it passed under Norse rule we are not informed, but King David accepted it as the most venerable Church in the earldom, when he defined the diocese of Caithness, and made this its Cathedral centre. Andrew, 'Bishop of Catanes,' appears on record in 1146"; but, in 1222, Bishop Gilbert built a new Church, and established a Chapter. "He

[1] Dr. Reeves, Culdees, pp. 164, 165.   [2] Dr. Reeves, Culdees, pp. 162-164.

found at his accession no more than one priest; he left his Cathedral endowed for five dignitaries and three prebendaries,"[1] and with his name is to be associated the virtual extinction of the Keledei in this diocese.[2]

Thus "in his restorations David I merely added a bishop to the existing societies at Brechin, Dunblane, Ross, and Caithness; while in the earlier sees of St. Andrews and Dunkeld he superseded the Keledei by instituting chapters of regular canons. The encouragement of their lax and impotent system would have ill accorded with the vitality and reforming spirit which pervaded all his measures; and further as the representatives of the Celtic clergy, they were little likely to be acceptable to a prince who wished to infuse the Saxon element into the Scottish Church."[3]

In the West, LISMORE, an island six miles from Oban, seems to have been a home of the Culdees, but they can hardly be traced.[4] The Monastery was founded by St. Moluoc, an Irish bishop, who died in 592, and it "no doubt continued to exist through successive ages, until in the course of time, its society, in conformity with the progress of native monasticism, settled down into the condition which obtained for them the name of Keledei."[5] About 1200 the district was separated from the Bishopric of Dunkeld and formed into the Diocese of Argyll, and in Silgrave's Catalogue its chapter is called Culdean, but in 1249 the election of the bishop is vested in the canons of the Church. The old Church lands had come to be held by a layman as his private property, who assumed the name of Abbot, as is still testified by the extensive district opposite bearing the name of APPIN, which is simply the old word Abdaine, Abthane, Abthein, or Abbacy, denoting the territories of the old Abbey,

[1] Dr. Joseph Robertson, Abbeys, p. 49.
[2] Dr. Reeves, Culdees, 166, 167.
[3] Ibid., pp. 148, 149.
[4] Mr. Skene, Celtic Scotland II., p. 408.
[5] Dr. Reeves, Culdees, pp. 167, 168.

just as, widely separate from it, there is the other Appin named from the Church lands of Dull in Athol being held by the great lay-abbot of Dunkeld.[1]

These SEVEN Culdee homes became in course of time Episcopal seats, one reason doubtless being the importance of the places at the time, and another, probably a stronger reason, that they already possessed these corporations of Culdee clergy, who had endowments, and had been engaged for years in the constant round of divine service.[2] The Culdees became merged in the Cathedral chapters, but before the end of the thirteenth century they all disappear, except at St. Andrews, leaving the chapters composed of secular canons.

There were only other five or six Culdee homes in the whole country, and they "were never raised to the rank of Episcopal sees. This was owing to some secular influence or peculiarity of position. These merely retained their conventual character, with diminished importance, as being inside the jurisdiction of more favoured Churches, until in the course of events their societies were suppressed or died a natural death. In fact, the generality of Monasteries, both in Scotland and Ireland, were in a state of decrepitude at the beginning of the twelfth century, and those which survived for any length of time owed the continuation of their existence either to the superaddition of a bishop and chapter, or to their reconstruction on a new model."[3]

ST. SERF'S, in Lochleven, was one of the "earliest religious foundations in Scotland, and probably owed its origin to St. Serf in the dawn of national christianisation."[4] We have already spoken of its origin. One point, however, seems incapable of being determined. Wynton, who became its prior, identified

---

[1] See also Dr. Reeves, Culdees, p. 147.
[2] See Bishop Dowden, Celtic Church, pp. 202, 203.
[3] Dr. Reeves, Culdees, p. 14⁸.
[4] Ibid., p. 171.

"Brude, son of Dergard," the donor of the island, with Brude, son of Derili, who reigned from 697 to 706, and some think it may be this Brude, while Dr. Reeves [1] thinks this date too early, and considers it was another Brude who reigned in 842 for one year, especially as the writ says he was "the last of the kings of the Picts." The earlier date would connect this, the first mention of the Culdees in Scotland, with the time— 710 to 717—when Nectan tried to induce the old Columban clergy in Pictland to yield to the Roman missionaries, and found not only that this was impossible, but that the two Churches could not exist side by side with each other, so that, as we saw before, he banished the Columban clergy from his dominions. In Ireland we find Culdees devoting themselves to the care of the sick and of the poor, some of their heads being married, as celibacy had not yet become the universal rule,[2] and if this self-denying charitable spirit was present among some in the Celtic Church, it is possible that a few of the old clergy who came to bear the name of Culdees may have been allowed to remain in Pictland by Nectan, and in this early gift of St. Serf's island we may have the record of royal favour shown to some of their body. This, however, is merely a supposition. Besides the gifts we mentioned before, the Culdees at St. Serf's about 1120 received a grant of the lands of Admore from Ethelred, a younger son of Malcolm III. and Margaret, and lay-abbot of Dunkeld. In this he followed the example of his father and mother in their gift of Ballechristin, and his deed says that "he gives the lands with more affection since this possession was given him by his parents while he was yet in boyhood."[3] A few years after, his brother David I and the Bishop of St. Andrews, by writs that we shall afterwards

[1] Dr. Reeves, Culdees, p. 243.   [2] Dr. Reeves, Culdees, p. 128, 137.
[3] Reg. St. And. Priory, p. 115.

detail, gave over all that these *Chelede* possessed — island and monastery, churches, lands, mill, and all pertinents, even the vestments in which they performed their services, and their little library of seventeen books, the names of which we shall mention particularly—to the newly-founded Augustinian Canons at St. Andrews, that a priory of this order might supplant the old "Culdee" Abbey of the island. We learn that by 1248— the same year as at Brechin and three years after Monymusk —this change had been fully accomplished, and we hear no more of the Culdees of Lochleven.[1]

ABERNETHY, on the Tay, in Perthshire, was for a time the capital of the southern Pictish kingdom. It was a very ancient centre of Christianity, and an old Pictish Bishopric. It is said that Ninian planted the first Church here about 400, and that Columba refounded it about 580. The Church was first dedicated to St. Bridgid of Kildare, to whom were granted the lands and tithes which the priors and canons enjoyed from ancient times. Its Round Tower is an abiding record of its early connection with the Irish Church, and was built probably about 850, one thousand years ago. It is seventy-two feet high, and is believed to be of an older type, and earlier in date than the only other one in our country at Brechin, and could have been the work of Irish Clergy alone.[2] "In illa ecclesia (Abirnethy) fuerunt tres electiones factæ, quando non fuit nisi unus solus episcopus in Scotia"[3] Thus Abernethy gave three successive bishops when there was but one solitary bishop "in Scotia." Evidently this was after the power had passed from Dunkeld, and before the seat of the one bishop was transferred to St. Andrews whose Culdees then became the electors.

---

[1] Dr. Reeves, Culdees, pp. 169-171, 242-250; Mr. Skene, Celtic Scotland II., pp. 388, 389.

[2] Mr. Skene, Celtic Scotland, II., 309; Dr. J. Anderson, Scotland in Early Christian Times, p. 35.

[3] See Dr. Reeves, Culdees, p. 251.

The statement just quoted from the writ has given rise to difficulty—especially in regard to the form of Episcopacy then existing. We have seen that in the "Columban" period, there were many bishops throughout the country, and if there was only one at this time, a great change must have taken place, perhaps in regard to jurisdiction, and when the solitary bishop died, it has been asked what episcopal authority was left to consecrate his successor, and whether this was done simply by Presbyters. Abernethy became a Culdee Abbey, and Culdees are found in it about 1120, for Ethelred's writ, mentioned in regard to Dunkeld, was confirmed there, and among the witnesses to it are the names of two who were sons of priests of Abernethy, and three other priests, two of whom were Culdees, thus showing secular "married" clergy existing there side by side with Culdee priests. About eighty years after an hereditary lay-abbot named Orm, the founder of the baronial house of Abernethy, and after him his son and grandson appear dividing the lands and tithes with the prior and Culdees who performed the religious duties. "The finishing blow was struck in 1272, when the priory was converted into a society of Canons Regular."[1]

At MUTHIL, "the capital of the Earldom of Stratherne," near the river Earn, north of Dunblane and three miles from Crieff, we find Culdees with their prior from 1178 to 1214, charters between these dates being recorded, which are witnessed by three priors, whose names are given, and other clergy, but we know little of the early history of this Church.[2]

At MONIFIETH, on the north shore of the Firth of Tay, "Culdees are once mentioned, and then pass away for ever." Malcolm, Earl of Angus, grants to the Abbey of Arbroath "the

[1] Dr. Reeves, Culdees, pp. 171, 172; Mr. Skene, Celtic Scotland II. pp. 397-400.
[2] Ibid., pp. 175, 259, 260; Mr. Skene, Celtic Scotland II. p. 404; Dr. Joseph Robertson, Spalding Club Miscel. v. p. 58.

E

Church of Monifod with its chapels, lands," &c., which is confirmed by King William. About 1220 he grants the land of the Abthein of Munifeth to the son of Bricius, priest of 'Kerimure,' which Matilda, Countess of Angus, his daughter, confirms in 1242, the vicar of the parish witnessing her charter, and then the Countess Matilda grants to the Abbey of Arbroath "the land on the south side of the Church which the Keledei held in the life-time of her father, with a croft at the east end of the Church"; and finally Michael, the lord of the Abbathania holds this croft in feu-farm from the Abbey. Thus the old abbacy is granted to the son of a priest who then calls himself Abbot, while the Church is served by a vicar, and a descendant appears, as in other cases, with the simple designation of "de Monifoth," and calls himself lord of the Abbathania or territory of the Abbacy, so that the ancient Monastery had now passed into the hands of an hereditary lay-abbot. We hear simply of "the expiring remnant of an ancient society, whose endowments were lost in part through the vicious administration of their secular affairs, while the remainder was handed over to a neighbouring Monastery, whose practice was considered more orthodox and its recognition of Anglo-Norman law more express."[1]

Here, at MONYMUSK, we shall find that the first-recorded grant to the Culdees was made by a Celtic Earl of Buchan about 1130. Details of all the other known grants will be given. A record of date 1211 will also be given in full telling of the constitution of the society at that time. "This society, which consisted of secular priests, thirteen in number, was probably the representative of an ancient monastic foundation. Its early connection, however, with St. Andrews reduced it to a condition of secondary importance and deprived it of the presence

[1] Dr. Reeves, Culdees, p. 176; Mr. Skene, Celt. Scot. II., 394, 395; Dr. Grub, His. I., 243.

of a bishop, whose place was to some extent supplied by a Prior or Master." When the Culdees made an effort to assume the condition of Regulars the Bishop of St. Andrews resisted it, and they were compelled to adhere to their original discipline; but thirty-four years after the Culdees have disappeared, being transformed like the others, and are spoken of as "The Prior and Convent of Munimusc of the Order of St. Augustine," being still subject to the Bishop of St. Andrews.[1]

At IONA, but only at as late a date as 1164, we read of there being Culdees, their "Head"—not their "Prior"—being mentioned last of the four chiefs of the clergy there by whom the abbot was chosen. Thus they evidently formed a subordinate body, the Abbey never being Culdean, but having clergy of another order. The Register of Holyrood shows that soon after this, about 1175, even Iona was wholly or in part in the lay-possession of the King of Scots.[2] It is singular that this body of inferior rank in Iona and the unknown body at Lismore are the only Culdees of whom we have any record in the whole West of Scotland, where there were so many religious houses, showing that Columban influence had nothing to do with the origin of the Culdees, and that the great mass of Columban Monasteries throughout the country are to be distinguished from Culdean homes.

Unlike the seven houses we joined together, St. Serf's, Abernethy, and Monymusk had no local connection with any bishop's see, so that their Culdees were in course of time simply transformed into Canons Regular. The Culdee s at Muthil and Monifieth seem to have disappeared altogether— probably owing to their neighbourhood to Dunblane and Arbroath—while at Iona "they probably joined the monks of

[1] Dr. Reeves, Culdees, p. 174. [2] Dr. Reeves, Culdees, pp. 168, 169: Dr. Grub, History I., 243.

the Benedictine Abbey of which the present ruins are the remains."[1]

It may be of interest to mention the facts we have been able to collect regarding the Churches at these thirteen places without anticipating materially what is to be said about the date of the building of our own Church.

One sees the little island of ST. SERF'S when crossing Lochleven to visit the remains of the castle on the other well-known island where Mary Queen of Scots was confined, and one is sorry to see " its desolate bareness," and that the ruined walls of the ancient Abbey are quite dishonoured.

The site of the Culdee Church at ST. ANDREWS, once the Chapel Royal of Scotland, "is still visible between the Cathedral and the sea,"[2] and of it Dr. A. K. H. Boyd writes— "The Church of St. Mary of the Rock is now the most desolate among the many ruins of a city of ruins."[3]

At LISMORE the remnants of the walls of the Cathedral are of a later date, for the bishopric founded in 1222 had its first seat at Muckairn, on the south shore of Loch Etive. It was the smallest of our Cathedrals, fifty-six feet long by thirty broad, "perhaps the humblest in Britain." It has no aisles, and seems to have had neither transepts nor nave.[4]

The "aisle-less choir" of DUNKELD Cathedral is used as the Parish Church, but, "although the piers of the nave seem Romanesque," it was not built till between 1318 and 1337,[5] long after the Culdees were superseded.

The Cathedral of St. Peter and St. Boniface at ROSEMARKY or Fortrose was the finest of the few northern Cathedrals of the

---

[1] Mr. Skene, Celtic Scotland II., 417.
[2] Principal Shairp, Sketches, p. 90.
[3] St. Giles, p. 62.
[4] Dr. Joseph Robertson, Abbeys, p. 78.
[5] Ibid., pp. 76, 77.

Decorated age. "The style is the purest and most elaborate Middle Pointed; and the whole Church, though probably not one hundred and twenty feet long, must have been a gem of the very first description."[1] But it was not built till the beginning of the fourteenth century, and the only remains of it are the south aisle and part of the chapter-house.[2]

At DORNOCH, Gilbert de Moravia, Archdeacon of Moray, became Bishop of Caithness and Sutherland in 1223, and is said to have built the Cathedral not only at his own cost but with his own hands. It was ruined by a clan feud, being given to the flames during a war between the Murrays and the Mackays in 1570. His Church survived to our time, though much decayed and partly ruined, and Dr. Joseph Robertson says that its restoration about 1837 was unhappily not entrusted to competent hands.[3] Bishop Gilbert's Cathedral was thus built after Culdee times.

At MONIFIETH the Culdee Monastery and Church were on or very near the site of the present Parish Church, which was built in 1812. The old pre-Reformation Church which had a crypt underneath it was cast down, as it was worn out, a few of the sculptured stones being afterwards recovered and preserved by the present minister, Rev. Dr. J. G. Young.

At IONA it were vain to look for the home of the Culdees as we have so little knowledge of them there. "The oldest structure in the island is St. Oran's Chapel, a small building of twenty-eight feet eight inches by fifteen feet ten inches, roofless and decaying. It has not an east window, and its great object of interest is the Romanesque circular-headed west door. It was probably built by Queen Margaret's liberality."[4]

Thus in these eight of the thirteen places there are either

---

[1] See Dr. Joseph Robertson, Abbeys, p. 74.
[2] Mr. Stephen, History, p. 272.
[3] Abbeys, pp. 93, 49.
[4] Dr. Reeves, Adamnan, p. 415.

only decaying ruins or no traces at all of the Churches of the Culdees.

The Round Towers of ABERNETHY and BRECHIN stand unique in their associations with the early Christian missions in our land. There is no question that such towers were built not as places of worship, for which they are quite unsuited, but to be a refuge for the clergy and a place of security for their sacred treasures against attacks by the Norsemen. At Abernethy some very primitive sculptured stones have been found in the churchyard near what is believed to be the foundation of a very ancient Church. Of the old buildings, however, nothing remains but the Tower. "The Cathedral at Brechin was built on the very old foundation of the Irish Church beside the Round Tower, but it dates from about the middle of the fourteenth century.[1]

At MUTHIL the Church is a recent one, but there remains a square belfry of three unequal storeys, in some of the upper windows of which there are traces of Norman or Romanesque architecture. The Cathedral at DUNBLANE has recently been most reverently restored. Its square tower is its oldest portion, and rises one hundred and twenty-eight feet high, the first four stages being Norman or Romanesque work of about the year 1140, its upper section being of later style. "The bishopric was restored by David I, and the tower would seem to have been built about that time."[2]

We can hardly include Iona among the Culdee homes, with the square tower of its Benedictine Abbey, but supposing we do so we reach in this little inquiry the unexpected result that our own tower, in its "lower part" at least, may be united in our thoughts with the earlier Irish Round Towers of Abernethy and Brechin, and with the probably contemporary Norman

---

[1] Mr. Stephen, History, p. 276.   [2] Dr. Joseph Robertson, Abbeys, p. 49.

square towers of Dunblane and Muthil, and with the tower at Iona, as lifting up our eyes to heaven, when we come here to worship God, and when we look at it while going about our common work—even as it pointed the Culdees of old to Him who has been our refuge from one generation to another—while our Church itself can have only one or two companion "Culdee" Churches in all our land, in which worship is now offered within walls that heard the praises of those who bore this distinctive name. Even if the Culdees, as it appears to some, were sent to Monymusk "by the Bishop of St. Andrews only towards the end of the eleventh century,"[1] say about 1080, "at which date, at all events, it was affiliated to the Church of St. Andrews, and partook of its discipline as an institution of Keledei,"[2] we hope to show that "portions" at least of the Church that was soon after built for them, remain, and that we are worshipping on the same spot as they, although ruin has unfortunately been the lot of nearly all the other "Culdee" Churches in our land.

In regard to the doctrine and worship of the Culdees, "there is no reason to suppose that they differed in any material point of faith, discipline, or ritual from the other clergy of the British Islands and Western Christendom. Their name was their only peculiarity."[3] "Nowhere is there the slightest foundation in any really authentic document for any supposed peculiarities of doctrine or of Church government"[4] in their system, as has been often imagined. We shall mention the different manuscript books that composed the little library at St. Serf's, which prove that in doctrine and ritual and manner of worship they differed in no way from the rest of the

[1] Dr. Joseph Robertson, Chambers' Ency.
[2] Dr. Reeves, Culdees, p. 173.
[3] Dr. Joseph Robertson, Chambers' Ency.
[4] Smith's Dictionary.

Christian Church, even the vestments they wore in service suiting the Augustinian monks who took their place. Mr. Stuart, in his preface to the " Book of Deer," says—" There is no reason for thinking that the Culdees differed in their doctrinal views from those which prevailed in the Church around them. At Monymusk it would seem that the old body made an attempt at self-reformation, and wished to be regarded as Canons without being subject to the ecclesiastical rule thus involved. The attempt indicates the strength of the current which had set in for the new institutions, and the slightness of the external difference which kept the bodies asunder." [1]

Since we have "record evidence" of only these thirteen Culdee homes in our country, it need hardly be mentioned that there were also a great many other religious houses throughout all the provinces that had nothing to do with the Culdees as a distinctively named body.[2] In our own district, for instance, to speak only of rural houses, there were never any Culdees at Deer, which was personally founded by St. Columba, or at Turriff, which was founded by St. Congan in the next century, both of which retained their ancient Celtic character unimpaired down to the time of David I who began to reign in 1124. Nor were there ever Culdees at Mortlach, another Columban house, founded by Moluoc of Lismore before 600. Monymusk was the only " Culdee home " of which we have any record between Monifieth near Dundee and Rosemarky on the other shore of the Moray Firth, and it is only when we remember that "the name Culdee became at length almost synonymous with that of secular Canon," [3] and also that the name "is said to have been given by the common people to priests of

[1] Book of Deer, p. cxxii.
[2] See Dr. Grub's History I., p. 243 ; Dr. Joseph Robertson's Abbeys, p. 28.
[3] Mr. Skene, History II., p. 277.

all kinds without discrimination,"[1] that we can account for their name being identified with the whole period in which their few homes are found, and for its being even trajected into a longer and more distant period during which they had no existence at all.

When we first meet with them in our own parish about 1130, the Culdees were already settled here and were receiving property as a monastic body. In our early writs the different grants of lands, &c., are made to the " Keledei serving God at the time, and who shall afterwards serve God in the Church of St. Mary at Monymusk," thus connecting them very specially with the Church which we shall find was used both for the parish and the priory. Although this dedication was unknown in Columba's time, it in no way proves that the settlement here was not of "Columban" origin, for the "Culdee" Churches at St. Andrews and Abernethy, both among the earliest centres of the Columban Church, came to have the same dedication.

"Whatever may have been their original institution and discipline, the Culdees in the time of David I (1124 to 1153) lived in a manner that must have been inconsistent with any monastic or collegiate discipline."[2] "The name came to signify not as at first special asceticism, but precisely the reverse."[3] "Married men were as eligible to be Culdees as single; and though they could not take with them their wives and children into their conventual residences, yet it would seem they returned to their families as soon as their period of service was over."[4] At least this seems to have been the case at St. Andrews, and an account shows it may have been the same at Dunkeld. The same is found at Durham and at Hexham on

1 Dr. Joseph Robertson, Stat. Ecc. Scot., p. ccxiv.
2 Mr. Cosmo Innes, Middle Ages, p. 111.
3 Smith's Dictionary.
4 Principal Shairp, Sketches, p. 59.

the Tyne, and also on the Continent about this time. The Canons at Winchester in the tenth century were married, and so too generally in Saxon England, and it was Margaret's adviser, Lanfranc, who completed the change there.[1]

"It was the fate of the ancient Columbite foundations in Scotland to fall before the reforming vehemence of David I, the most zealous of Romanists."[2] An active war was commenced in his reign against the Culdee homes, and every effort made either to transform them into Augustinian Canons, or to suppress them entirely. "Although there may have been here and there a few convents that maintained the older and stricter system of Columba, and though there certainly were solitary hermits of severe life scattered over the country, yet the general religious system was in its last decrepitude."[3]

We are thus brought to the period of the introduction of the monastic orders of the Church of Rome, which was connected with the revival of deep religious feeling in many parts of Europe, leading kings and nobles to found convents and endow them with lands, and build for their inmates beautiful edifices. "A powerful motive for liberality," as we shall find from our own writs, "was the reward which they believed this would secure for them; and benefactions were usually bestowed for the salvation of the souls of the donor, his parents and ancestors, his children and descendants, as well as for the glory of God and the honour of the blessed Virgin or of the saint to whom the house was dedicated."[4]

Thus the discipline and rule of the Church in our country became entirely changed. National peculiarities were abrogated, marriage of the clergy, secular and monastic, was

---

[1] Dr. Joseph Robertson, Stat. Ecc. Scot., pp. ccxviii, ccxix.
[2] Mr. Cosmo Innes, Reg. Epis. Aber., p. xi.
[3] Principal Shairp, Sketches, p. 60.
[4] Dr. Campbell, 'St. Giles',' p. 76, 77.

forbidden by decrees of the Council of 1139, and the authority of the Church of Rome became supreme. The close of the thirteenth century saw the suppression of the name and system of the Culdees. By 1245 the Culdees here have become Augustinian Canons, whose "discipline was less severe than that of monks properly so-called, but more rigid than that of the secular clergy,"[1] and henceforth the name Culdee is no longer known in our Priory or Church.

[1] Dr. Joseph Robertson, Chambers' Encyc.

CHAPTER IV.

MALCOLM III AND QUEEN MARGARET.

IN his preface to the "Book of Deer" Mr. Stuart[1] gives an account of the early population of our country separated into clans under the rule of the "Mormaer" (answering so far to our 'Earl'), with chiefs, &c., and shows that the patriarchal polity had not yet given way to the feudal kingdom. But "a great consolidation of the power of the supreme king, especially during the reigns of Malcolm II and his father Kenneth, took place by conquests over the provincial rulers," Malcolm II reigning from 1005 to 1034, the last and probably the greatest of the kings of the MacAlpine line. "This resulted not merely in the royal aggrandisement in a political view but in a great addition to the property of the king. When the importance of the supreme head came to be more prominent than at an earlier time and his power recognised, considerable portions of land in the newly annexed districts were reserved for the use of the Crown. It is thus that we can account for the numerous estates throughout Pictland held in demesne by the kings of Alba which appear in the records of later times, out of which they founded Monasteries and endowed Churches; *see as an instance the remarkable grant by Malcolm III of the lands of Keig and Monymusk to the Church of St. Andrews.*"

The occasion of this grant was Malcolm's passing on to the Spey to quell a rebellion in Morayshire. When encamped at Monymusk he inquired whether there were any lands in the district belonging to the Crown, and was informed by his

[1] Book of Deer, pp. lxxv, lxxvi.

Treasurer that he was encamped on such. He then vowed that if his expedition were successful, he would in gratitude bestow the lands on the Church. The Record of the gift is of later date, but "it is certain," says Mr. Skene,[1] "that Malcolm Canmore did make an expedition against the race of Moray in 1078, from which he returned victorious." It is important to observe that the practice referred to explains how there came to be Crown lands in this distant part. With this gift in 1078 begins the known history of our district, connecting Keig and Monymusk from the first with St. Andrews, which was the only see then in the country and under which our Priory continued to the Reformation, although the see of Aberdeen was founded about 1139.

"The history of Scotland properly so-called begins with Malcolm Canmore,"[2] more than four hundred years after Columba's time. He is the Malcolm of Shakespeare's drama, the son of the gracious Duncan. He had to flee to England, and "grew up into manhood under Edward the Confessor's benign protection—standing before the Confessor's throne, consorting with the Confessor's knights, sitting at the Confessor's table."[3] He returned in time to avenge the death of his father, who had been murdered at Bothgowan, near Elgin. Macbeth had been Mormaer of Moray, and after slaying Duncan reigned over Alba for seventeen years. We have mentioned his gifts and Lady Macbeth's to the Culdees of St. Serf's. Afraid to fight at Dunsinane, he fled over the Mounth and across the Dee to Lumphanan, where he was slain 5th December 1056, "Macbeth's Cairn" still marking the spot, and his head was brought to Malcolm at Kincardine O'Neil. Malcolm's life was much occupied in wars with William the

[1] Celtic Scotland II., p. 389.
[2] Iona, p. 54.
[3] Palgrave's England and Normandy IV, p. 311.

Conqueror and William Rufus, and it was while engaged in one of these that he and his son Edward, his acknowledged heir, perished at the siege of Alnwick. "All through his life was a busy troublous one, sweetened only by the calm presence of his wife—for his country was seething with change. He was the last of the old order—the introducer of the Scoto-Saxon."[1]

"No other event was more momentous to Scotland than the coming of Margaret in 1068. It marks the beginning of a new era. For by her own life, and through her descendants who followed in her steps, she changed the whole future destiny of the land which adopted her."[2] Margaret—the Saxon but half-Norman princess,[3] the representative of Alfred the Great, grand-daughter of Edmund Ironside, niece of Edward the Confessor, sister of Edgar Atheling who was son and heir of the English King Edmund—fleeing from the wrath of William the Conqueror, became Malcolm's second wife "in the spring of 1069."[4] It was the Culdee Bishop at St. Andrews, the second Fothad, who performed the ceremony at Dunfermline, which was Malcolm's chief residence, and where "the crumbling moss-grown walls" of the fort to which he brought his bride are still to be seen.[5] She was then twenty-four, and she died when forty-seven. Malcolm, when himself an exile, had received much kindness from her uncle. Her coat of arms is displayed on the ceiling of the Cathedral in Old Aberdeen, and they are the arms of the Confessor, assigned to him years after he died, and they show how well her relationship to him was remembered. She is said to have been the most beautiful woman of her time; she was also of great beauty of character, uniting saintly piety with the domestic virtues, wise too in exercising "the arts of 'continental' civilisation which were

[1] Principal Shairp, Sketches, pp. 51-55.
[2] Ibid., p. 48.
[3] Dean Stanley, Lectures. p, 32.
[4] Mr. Skene, Celtic Scotland II, p. 344.
[5] Principal Shairp, Sketches, pp. 47-50.

Malcolm III and Queen Margaret. 63

then just taking root in England," her mother being Agatha of Hungary.[1] "Her portrait as it is drawn in the pages of Turgot, her friend and spiritual adviser, commends her to our admiration as one of the purest, the most humble and beneficent of women ; while, as a queen, she appears to have combined with her personal graces, admirable majesty of conduct and true love of her adopted country."[2] Such was her influence for good on King and Court, clergy and people, that "her memory is worthy of being associated in the heart of the Scottish people with that of Columba."[3] She often visited the hermits who were found in various parts of the country, and entreated their prayers. Lochleven is but a short distance from Dunfermline, and in the Register of the Priory of St. Andrews[4] there is preserved a record in which she is joined by name with her husband in a gift to St. Serf's:—"Malcolmus Rex et Margareta Regina Scocie contulerunt devote villam de Ballecristin Deo Omnipotenti et Keledeis de Lochleven cum eadem libertate ut prius"—"the 'villa' or village probably including the gift of the Church, as on similar occasions."[5]

Her illuminated Book of the Gospels, valued by her as the most precious of all her manuscripts, its case being adorned with gold and gems—a small volume of thirty-eight leaves of vellum, was once lost as they crossed a river, but was recovered, her biographer says miraculously. Strange to say, it has been preserved to this day, and was purchased for the Bodleian Library at Oxford for £6, having been sent without anyone's then knowing its value, in July 1887, from the Parish Library of the Village of Brent Ely in Suffolk, for public sale in London. A page of its illumination is given in Green's "History of

---

1 Dean Stanley, Lectures, p. 38.
2 Book of Deer, p. cxi.
3 Montalembert, p. 144.
4 P. 115.
5 See also Dr. Grub's His. I, pp. 190, 191 , Mr. Skene, Celtic Scot. II, pp. 344, 351.

England,"[1] and its genuineness is put beyond question by what is stated in a Latin poem of twenty-six hexameter lines written on an old fly-leaf, and coinciding with what Turgot says regarding its loss.

"The Church of St. Columba, sadly fallen from the days when it called forth the glowing praises of Bede, lived only as a barren and sapless branch in her time. Its chief temporal possessions had become the heritage of laymen. Its wealthier priests were an hereditary caste, living in ease and sloth, and transmitting their benefices to their children."[2] "The royal house into which she had married owed its origin to Crinan, the lay-abbot of Dunkeld and Dull (of whom we have spoken), and was enriched with other possessions of the Church, such as the Boar's Chase near St. Andrews, and one of her own sons, Ethelred, when only a boy succeeded to Crinan's lay-abbacy."[3] "Monasticism throughout Europe and in England had been quickened by a fresh revival, and she had become keenly alive to the new fervour."[4] By her piety, tact, and energy she was able to accomplish great changes. The Celtic Clergy met her in several Councils. Once in 1074 they listened during three days to her reasonings, which were translated out of her Saxon tongue by her husband, who could speak English, French, and Gaelic with equal ease—Gaelic being naturally the only language the Clergy could speak. The sacred observance of the Lord's Day had almost ceased, and it is to her that our land owes its restoration. One deeply-rooted feeling was a reverence filled with awe for the Sacrament of the Supper, growing to such a pitch that it had almost ceased to be celebrated or was celebrated without anyone's partaking of it. Combined with this there was "such a superstitious regard for the sanctity of Easter

---

[1] Vol. I, p. 356.
[2] Dr. Joseph Robertson, Abbeys, p. 25.
[3] Mr. Skene, Celtic Scot. II, p. 350.
[4] Principal Shairp, Sketches, pp. 61, 62.

that it was the practice not to partake of the Eucharist on that day."[1] Lanfranc, the great Lombard Archbishop of Canterbury, was Margaret's friend and adviser, as Anselm became of her sons. "He was more than her counsellor—he was her chosen spiritual father, and he claimed to be Primate not merely of all England but of all Britain."[2] He is said to have sent three of the Canterbury clergy to give her counsel in her resolution to reform the Celtic Church, and "it is strange to find him waging the same war against the vices of the Saxon clergy in England as she had to carry on against those of the Celtic clergy in Scotland."[3] The Church estates were recovered from their unauthorised owners in course of time, and were bestowed on the new Abbeys with their Canons Regular which her sons founded. Close beside the little "Culdee" Monastery at St. Andrews rose, as we have mentioned, the rich "Priory of Augustinian Canons," first endowed by Robert, Bishop of St. Andrews, about 1144. It was confirmed as the electoral Chapter of the bishopric by the Pope some three years after, and "soon took its place as the first in rank and wealth of the religious houses of Scotland, and its Prior with the ring and mitre and symbols of Episcopacy had (in James I's time) rank and place in Parliament above Abbots and all other Prelates of the Regular Clergy."[4] It was to this Priory at St. Andrews that the Priory of Monymusk became subordinate, and the Culdees here were in course of time transformed into a similar body of Augustinian Canons, as were likewise the Culdees of Abernethy on the Tay, and very specially those at St. Serf's on Lochleven—such Canons forming a class midway between the monks and the "Secular" Clergy who answered in a certain way to parochial clergy and were not bound by monastic vows.

[1] Dr. Joseph Robertson, Stat. Ecc. Scot., p. xxiii.
[2] Ibid., p. cccx.
[3] Principal Shairp, Sketches, p. 62.
[4] Reg. St. And. Priory, p. xiii.

It was Queen Margaret who also introduced "Romanesque" architecture into Scotland, a style that would have been called 'Saxon' in former times and 'Norman' some years ago,[1] and of which our Church bears traces.

She and Malcolm both died in November 1093, eight hundred years ago. In the same year died the second Fothad who had married them, the last Celtic Primate, the last native "Bishop of Alban," ruling from 1059 to 1093, and with him may be said to date the passing away of "the Celtic Church" in our land. His place remained empty for fourteen years, for it was a time of strife and transition. Then a line began bearing the title of "Bishops of St. Andrews," and Turgot, Margaret's biographer, who had been her friend and Chaplain, Prior of Durham, was selected first to bear the title. "The Scottish Church had hitherto owed nothing to the see of Rome, and had held little communication with it."[2] It now found a claim made by the see of York to supremacy over it which gave rise to much controversy.

Malcolm and Margaret had six sons and two daughters. One daughter, Maud, became the queen of Henry I of England in 1100. Her monument is still at Winchester:—"Maud the good Queen." The other, Mary, married Eustace, Count of Boulogne, who with his brother Godfrey was among the chiefs of the first Crusade, and their daughter Matilda became wife of Stephen, King of England. Three of Malcolm and Margaret's sons were successively kings of Scotland—'the meek Edgar' from 1097 to 1107, 'the fierce Alexander' from 1107 to 1124, and 'the saintly David' from 1124 to 1153. They continued the work she began, extinguishing the remaining Celtic peculiarities by introducing the system of parishes throughout the country as had already been done in England, founding new dioceses,

[1] Dr. Joseph Robertson, Abbeys, p. I.   [2] Mr. Stephen, History, p. 241.

bringing in the different monastic orders, absorbing the Culdees into the Roman system by changing them from Secular to Regular Canons, all leading to a more rapid yet less violent overthrow of the clan system both in Church and State than could have been otherwise anticipated.[1] "The Church which they thus erected was to all intents and purposes an English Church in place of the old Celtic Church,"[2] and "the Celtic Church that had grown from seed scattered by a handful of errant missionaries until it overshadowed the whole land, was now replaced by the Romanised Christianity brought from England by the Saxon Margaret and her three sons."[3]

[1] Mr. Skene, Celtic Scot.; Book of Deer, p. cxii.
[2] Dean Stanley, Lectures, p. 39.
[3] 'Saturday Review,' 29th June, 1878.

CHAPTER V.

THE BUILDING OF THE CHURCH AND PRIORY.

WHEN a Monastery was founded and placed under a Bishop, or counted a cell of another Monastery, it became a PRIORY; when it was independent, it was called an ABBEY, the Abbeys of the same order being subject to a Superior or Provincial. The Priory of Monymusk was under "The Priory of the Cathedral Church of St. Andrews," such Priory being founded by David I. and Robert, Bishop of St. Andrews, and being itself subject in a certain sense to the Bishop of St. Andrews. The other cells of the St. Andrews Priory were the Priories of St. Serf's on Lochleven, St. Mary's Portmoak in Kinross, and the Isle of May at the entrance of the Firth of Forth, about six miles off the coast of Fife, afterwards transferred to Pittenweem in Fife. The Priory here was thus the only distant one, the others being within easy reach of St. Andrews. In early times St. Andrews was the only see in the country. "The diocese extended from the English border almost to Aberdeen, but the possessions of its Priory went even beyond this ample diocese, and included property in land as well as tithes in the fastnesses of Mar, and beyond the Grampians,"[1] as our Priory was.

If Monymusk was a Columban or a somewhat later settlement, the stone Church and Monastery would doubtless be built on the same spot as the former wooden ones, and here both Church and Priory stood within a few yards of each other. Thus at Iona, "St. Oran's Chapel has this great interest that

[1] Reg. St. Andrews Priory, p. xiii.

in all probability it marks the site of the still humbler Church of wood and wattles in which Columba worshipped."[1]

Not a vestige of the Priory remains. We shall find that it was accidentally burned down a few years before the Reformation, and became ruinous. In 1211 it was enacted that it should consist, as was usual, of an oratory, a refectory or dining hall, and a common dormitory, and that it should not have a separate cemetery. We find also reference made in the writs to a chapter-house. Further details are wanting, but there is the impression of the common seal of the Monastery attached to a deed in Monymusk House, that has been engraved for our title-page. It shows four buildings branching out from a centre on which a spire is placed, the whole being in the form of a St. Andrew's Cross, but how far this represents the Monastery one cannot say. There would also be a Priory School, for every Monastery is said to have had a school, and of it there seems to remain a singular record in the now-forgotten name of a piece of ground in the village that once formed an endowment in connection with it. Dr. Joseph Robertson in his remarkable essay "On Scholastic Offices in the Scottish Church in the Twelfth and Thirteenth Centuries," writing of 'scolocs' or 'scholars' in the sense of 'ecclesiastical clerks,' says,[2] "It may have been its appropriation of old to the support of 'scolocs' that gave name to . . the 'Scollatis-land' at Monymusk in Mar, an early possession of the see of St. Andrews." He then gives two references to the "Inquisitiones Speciales" of Aberdeenshire :—

210. Oct. 31, 1628. Dom. Gul. Forbes de Monymusk . . in tenemento olim vocato Scollatis-land, olim vocato Forsythe's land in villa de Monymusk.

[1] Iona, pp. 85, 86.   [2] Spalding Club Misc. V. p. 67.

324. Dec. 15, 1654. Sir John Forbes of Monymusk. . . The tenement callit Scollatis-land, somtyme callit Forsyth's-land, in the toune of Monymusk.

In the "service" of Sir William Forbes as heir to his father, Sir John, Oct. 5, 1702, the same land is evidently referred to, although its meaning had been lost, *ll* being changed into *tf*, as "the tenement of land commonly called Scotfatis-land . . lying in the village of Monymusk."[1] Speaking of the early Columban Church, Mr. Stephen says that the 'senior' brothers, among other duties, "were engaged in teaching the students, the 'juniores' or 'scolocs,' who always formed a wing, and not the least important wing, of a Celtic Monastery."[2]

There would be also the sick-room, the kitchen, and the guest-hall with sleeping-rooms adjoining it. At St. Andrews the number of guests was limited to six, while a chaplain and two hospitallers attended the sick. We are told that there were two gardens, of which the schoolmaster's is one. Until lately it was unusually large, owing to its origin, and was secured to the teacher notwithstanding a lawsuit, the Court declaring that while there was then "a minimum" prescribed, there was no "maximum." There was also a croft equal to ten bolls sowing, as well as pasture for six horses and fifteen sheep. The buildings lay immediately within the entrance wicket-gate, in the plantation on the east side of the schoolmaster's garden.

A Church remains; everyone sees that it is an ancient building; what we have to do is not only to describe it, but to try to learn from its structure what may be its approximate date. Perhaps it may be gathered from the following statement that, as Mr. Walcott says,[3] 'portions' at least of the original

---

[1] Ant. A. and B. III. p. 504.
[2] History, p. 98.
[3] Ancient Church of Scotland, p. 26.

stone Church are still preserved, although the building is greatly altered, and that our Church bears 'traces,' to use Dr. Joseph Robertson's word, of being, in these 'portions,' one of the earliest sanctuaries in our country and one of the few Churches now remaining in which worship has never ceased being offered to God week by week, and the Sacraments administered, from the time the ancient Church was built, perhaps about seven hundred and fifty years ago, for as a whole it has never been in ruins. If so, its sacred associations may perhaps be further enhanced by the thought of there being some little probability that the stone Church, of which these 'portions' remain, may have taken the place of one or more oaken Churches, where worship may have been offered from a time perhaps not long after Columba's mission, now one thousand three hundred years ago. On ancient Churches there are never any dates engraved to record the time of their erection, nor are the names of founders or architects ever inscribed upon them, so that in the absence of rare historical evidence we have to gather an approximate date from various special indications in the buildings themselves.[1]

The Church being dedicated under the name of St. Mary, it is frequently called by this name in the writs that are preserved in the St. Andrews Register—"ecclesia beatæ Mariæ de Munimusc." It consists of a square western Tower, a Nave in which we now worship, and a Choir or Chancel, without any transepts. We shall find that the distinction between the Choir and the Nave was carefully observed in ancient times, the Choir, for instance, being specially mentioned in the record of the installation of one of the Priors.

The tower is said to have been about eight feet higher than at present. It is now fifty-one feet three inches high. About

[1] Dr. Joseph Robertson, Abbeys, p. 47.

seventy years ago it was lowered about fourteen feet owing to the top part's bulging outwards, and a slated spire was then erected, which became dangerous, and was taken down four years ago. The shape of the present coping is thought to be somewhat like the original. The west front of the tower measures twenty-two feet in width, and its south side nineteen feet at the ground, but the tower is contracted a little under the line of the roof of the Church in a way not unusual. Tradition says that Malcolm III, standing as in the middle of the floor, marked the four corners of the tower with a spear. Its sandstone edging-stones were probably brought all the distance from Kildrummy quarries, as no sandstone is found nearer. On the two sides of the west front these stones go up only a certain distance, twenty-five feet on the left-hand side, and eighteen feet six inches on the right-hand side. It is probably these twenty-five feet that some persons reckon the 'portion' that remains of the original tower. Some edges of the Church have ordinary stones, so that the sand-stone had evidently to be used sparingly. The granite used in the building is not the same as the common blocks in the fields or in recently-opened quarries. The tradition is that it was taken from Tombeg farm, and that the stones were passed from hand to hand down the hill, which seems very unlikely, and that the head-mason, as he looked back from the Tombeg hill on the finished tower, exclaimed that if he had received a few merks more he would have been properly paid. The mode of building, as seen both outside and inside, is primitive, the stones often not overlapping the joints in the successive courses, but depending for security rather on the great thickness of the walls and the strength of the mortar, which is said in some buildings to have been poured in molten, and which is often harder and more enduring than the stones themselves. Old narrow windows, with

The Building of the Church and Priory. 73

sandstone edgings, that have been built up, are still to be seen in the tower, but inside there is the usual wide bevel. Mr. Walcott says[1] "The original Church was erected by King Malcolm III . . in 1080, and was affiliated to St. Andrews. The Norman basement of the tower . . remains." The present bell, like some others in the district, as at Cluny Church, was made in Old Aberdeen, and bears the inscription "Ica Mowat me fecit vet. ABD 1748. In Usum Æcclesiæ de Moniemusk Sabbata pango funera plango" (I fix the Sabbaths, I bewail at funerals). This it has done for nearly a hundred and fifty years. The tower door is still called "The Civil door of the Church," reminding us of its being the door for the laity, the 'Cives,' in contrast with the Chancel Arch and the Priests' door. This is the reason too of there being no ornament on the Nave Arch. It is only recently that the vaulted ceiling and walls were plastered; formerly they were in the rough-built state, and in the floor beside the Nave Arch there is a stone with a mason's mark. Immediately inside the Nave on the right hand there is a small recess in the wall.

At one time there was a Priory Church dedicated to St. John the Evangelist.[2] This may have been the Oratory mentioned in the record of 1211, for from other writs it appears that the Church of the Monastery was the Chancel of the present Church, being close at hand. The walls of the Chancel were originally rather higher than at present, and marks of an old roof are visible on the gable of the Nave, as are also marks of a former roof of the Nave on the east front of the tower. By outside measurement, as it is at present, the whole eastern part, including the portion that has not a roof and that is the burial-place of the Grant family, is one foot longer than the

[1] Ancient Church of Scotland, p. 322.　　[2] Collns. A. and B. p. 171.

Nave, being about fifty-three feet three inches. One has difficulty in thinking that the original Chancel would be so very large, but we have to recollect that it was in reality the Church of the Priory. It will be mentioned presently that Mr. Muir of Leith gives as the dimensions of "the Chancel, somewhat curtailed, sixteen feet five inches long by fourteen feet nine inches wide." These are virtually the dimensions of the part that is now roofed and used as an entrance to the Church, and this would have given sufficient room for the Prior and his twelve associates. There is no tradition that the part without a roof was added in later times, and one of our oldest parishioners recollects that her parents used to speak of seeing the whole under one roof, and of there being access to the whole from the Nave. Although there appears to be some difference in the mode of building on the east side of the door in the north wall, the stones used are of a somewhat similar character to the others, while those in the modern addition to the Nave are quite different, except where old stones have been used. If the whole eastern part was actually the Chancel, it had been of an unusual size, for the number of square feet in the Nave and in such part is respectively about 963 and 820, the inside measurements of the original Nave being about 47 feet by $20\frac{1}{2}$ feet, while of the whole eastern part the inside measurements are about 53 feet by $15\frac{1}{2}$ feet. The clergy in the Priory and the parishioners worshipped together in one Church, but they were separated at the Chancel Arch, and in the Chancel there would be frequent worship every day, as the Canonical hours would be observed. We shall find that the parish had a separate vicar or parson to minister specially to it, for the Culdees were not parochial clergy and had no cure of souls, and in the decree of 1211 they were enjoined under the authority of the Pope to do nothing to the prejudice of the parish Church. The little door in the south wall of the Chancel, close to the Arch, is evidently recent, but it may have been simply enlarged at some time, in which case its ancient character has been obliterated. It is the same with all the windows of the Nave. If the whole eastern part formed the original Chancel, the door in the north wall was probably " the priests' door," giving them direct access from the Priory, which was separated from it by only a few yards obliquely across the present school play-ground.

This door has sandstone facings on the outside, and is not placed in the middle of the wall, but makes the east end five feet longer than the other part by outside measurement. On this wall there is no sign of any window, and the thick ivy on both the other walls makes examination difficult, and on the inside one cannot see any traces of windows. If the present division however shows the approximate size of the original Chancel, as Mr. Muir indicates, the Prior's seat would be placed at its east end beside the present window, and he would stand there with all the clergy on either hand, and when the Bishop of St. Andrews visited the Priory, as spoken of in the record of 1211, he would occupy this position, and administer the Communion.[1] If there was no east window in the Chancel, there would be an indication of great antiquity, as it was only afterwards that the east window became of so much importance in architecture. There is none in the Church of Birnie, or in St. Oran's Chapel at Iona, which was doubtless built by Queen Margaret's liberality.[2] In the absence of glazing, the narrow windows would be fitted with moveable frames, on which parchment or transparent skins would be stretched. At Birnie the lack in the original windows of any ancient groove for inserting glass is very noticeable.

[1] See Church of Birnie, pp. 26, 27, 28.   [2] Dr. Reeves, Adamnan, p. 415.

There are three Norman or Romanesque arches:—(1) the western tower door; (2) the Nave arch, which is plain because it admitted only the laity, and is now much decayed; and (3) the Chancel arch, which is more ornamental. As it requires one who is acquainted with the special terms in use, to describe these arches, we may quote the account of the architecture of the Church given in a small book that is one of the works placed by Dr. Joseph Robertson at the head of his celebrated article in the Quarterly Review of June, 1849, on "the Cathedrals and Abbeys of Scotland," which was published separately in 1891,—" Descriptive notices of some of the Ancient Parochial and Collegiate Churches of Scotland by J.S.M. [Mr. Muir of Leith] London, J. H. Parker, 1848.

"St. Mary's Monymusk. Orientation E.S.E. One of the few Norman examples among the inland parishes of Scotland between the Forth and Spey. Seems to belong to an early period, and consists of—

> A Chancel, somewhat curtailed, sixteen feet five inches long by fourteen feet nine inches wide;
>
> A Nave, forty-eight feet eight inches long by twenty feet seven inches wide;
>
> A square tower of three undivided stages, seventeen feet three inches long by fifteen feet one inch wide.

"Infringements and repairs have obliterated nearly all the details of the structure within and without. Both roofs are considerably underdrawn, walls of Chancel have lost two or three feet of their original height, and a large part of that on the north of the Nave is destroyed by an addition. On the West face of the tower under the belfry is a small blocked round-headed light, and below it a plain round-headed doorway with a trigonal hood carried immediately over the vousoirs and ending abruptly at the spring of the arch. Besides the

The Building of the Church and Priory. 77

belfry arch which is of two orders much wasted and partly blocked, the only feature in the interior is the Chancel Arch of two semi-circular orders, uniform on both sides, and singular perhaps in being without a hood. The exterior arch is moulded into a quarter hollow and a heavy three-quarter quirked edge-roll; the sub-arch is square-edged and quite plain. Respectively the jambs present the ordinary arrangement of three half-round bearing shafts, the middle one being of much larger size and placed in front to meet the projection of the soffit-rib. In the character of the abaci and capitals no peculiarity is observable, the under edges of the former are turned off by a broad chamfer, and the latter have their double escalloped faces divided, not by the usual channel, but by a conical-shaped roll, the base of which unites with and dies into the heavy annular neck-moulding under the cushion. The central shaft and capital in the north jamb are wanting; the bases are sunk in the flooring, and the crown of the external arch is concealed by the gallery. The depth of the two arches is two feet nine inches, and the width of the aperture between the responds is nine feet."

As regards the date of building, the examples of the earliest Church architecture in our country are mentioned in his essay by Dr. Joseph Robertson, who was the highest authority on this subject. He says that there was "perfect sameness of ecclesiastical architecture on both sides of the Tweed during the twelfth and thirteenth centuries, or throughout the epochs of the Norman or Romanesque and the Early English or First Pointed styles. During these ages cathedral and convent church and chapel rose everywhere in Scotland fashioned on English models, by English hands, and under English oversight. St. Margaret built a church at Dunfermline, the spot where her auspicious nuptials with the King of Albany were celebrated, but of her ancient Abbey Church there now remains nothing but the Romanesque nave, which was consecrated in 1150 [fifty-seven years after her death]. The little Romanesque Church and square tower at St. Andrews, which bear the name of St. Rule, have, so far as we know, no prototype in the south; but no one acquainted with the progress of architecture . . . will have much difficulty in identifying the building with the small 'basilica' reared by Bishop Robert, an English canon regular of the order of St Augustin, between the years 1127 and 1144." . . . "The conventual Churches of Kelso [begun in 1128] and of Jedburgh exist but in broken ruins; but enough of both is spared to show that they were noble examples of the more advanced Romanesque. [They were destroyed by the English soldiers of Henry VIII in 1544, 1545, along with others of our most beautiful Churches and Abbeys such as Melrose, Dryburgh, Coldingham, Newbattle, Holyrood, &c.] There are traces of Romanesque work in Dryburgh, in the tower at Dunblane, in Iona, Coldingham, MONYMUSK. . . The Romanesque had the same duration in Scotland as in England, except that in the north perhaps only one edifice—the Church built by St. Margaret at Dunfermline—arose before the year 1100. But the date was the same at which in both countries the style began to show that change of character which issued in the First Pointed. The transition appears in the Choir of the Cathedral of St. Andrews, which was founded in 1162."[1]

Thus Dr. Joseph Robertson joins our Church in one sentence with Dryburgh, Dunblane, Iona, and Coldingham, drawing his evidence from the building itself, without any reference to tradition. His reasoning may be expressed in a

[1] pp. 32-41.

few words:—St. Margaret built her own Church at Dunfermline, the nave of which is perhaps the only existing Church in our country that rose before 1100; of the Augustinian Priory of St. Andrews, to which our Priory was annexed, there remains the small Church of St. Rule's, with its square tower of Romanesque style like our own; it was built between 1127 and 1144; and the transition to the next style, the First Pointed, is seen in the Chancel of the Cathedral that stands beside it, and that was founded in 1162.

Does it not seem probable then that if our Church, being under the St. Andrews Priory, had been built after 1162, it would have borne 'traces' of the later and finer style of the Cathedral rather than of the old Church and tower whose style was being discarded, and which was small compared with 'the vast adjacent pile, the grandest of all our Cathedrals'? and does it not seem natural that, though St. Rule's Tower is twice the height of ours, yet being the mother-church of our Priory, ours should be of a somewhat similar character? and may we not, with some show of reason, infer that though the building here was on a humble scale compared with it, yet 'portions' at least of our Church and tower may have been built before 1162, the date of the next style, as shown in St. Andrews Cathedral, and that through these 'portions' it has 'traces' of being among the oldest Churches in our country, and one of the few Churches remaining in it in which worship has been offered in an unbroken line of more than seven hundred years? In addition to this evidence from the building itself we shall find that in the record of 1211 the Bishop of St. Andrews is called the founder of the Priory, and also that a gift of land was made to the Culdees here by the same Bishop Robert who built St. Rule's Church and tower. Now the Romanesque style, introduced by Queen Margaret, was followed for only about sixty years, so that any clergy here, though their successors came to be the architects and builders of their times, must have been unskilled in a style so foreign to the country and so new to them, as the Romanesque, and thus either clergy, or master builders, or skilled workmen, however few, who had been employed at St. Rule's Tower, or perhaps even at Dunfermline Abbey Church, may have had to come to this distant place to instruct the local builders and, to use Dr. Joseph Robertson's illustration,[1] is there any "violence in the conjecture that the same head may have planned or the same hands have hewn" parts of all three? Some of these builders may perhaps have been unaccustomed to hew shafts and arches and corner stones in our obdurate granite, different tools being still required, and may have had to send to Kildrummy for the freestone. At a time when roads were unknown as we have them, and when oxen were employed for dragging burdens along the rough tracks or for bearing them on their backs, how earnest must these men have been in beautifying the House of God when they brought its ornamental stones from so distant a quarry! "It is believed," says Dr. Campbell of Balmerino, "that those magnificent structures, whose ruins now cover the land and excite so much regret in the mind of every lover of art, were the work of Freemasons, who according to the best established accounts, originated in the middle ages, and travelled about from one country to another as their services were required. This opinion is strengthened by the fact that many and even close resemblances can be traced both in the plans and minute details of structures remote from each other. Wherever an Abbey or Cathedral was to be erected, a lodge of Freemasons, governed by their own laws and enjoying important privileges, settled in

[1] Abbeys, p. 33.

the neighbourhood. The designers of those splendid buildings were however generally the monks and churchmen themselves, who were devoted to the study of Architecture as well as the various arts connected with the ornamentation of Churches."[1]

There is one parish Church not mentioned by Dr. Joseph Robertson, that of Birnie, within three miles of Elgin, a district abounding in the finest sandstone. It has a beautiful round Chancel Arch closely resembling ours, with very similar capitals, but it is in much finer preservation. It is claimed for it that it was built not later than 1140. It has been recently repaired, and worship in it has never been interrupted. It has not a tower, but consists simply of a Nave forty-one feet by eighteen feet, and a Chancel sixteen feet by thirteen feet— almost the size Mr. Muir gives for our Chancel, though he adds "somewhat curtailed." In the Chancel at Birnie there is no window in the east end which "suggests the early basilican Churches of Italy, and points to a time before the east window became a special effort in architecture." The "Priests' door" in it is on the south side, there being no special reason for its being on the north side, as facility of access from the Priory might make it natural here.[2]

Of the clergy of the twelfth century, Dr. Joseph Robertson says, "They were the schoolmasters, the statesmen, the lawyers, the bankers, the engineers, the artists, the builders, the glaziers, the agriculturists, and the gardeners of the age."[3]

When thinking of the order of worship in the Church after Queen Margaret's time, we have to remember that "of the Scottish Bishoprics all, save three or four, were founded or

[1] Balmerino, pp. 51, 52; referring to Wilson's Prehistoric Annals, p. 639; Tytler's History of Scotland, Chap. VI.
[2] The Parish Church of Birnie, 1891, p. 12.
[3] Chambers' Encyc. David I.

restored by her son David I (1124-1153), and that their Cathedral constitutions were formally copied from English models. So too St. Oswald's at Nosthill, near Pontefract, in Yorkshire, was the parent of Scone, and through it of St. Andrews and Holyrood." The "Use of Sarum" (Salisbury) arranged by Bishop Osmund in 1076, and completed in 1085, "obtained generally throughout Scotland,"[1] as well as in England, Wales, and Ireland. Every vestige of the old Celtic Church individuality was swept away. "The service books, vestments, services, and festivals, were now all in accordance with the Roman order. All through the mediæval period Scotland was entirely dependent on England, and perhaps to a slight degree on Ireland for its service books, especially on Sarum, whose Breviary and Missal were in all but universal use." Unfortunately, "the Church services, which enshrined what were at once the warmest, tenderest, and most devout affections and aspirations of the human heart, were all embodied in Latin, which was entirely unknown to the people."[2] In our Collection of Hymns, No. 91, "Come, Holy Ghost" (which we also sing to an ancient tune), No. 170, "Jesus, the very thought of Thee," which is given in another translation in No. 190, "Jesus, Thou joy of loving hearts," and No. 283, "Now that the daylight fills the sky," are taken from Latin hymns in the Sarum Use. Mr. Moorsom in his "Companion to Hymns Ancient and Modern,"[3] gives a list of those to be found there. The hymns were sung or chanted in Latin by the priests and trained choirs.

In addition to the Church, there was an Oratory or little Chapel for the Prior, also called St. Mary's, on Balvack, a

[1] Dr. Joseph Robertson, Abbeys, p. 27.   [3] p. 187.
[2] Mr. Lippe, Wodrow, pp. xx-xxii.

farm that we find belonged afterwards to the parson of the parish; another near Todlochy, about two miles westward from the Church;[1] and a third on the other side of the Don near Abersnithock, now Braehead farm, the little spot close to Lord Cullen's being still enclosed with its beeches, which was dedicated to St. Ffinan. This is of great interest, for the name of this Welsh saint, who came from St. Asaph to help in spreading the Gospel in this distant district, survives among us in the name of a whole parish, 'Llanffinan,' now spelled Lumphanan. If he did not himself preach the Gospel in our own parish, which he may have done, his name was held in reverence by the early clergy here, who dedicated this Oratory to God under his name. Professor Rhys of Oxford says[2]— "When Columba was busy among the Picts on the Tay, his contemporary and friend Kentigern" [St. Mungo, the founder of the see of Glasgow, the founder also of the see of St. Asaph in Wales; it is recorded that he and Columba met once in conference at Glasgow.] "appears to have gone on a mission beyond the Mounth" [the Grampians on the south side of the Dee. Mungo had been forced to flee to Wales for refuge. As he went south he preached in the district round Carlisle, where the Church of Crossthwaite at Keswick, and no fewer than eight others are dedicated under his name. When he was recalled to Glasgow in 573 or 574 by the new king, who was a Christian, he is said to have brought with him from Wales a little army of missionaries numbering no fewer than 665;] "and," continues Mr. Rhys, "that Welsh missionaries had carried on work of a lasting nature among the Transmontane Picts is proved by a group of dedications in the upper Valley of the Dee, among which are found Kentigern's own name and that of Ffinan, whose Church in Anglesey is called Llanffinan,

[1] Colln. A. and B. p. 585.   [2] Celtic Britain, pp. 172, 173.

while that of his in Scotland gives its name to Lumphanan, a place of some note in Pictish history," Macbeth being killed there by Macduff.

There is another striking coincidence. Glengairden on Deeside was dedicated to Kentigern, Migvie as well as Lumphanan to St. Ffinan, and Midmar to St. Ninan, a disciple, some say a cousin of Kentigern's. Strange to say, adjoining Llanffinan in Anglesey is Llaninan, so that two Welsh saints, Ffinan and Ninan, fellow-workers with St. Mungo, have left their names associated with two adjacent parishes in such far-separated parts as Anglesey in Wales and the Presbytery of Kincardine O'Neil in Aberdeenshire, while one of them is also commemorated in our own parish. So laborious was Kentigern in his preaching, and so long remembered that there used to be a proverb in our district, " Like St. Mungo's work, which was never done "—the type of an endless task.

A sculptured stone was found some years ago in a field on the farm of Nether Mains, about a mile from the Church. It bears the figure of a Celtic Cross—the four parts of which are nearly equal in size, with an interlaced projection for the shaft at the foot. Below the cross is a figure that seems to resemble an open box with a kind of hinge on which it may be turned round so as to close the two parts, and having at the other end an ornamental holder by which it may be suspended. This may be meant to represent a box in which might be carried some relic or sacred treasure. Beneath this is a circular figure within which there is what looks like a flower, and on the right and left of the circle are two small rings. An engraving of the stone is given in the Spalding Club volume, "The Sculptured Stones of Scotland," plate VIII.

The sculptor of the Cross may have lived earlier than the foundation of the Priory, and it may have been placed at the

distance we have mentioned from "an oaken Church with its thatch of reeds" to indicate the privilege of sanctuary or for some sacred purpose, or perhaps "to mark, as was customary, the boundaries of lands."[1] There is no tradition of there having been any right of sanctuary attached to our Monastery— a right that did not come to a religious house as a matter of

[1] Dr. Campbell, Balmerino, p. 83.

course, but that had to be regularly sanctioned. "It is not many years since the removal of the Crosses which guarded the sanctuary of Dull in Athol, that venerable Church which numbered St. Cuthbert among its disciples, the father of our kings among its abbots, and within whose precinct the regicide was safe. Four stones, each graven with a St. John's Cross, still stand at the four corners of the girth which surrounded the Church and preceptory of the Knights Hospitallers of St. John at Torpichen, near Bathgate, where the girth measured a mile on every side. Like the girths of Lesmahago, of Tain, of Dull, of Torpichen, the girth of St. John of Beverly was marked by crosses."[1]

[1] Dr. Joseph Robertson, Stat. Ecc. Scot. II. p. 262.

CHAPTER VI.

THE ENDOWMENTS OF THE PRIORY
AND
THE CHANGE FROM CULDEES TO CANONS REGULAR
AS RECOGNISED BY POPE INNOCENT IV.

1078 TO 1245.

IN considering the endowments of the Priory we have first to think of the large grant of land made by Malcolm III in 1078. Its record was originally inserted in the Register of St. Andrews, and has been taken "from a paper in the charter chest at Monymusk House, in the handwriting of the sixteenth century, collated with an older but less perfect copy in the charter chest at Whitehaugh."

The marches of the Episcopal lands of Keig and Monymusk granted to the Church of St. Andrew by Malcolm, King of Scots, as contained more fully in the charter above drawn up. Extracted from the Register of St. Andrews by Mr. Walter Bannantyn.

And the said King assigned to the said Church the said lands by the underwritten marches and caused them to be reduced to writing.

The first march begins at the brook which is called Toen [Ton], so called because a certain woman of the name of Toen [Ton] was submerged in that brook and drowned, and so as far as the brook called Kolcy and so by following from Kolcy as far as the river that is called Don, and so holding the Don as far as the rivulet towards the north that is called Fowlesy and so by following from the Fowlesy as far as Coritobrich, which is interpreted the valley of the fountain, and from Coritobrith to Lawchtendaff, which means in Latin, a place where a man was killed, to the turning point of the four royal roads, and so towards the east as far as the top of the mountain that is called Sclenemingorne, which is interpreted the haunt of goats, and so towards the east as far as the Standing Stones near Albaclanenauch, which means in Latin the field of sweet milk, and along the road as far as the top of the mountain that is between Keig and the Garioch, and so by dividing the separate hills into two parts as far as Benachie, namely one part to the property of the Garioch, and another to the property of Monymusk Likewise by dividing Benachie into one part to the property of Monymusk and another to the Garioch And from Benachie as far as Alde Clothi, which means in Latin the Rocky Rivulet, and from that place as far as Brecachath, which is interpreted a field marked by colours, on the right, and from Brecacath as far as the brook which is called Urcewy, and by following from the Urcewy as far as Cosalde and from Colsalde to the head of the wood which is called Trenechinen which means in Latin Wood extended straight, and towards the south as far as one fountain from which one rivulet flows which is called Dœli which means "Carbon" in Latin owing to its blackness, and so by following from Dœli as far as the river Don, and from the Don towards the south as far as the first march which began at the brook that is called Ton.

And such are the marches that King Malcolm left on account of the victory granted him, to God and the Church of the Blessed Mary of Monymusk, giving the blessing of God and S. Mary to all who preserve the rights of that Church.[1]

[1] Collns. A. and B. pp. 171, 172.

We have seen the importance that Mr. Stuart in the "Book of Deer" attaches to this grant. That the lands were given in possession to the Church is proved by all their subsequent history, but the copy of the deed necessarily belongs to a later date, for "we have no extant Scotch writing so early as the reign of Malcolm Canmore. The oldest Scotch writing extant is a charter of David I (1124 to 1153) to the monks of St. Cuthbert of Durham, which is kept in the treasury of Durham, and is in perfect preservation."[1] Dr. Reeves however says,[2] "The place in history held by Monymusk is due to its connection with St. Andrews, for as to the story of its foundation by Malcolm Cennmor, it rests upon the doubtful authority of a boundary charter, and the more questionable assertion of Hector Boece."

In a paper contributed in 1865 to the Proceedings of the Society of Antiquaries, Edinburgh,[3] the late Rev. Alexander Low, Minister of Keig, gave an account of the boundaries and localities mentioned in this charter as far as he was able to identify them. The lands are expressly called 'the Episcopal lands of Keig and Monymusk,' and are intersected by the Don. Beginning near the Mansion House of Whitehaugh the boundary seems to run to the top of Brindy Hill, then along the ridge of the Benachie range, turning downwards by Braco to the moss of Fetternear until it reaches the Don. At this point the charter mentions the name of Dœli, which is still the contracted form of Dalmadilly, near the Kemnay Quarries. Then the march is said to run by the burn of Ton which is the present boundary between Cluny and Monymusk, and passing Tillyfourie it goes by the burn of Banley, through part of Tough until it again touches the Don. The boundaries thus enclose a large part of the parish of Keig, parts of the parishes of Oyne

[1] Mr. Cosmo Innes, Middle Ages, pp. 78, 79. [3] Vol. VI. pp. 218-232.
[2] Dr. Reeves, Culdees, p. 253.

and of Chapel of Garioch, and perhaps of Kemnay, the whole of the parish of Monymusk, and a part of the parish of Tough. They form a four-sided figure, Mr. Low estimating the northern line to be about fourteen miles long and the western about twelve miles. The charter particularly names 'the Church of St. Mary of Monymusk,' so that it was already in existence, but it does not mention the Priory, which may not have been built at the time. The chief part of the rental of so large a district doubtless went direct to St. Andrews, but the farms of Abersnithock, now Braehead, Ramstone, Ardniedly, Balvack,[1] and Mains of Monymusk are afterwards specially mentioned as belonging to our Priory, and we shall also find a large number of farms in other parishes mentioned by name in a rent-roll at Castle Forbes, as belonging to the Priory down to the time of the Reformation.

This Priory having been placed under the Priory of St. Andrews, and perhaps emanating from it, had the advantage of having a number of its writs preserved as they would not otherwise have been, and in a way that leaves no question as to their genuineness. They are entered in the " Register of the Priory of the Cathedral Church of St. Andrews," which was printed in 1841 and presented by Mr. Tyndall Bruce to the Bannatyne Club. The original MS. is preserved in the Library of the Earl of Dalhousie (Lord Panmure) and was produced in court December 22nd, 1413, by the historian Andrew of Wynton, who was Prior of St. Serf's, in vindication of the rights of his house. " The declarations of title, and the controversies which grew out of the relations of Monymusk with the church of St. Andrews, rendered it a matter of importance to have its early muniments preserved, and accordingly a small collection of its charters was transferred into the Register of the Priory, where

[1] Collns. A. and B. p. 171.

The Chartulary of Monymusk. 91

they remain in a compact and separate group."[1] In his preface[2] Mr. Cosmo Innes says, " Only second in interest to the Hermits of Lochleven is the Priory of Monymusk, also an ancient seat of the Culdees, which likewise merged in our Priory of St. Andrews, and brought into its possession the fruits of the munificence of the old lords of Mar." The writs as well as other records have been printed under the different parishes with which they are connected, by Dr. Joseph Robertson in his "Collections on the Shires of Aberdeen and Banff," and his "Antiquities," for the Spalding Club. Abstracts are also given by Dr. Reeves in his work on the Culdees.[3] We shall try to translate them from the mediæval Latin and give them in historical order. They take us back to a period of which we know little, but as far as they go they bring us into the range of authentic history connected with our own parish.

The first is a grant by Gartenach, Earl of Buchan, whose date can be fixed as about 1120 or 1130, only forty or fifty years after Malcolm's great gift, his grandson Roger confirming it 'about 1170' (Dr. Reeves), ' probably before 1179 ' (Dr. Joseph Robertson).

Roger, Earl of Buchan . . let it be known that I have . . confirmed to the Culdees of Munimusc every year from Foedarg xx measures of barley grain, and x stones of cheese, and from Foleyt xx stones of cheese and iv measures of barley and a sheep (a wether), for perpetual charity, as Gartenach, my grandfather, gave the foresaid charity to them, and granted also that these amounts be brought to Munimusc by the feast of All Saints [say Nov. 1st]. In witness, &c.[4]

1 Dr. Reeves, Culdees, p. 253.
2 Reg. St. Andrews Priory, p. xvi.
3 Dr. Reeves, Culdees, pp. 253-259.
4 Reg. St. And. Priory, p. 370; Collns. A. & B. pp. 172, 173.

This is the first mention in history of the Culdees here, and they are simply called "the Culdees of Munimusc."[1] Dr. Reeves says,[2] "The opening document affords evidence of their existence about the year 1131." Earl Gartenach is otherwise known. A grant of lands for the consecration of a Church was made to the Monastery of Deer by "Gartnait," son of Cainnech, the mormaer, the date of which is the "eighth year of the reign of David I," 1131 or 1132, to which there were witnesses, Nectan, first Bishop of Aberdeen (1125 to 1154), Leot or Leod, Abbot of Brechin (a lay-abbot, for he and his grandson Dovenald, who was also abbot, alienated portions of the Church property there), Ruadri, mormaer of Mar (created first Earl of Mar by Alexander I, 1107-1124), Matadin the Brehon or Judge, Domongart, the 'ferleginn' (the man of learning, the reader, or scribe) of Turriff, and others.[3] This grant brings together the mormaers of Mar and Buchan, who doubtless owned between them a large part of Aberdeenshire, and here we have also the first historical notice of the Bishopric of Aberdeen. The Monasteries of Deer and Turriff are also here mentioned together, two very early Columban foundations, the scribe of the latter retaining his old Irish title. Gartnait, mormaer of Buchan, also appears in the foundation-charter of the Monastery of Scone about 1120 as 'Earl' Gartnait, and Ruadri, who in Gartnait's grant is styled mormaer of Mar, also appears in the same charter as 'Earl' Rotheri, just as in our deed Roger is called 'Earl' (Comes).[4] The name Gartnait had evidently been handed down for five hundred years in the family of the Celtic mormaers of Buchan, for a portion of land that Columba received from the Pictish ruler had as one of its boundaries 'the stone of the portion of Garnait's son.'[5]

[1] See Mr. Skene, Celt. Scot. II. p. 390.
[2] Culdees, p. 253.
[3] Book of Deer, pp. lv., cxxxiv.
[4] Book of Deer, p. lxxxii.
[5] Ibid., lxxxiii.

Earl Roger, Gartenach's grandson, who confirmed the grant to our Priory, was a Comyn or Cumin, representing through the female line the old Celtic chiefs of Buchan, but he himself was of Norman descent. In 1219 one Earl brought Cistercian monks from Kinloss (near Forres) to Deer, and it is the ruins of his Abbey that remain ; while in 1273, another Earl founded the almshouse at Turriff. After 1257, their party gained wide influence, there being thirty-two knights and three earls of the great race of Comyn. It was one of them, Sir John, the Red Comyn, that Bruce killed at the high altar of the Greyfriars Church at Dumfries in 1306. They paid a heavy penalty after the assertion of Scottish freedom, for the part they had taken against Bruce. They were Lords of Badenoch as well as Earls of Buchan, and they lost both. So wasted was the Earldom that soon there was no memorial left of it save "the orisons of the monks of Deer."

Two words used in this grant are of much interest. 'Cudri' is evidently a Latin form of the Celtic word given by Dr. Jamieson in his dictionary — "Chudreme, or cudreme, the designation of what is called a stone-weight." He quotes a charter of St. Andrews in which the word actually occurs in connection with cheese, viz., payments made by certain churches 'triginta panes decoctos, cum antiqua mensura farinæ ibi apposita, triginta caseos quorum quilibet facit chudreme.' The chudreme is said to be the Irish cudthrom (the 'th' being quiescent) which signifies weight. Clach-ar-cudrim means literally a stone-weight. David I. granted to the Monastery of Cambuskenneth 'viginti cudremos caseis' out of his rents at Stirling. The other word, "Multonem" is our familiar 'mutton' slightly disguised (multo, muto, and molto), and is of frequent occurrence in charters—strictly meaning a wether, though often used generally for sheep. 'Unum multonem' is a common grant in charters apparently, sometimes ' multones et agnelli.'

We shall find that the farms of Foedarg and Foleyt continued their payments to the Priory, but we are unable to say in what parish they lay. We learn afterwards that Wester-Fowlis, in Leochel, belonged to the Priory, and there may be a connection between it and Foleyt. One ancient name, however, of Fowlis was Fouellis.

The next endowment that we know of, was made by Bishop Turgot's successor, Robert, who was Bishop of St. Andrews for over thirty years, from 1127 to 1159. We learn of it from the "Agreement" of 1211 which shall be given afterwards.

> The foresaid Culdees shall henceforth possess for ever the half-ploughgate of land by name Eglismenythok which they have had by the gift of Robert, of good memory, Bishop of St. Andrews, as freely, fully, and quietly as they have possessed it from the time of the said Bishop Robert even to these times.[1]

The local denominations, a ploughgate of land etc., are very early indications of some general valuation of all the lands in the Kingdom.[2] A carucate of land was reckoned as much land as a plough could till in one year—equal to about one hundred and four acres, so that this grant would be about fifty acres Scots. "The Scotch plough of the thirteenth century was a ponderous machine drawn, when the team was complete, by twelve oxen."[3] 'A ploughgate of land' is the amount mentioned in the charter of the erection of the parish of Ednam, the first parish of whose endowment the record has been preserved. The Culdees were to hold the land 'freely, fully,' etc., for "rents, tributes, and customs were taken by the officials from those over whom they ruled and were inherent in the possession

---

[1] Reg. St. And. Priory, p. 369; Collns. A. and B. pp. 175, 176.
[2] Book of Deer, p. civ.
[3] Mr. Cosmo Innes, Middle Ages, p. 139.

of land, unless a special 'freedom' was conferred by competent authority."[1] We shall find frequent mention made of this farm. The late Rev. Dr. Taylor, minister of Leochel-Cushnie, was wont, we believe, to claim it for his parish, but Mr. Macdonald, author of "Place Names in Strathbogie," is inclined to think that it lay in our own parish and may have been near Abersnithock, now Braehead. The Priory did receive grants of land in Leochel, but it is difficult to see how the Bishop of St. Andrews possessed any lands there, as it was beyond the bounds of Malcolm III's gift. There is some confusion in Mr. Skene's remarks in connection with this name. "The possessions of the Culdees at Monymusk included those Northern Churches which were connected with the legend of St. Andrew, or were dedicated to him, as Kindrochet in Mar, Alford and Eglismenythok in Angus," and afterwards he says that within the parish of Monifieth "was the chapel of Eglismonichty, dedicated to St. Andrew.[2] But Alford was not in Angus, and it will be seen afterwards that though Eglismenythok may have originally owed its name to its being dedicated to a saint who is now quite unknown, it came to be simply the name of a farm.

Bishop Robert who made this grant has much interest centred round him in regard to the Culdees. He was an Englishman, a canon of St. Oswald's, near Pontefract, and became Prior of Scone in 1115. The Celtic Monastery there was of great antiquity, but Alexander I. changed it into an Abbey of Augustinian Canons whom he brought into Scotland for the first time from St. Oswald's. Robert became Bishop of St. Andrews in 1127, and in conjunction with David I. about 1144 reared the small 'basilica' and tower of St. Rule's for a Priory of Augustinian Canons whom he brought from his old home at Scone that they might supersede the Culdees, as we have

[1] Book of Deer, pp. lxxxvii, lxxxviii.   [2] Celtic Scotland II. pp. 390, 395.

mentioned before. We may, however, think of him chiefly in connection with St. Serf's. "The little Isle of St Servanus in Lochleven," says Mr. Cosmo Innes in his preface to the Register of St. Andrews Priory,[1] "contained one of the Culdee foundations that for centuries of darkness and violence kept alive the lamp of a civilising religion; and we are indignant when the Saintly David and his friend Bishop Robert expel them from their quiet dwelling to make room for the new churchmen. The Bishop is content to give to others their heritage, their Church vestments, and their little library of seventeen Christian books. But the King insults them in their distress." His charter is preserved in the original Latin, and a fac-simile of it is given in the Register. It is witnessed by Bishop Robert and by Andrew, first Bishop of Caithness, of whom Mr. Stephen says[2] that "he was a witness to so many charters in different parts of Scotland that he must have been a frequent absentee from his diocese."

David, King of Scots to the bishops, abbots, &c., greeting, know that I have granted and given to the canons of St. Andrews, the island of Lochleven, that they themselves may there institute the canonical order. And the Culdees who shall be found there, if they are willing to live as Regulars, may remain at peace with them and under them, but if any one of them is inclined to offer resistance to this I will and ordain that he be expelled from the island. Witnesses, &c., at Berwick.

Bishop Robert soon carried this into effect, and made the possessions of the Culdees into an endowment for the new Augustinian Canons. His writ is of unusual interest.[3] "Their little store of seventeen books was evidently thought of much

[1] p. xv.
[2] History, p. 273.
[3] Reg. St. Andrews Priory, p. 43.

importance, for the bishop distinguishes each of them separately. We have not many instances of books conveyed by charter, and we here learn what may have been some of the MS. books that were to be found in our own Priory at the time. Dr. Joseph Anderson[1] gives the catalogue of the Scottish MSS. in the library at St. Gall in Switzerland compiled about 829, containing about thirty-two treatises, "the earliest document from which the nature of the books in use in a Celtic Monastery may be inferred."

To all sons of holy mother Church, Robert by the grace of God, the lowly servant of the Church of St. Andrews greeting and episcopal benediction . . . Let all know . . . that we have given . . to the Church of St. Andrews and to Robert the Prior, the Abbey of the island of Lochleven [then he details its different Churches with their tithes, as was mentioned before] for instituting Canons Regular in the Abbey . . along with the Church vestments which the *Chelede* themselves possessed, and with the following books a *pastoral* (or ritual); a *gradual* (or antiphonary); a *missal* (or liturgy book—these three being used in the public service of the Monastery); an *Origo* (perhaps the popular Origo Mundi) or *Origines* (some of the writings of Origen); the *Sententiæ* of St. Bernard, whose title is given '*the Abbot of Clairvaux*,' a commentary on the famous collection of theological subtleties (he was probably still living, 1091-1153; he is called 'the holiest monk that ever lived,' and wrote the hymns, 'Jesus, the very thought of Thee,' 'Jesus, Thou joy of loving hearts'; perhaps this was their newest book); a treatise *on the sacraments* in three parts or staves; a Bible or *portion of a Bible*, doubtless the

---

[1] Scotland in Early Christian Times, pp. 155, 156.

Vulgate of St. Jerome; a *Lectionary*, perhaps a collection of the portions of St. Paul's Epistles used at the Mass, or a book of the Epistles and Gospels; *the Acts of the Apostles;* the *four Gospels* after the text of St. Prosper, or it may be the Gospels and *some work* of *Prosper* of Aquitane, a follower of St. Augustine; *three books of Solomon* (Proverbs, Ecclesiastes, and Canticles); *glosses*, or a commentary *on Solomon's Song*; a work called *Interpretations of phrases* or *words;* a *collection of* religious *maxims;* an *exposition of Genesis;* and *excerpts of ecclesiastical rules.*

Among the witnesses are Gregory, Bishop of Dunkeld, and William, Abbot de Sancta Cruce, *i.e.*, Holyrood, which was founded by David I., and begun to be built in 1128, for Augustinian Canons Regular, to whom he presented the famous crucifix, the Black Rood, that belonged to his mother, Queen Margaret, and that was supposed to enclose a part of the true Cross.

Dr. Reeves says[1] that "the character of the books is just what might be expected in a small monastic establishment of that date, and the ritual works are those which were in general use"; while Mr. Stuart says,[2] "These works were suitable for any religious community in Western Europe, and were accordingly transferred to the Canons Regular for their use, a tolerably sure token that the differences between the bodies were less doctrinal ones than on points of rule and discipline." Mr. Stephen also says,[3] "The titles of some of the books are the best corrective of the notion that the Culdees differed in any respect either as to faith or worship from the Catholic Church of their time. The library was probably more extensive,

---

[1] Culdees, p. 249.   [2] Book of Deer, p. cxxiii.   [3] History, p. 270.

as the Lochleven Culdees had been frequently favoured with royal gifts."

St. Serf was the teacher of St. Mungo and the companion of Palladius, who is said to have died at Fordoun in Kincardineshire. Culross on the Forth was his principal Church, where he died at an advanced age about the year 540.[1] St. Sair's Fair, held in Culsalmond, shows that his fame extended to our district; the Fair was formerly held at Monkegie, now Keithhall.

We do not know for what reason Bishop Robert treated our Priory so differently from St. Serf's, bestowing on it the halfcarucate of land at Eglismenythok; but this may have been simply owing to the distance from St. Andrews.

We now come to the large benefactions of the Earls of Mar. "The ancient district of Mar," says Dr. John Mackintosh,[2] "was very extensive. Commencing near Aberdeen, it extended to Badenoch, comprising almost the whole of the valleys of the Dee and Don and the territory lying between them. It seems probable that the whole of this district was under the 'Mormaer' of Mar—this Celtic title being superseded by that of 'Earl' in the reign of Alexander I., 1107-1124." The coat of arms of the old Earls is displayed on the ceiling of the Cathedral, Old Aberdeen.

Gilchrist, the third Earl, was one of the principal benefactors of our Priory, 1170-1204 (Dr. Joseph Robertson) or 1199-1207 (Dr. Reeves). One of his charters still remains.

[G. Earl] of Mar to all honourable men [both cleric] and lay greeting. Let all of you know that we have given, granted, and by this our charter confirmed to God and the

[1] Dr. Reeves, Culdees, p. 242. [2] Hist. of Valley of Dee, p. 211.

Church of S. Mary of Munimusc and the Culdees serving in the same . . the Church of Leochel with all its tithes, privileges, oblations, revenues (ovencionibus = obventionibus) and with that whole half dauach of land in which the Church is situated, free from every secular exaction and service, according to the tithes there are and other offerings of the altar, in pastures, meadows, woods, and waters for the mill, and with all its rights, as divided both by marches and common pasture for free and pure, quiet and perpetual charity, from me and my heirs and my successors for the salvation and prosperity of my Lord King William and his son, and his loved ones, and for myself and all my progenitors and heirs and successors favouring this my gift. Wherefore I wish and enjoin that the said Culdees hold and possess the said Church as freely as any canons or monks or any other religious men in the whole kingdom of Scotland hold . . any Church or charity through the gift of baron or earl, &c.[1]

In two confirmations made by John (formerly prior of Kelso),[2] Bishop of Aberdeen, 1199-1207, we have mention made of this gift and also of two other Churches presented by the same Earl. The first confirmation is of importance, and if it had given a little more information, would have had much historical value.

To all sons of holy mother Church, John by the grace of God, the lowly minister of the Church of Aberdeen, greeting and sincere love in the Lord. Let all both past and present know that we have granted and confirmed by this our charter that gift which G[ilchrist], Earl of Mar, gave to his own Monastery which he built at Munimusc in the Church of S. Mary, in which Culdees formerly were, namely,

[1] Reg. St. Andrews Priory, pp. 373, 374 ; [2] Reg. Episc. Aberdeen, pp. xix, xx.
Colln. A. and B. p. 602.

the Church of Leochel with its lands and pertinents, the Church of Ruthven with its lands and pertinents [sometimes called Logy-Rothven or Logie-Rothman, supposed to be Logy in Mar],[1] the Church of Invernochin with its lands and pertinents ["this grant does not seem to have taken effect"].[2] Wherefore we will and grant that the said Monastery and the Brethren serving God in the same hold . . the said Churches and all their other lands and gifts which the said Gilchrist bestowed on them. . . . We also will . . that the said Monastery and the Brethren dwelling there be subject to no house nor yield subjection to any one except ourselves, and yield like subjection to us and our successors as other houses of religion throughout the kingdom of Scotland arranged in dioceses, ought to yield to their own Bishop.[3]

The second is the confirmation of the gift of a fourth Church made by the same Earl.

To all sons of holy mother Church . . John by the grace of God . . know that we in addition to the presentation of Gilchrist, Earl of Mar, have given, granted, and by this our charter confirmed to the *canons* of Munimusc, serving God in the same, and to serve in perpetuity, the Church of Afford with the half dauach of land pertaining to that Church in which the Church is situated, and with the tithes and oblations and all other rights pertaining to the said Church . . for perpetual charity. . . Wherefore we will that the said 'Canons' hold the said Church with all its pertinents as freely, &c., as any other Church is held by any religious men in our whole diocese, &c.[4]

[1] Colln. A. and B. p. 217.
[2] Antiq. A. and B. IV. 467.
[3] Reg. St. Andrews Priory, pp. 374, 375; Collns. A. and B. p. 173.
[4] Ibid., p. 375; Ibid., p. 588.

A further gift of Earl Gilchrist's is mentioned in the Agreement of 1211, of which we shall learn particulars afterwards. It contains the clause,

The lands that the same Culdees received by the gift of Gilchrist Earl of Mar without the consent of the said Bishop—namely Dolbethok and Fornathy.[1]

There are other writs making mention of the Churches— St. Andrews of Alford, St. Woloc of Ruthven, Invernochty in Strathdon, St. Mary of Nemoth, and especially St. Marnan of Leochel. St. Marnan's death is given as in 635, and "his stone-chair still looks down upon the Church which bears his name at Aberchirder,"[2] in Banff, while "the mainland abode of St. Woloc, a bishop of St. Columba's time is described in the Aberdeen Breviary as a mere wattle hut,"[3] 'casam calamis viminibusque contextam,' and his "baths are still to be seen beside his ruined Church in Strathdeveron."[4] "His well in the parish of Glass near Huntly was till lately resorted to as a place of pilgrimage,"[5] and there is still a burial ground at 'Wallakirk,' with the foundations of a Church, near Beldornie Castle.[6]

King William the Lion, who is mentioned in the first of Earl Gilchrist's writs was the grandson of David I., and reigned from 1165 to 1214. His reign was a long one of almost fifty years, and it was owing to an appointment he made to the Bishopric of St. Andrews that our country was made to feel for the first time, by the terrors of excommunication and interdict, what it was to be under the Roman obedience. The Pope, Alexander, whom he defied by his choice of a bishop, was the same that had humbled the great Emperor Frederick

---

[1] Reg St. And. Priory, pp. 370-372 ; Collns. A. and B. p. 176.
[2] Dr. J. Robertson, Abbeys, p, 19.
[3] Ibid., p. 16.
[4] Dr. J. Robertson, Abbeys, p. 19.
[5] Dr. J. Anderson, Scot. in Early Chris. Times, p. 194.
[6] Mr. Macdonald, Place Names, p. 113.

Barbarossa. "Churches were closed, sacraments were forbidden, even the dead were buried without religious rites, and marriages were celebrated among the graves of the churchyard."[1]

These confirmations were doubtless made by the Bishop of Aberdeen, because the various Churches were under his jurisdiction, and it is clear that the subjection of this Priory to the Bishop of St. Andrews "did not infer any breach of diocesan privileges, and we may readily believe that these were as yet too undetermined, and the old feelings of personal connection too common to render" the continuance of "such an arrangement in any way unsuitable,"[2] and yet the Bishop seems to express a certain degree of soreness in regard to this matter when he says—"We also will that the said Monastery and the Brethren dwelling there shall be subject to no house nor yield subjection to any one except ourselves." But his gentle protest was unavailing, for we shall see how completely our Priory continued subject to the Bishop of St. Andrews.

It is singular to find in so early a deed the Bishop of Aberdeen dropping the name 'Culdees,' and twice calling the clergy here by the title of 'Canons,' and this is probably the explanation of the word 'formerly' in the first confirmation, when he says, 'in the Church of St. Mary in which Culdees formerly were.' Even in his time, the name seems to have had an antique sound, and the clergy here were being recognised as Canons as if in natural course. The name Culdee is already dying out.

The Bishop's words are specially to be noted when he says that 'Earl Gilchrist made the gift to his own Monastery which he built at Munimusc in the Church of St. Mary.' It is as if

[1] Mr. Stephen, History, pp. 335, 336.   [2] Book of Deer, p. ciii.

Earl Gilchrist were the builder of the Priory, and as if our Church had been in existence before the Monastery was founded, and had Culdees previously attached to it.[1] How far these statements are to be pressed one cannot say. We must simply take them as they stand, and regret that we have not a little fuller information. They would fix the date of the Priory between 1170 and 1204, while they also imply that our Church was of earlier date than the Priory.

In connection with this it has to be mentioned that Kildrummy Castle was or became the principal seat of the Earls of Mar. We do not know whether there was a more ancient castle than the present one that is now in ruins, and that is called "the noblest of northern castles."[2] The 'snow-tower,' its oldest portion, is said to have been built by William the Lion, of whom we have spoken, in 1172, the very date that is before us, while the extent of the building and the fineness of the workmanship lead to the belief that the "castle was built by foreign masons, who were brought over to assist in the erection of some of our finest buildings."[3] It is built of freestone, and the freestone used in the arches and edging stones of our Church probably came from the quarries there.

In the writs we have frequent mention made of the half-dauach of land in which a Church is built. "This seems to have been the accustomed measure of the Church-land, settled long before existing records, in the dioceses of Moray and Aberdeen."[4] "Dabhach (davach), a measure of land, is originally a measure of capacity, and was applied to denote the extent of land which required a *davoch* of corn to sow it."[5]

The gift of the tithes or teinds, along with the Churches, is to be specially observed, as uniformly bestowed at this early

---
[1] See also Mr. Skene, Celtic Scot. II, p. 390.
[2] Mr. Cosmo Innes, Sketches, p. 79.
[3] Rev. Dr. Milne, Kildrummy Castle, p. 7.
[4] Mr. Cosmo Innes, Sketches, p. 7.
[5] Sir Herbert Maxwell, Scot. Land-Names, p. 165.

time—seven hundred years ago. They were given as a matter quite understood, and not needing to be explained or enforced. Such writs prove how completely tithes originated in private beneficence, and that they were never a tax imposed by the State in support of the Church. They are to be looked upon as the inheritance of the parishioners, that the poorest may receive as their own the ministrations of the Gospel without price.

We shall find other two churches afterwards given to the Priory, while "Danachudor" in the Deanery of Mar and "Kyndor," in that of Buchan, are also mentioned as being at some time under the patronage of the Priory.[1]

In the grant of these Churches with their tithes, lands, and offerings there is "the meeting of the old monastic system with the Latin system when parishes were erected."[2] Parochial Churches in the proper sense, mainly supported by tithes drawn from the district which they supply, were almost unknown till about the commencement of the twelfth century. Ednam, near Kelso, is the first parish of whose formation we possess a distinct record, the Church being built and endowed with 'one plough of land,' and then receiving the tithes of the Manor, in the time of King Edgar, 1097-1107. "In the old rent-roll of the Church of Glasgow there were Churches as well as lands mentioned, though nothing approaching to the parochial divisions."[3] "The ecclesiastical system which obtained in Scotland before the reformation of St. Margaret and her sons, was monastic, not parochial. This was gradually displaced by the parochial system as the Anglo-Norman colonisation of the country advanced."[4]

The gift of these Churches to our small Priory is a sample

[1] Mr. Walcott, Ancient Church, p. 114.
[2] Dr. Davidson, Inverurie, p. 18.
[3] Mr. Cosmo Innes, Sketches, p. 6.
[4] Dr. J. Robertson, Abbeys, pp. 27, 29.

of what has been described as the "curse of impropriations" that came to lie so heavy on our country.[1] "The monasteries became indeed and continued for some ages the centres and sources of religion and letters, the schools of civil life in a rough time, the teachers of industry and the arts of peace among men who . . used to be roused only by the sound of arms. But even the advantages conferred by them were of small account in contrast with the mischief of humbling the parish clergy. The little village Church . . was left in the hands of a stipendiary vicar, an underling of the great Monastery, ground down to the lowest stipend that would support life."[2] "As early as our records reach, it had become the custom for the patron of the Churches, with the consent of the Bishop, to confer them in property upon the great monasteries and religious houses of Regulars. Thus Paisley had its thirty parish churches, Holyrood twenty-seven, Melrose and Kelso each as many, and to such an extent did this prevail that in some districts two-thirds of the parish Churches were in the hands of the monks."[3] "In the reign of William the Lion, no fewer than thirty-three parish Churches were bestowed on the recently founded Abbey of Arbroath."[4] The earliest record that exists of this custom is in the gift by the Celtic bishops of the three Churches to the Culdee Abbey of St. Serf's in Lochleven. It is reckoned that at the Reformation seven hundred parishes were served by vicars, the greater tithes of corn, etc., going to the monks and bishops, while the vicar who performed the parochial duties got only the lesser tithes.

To return to Earl Gilchrist—he is found in records throughout the greater part of the reign of King William the Lion, from 1178-80 to 1204-11.[5] He witnesses King William's gift to

[1] Dr. J. Robertson, Abbeys, p. 84.
[2] Mr. Cosmo Innes, Sketches, p. 19.
[3] Mr. Cosmo Innes, Middle Ages, p. 132.
[4] Dr. Campbell, Balmerino, p. 67.
[5] Ant. A. and B. IV. p. 693.

the Abbey of Arbroath of the Brecbannach and the lands of Forglen. He himself receives a charter from David, William's brother, giving him as serfs "Gillechrist son of Gillekucongal, and two Gillecrists and Gillen and Gillemar his four sons."[1] In the St. Andrews Register we find "serfs conveyed, as was customary, as a pertinent of the land and sometimes given away without the land,"[2] and it records the indenture of one given to Earl Gilchrist's brother.[3] So too in England "the Bodmin Book of the Gospels records the manumissions of the serfs which the bishops were successfully urging upon the Lords down in Cornwall early in the tenth century."[4] Dr. Joseph Robertson says[5]—" In the old laws regarding serfs and the numerous conveyances of them, preserved in the chartularies of an early date, we can trace no admission or claim of right raising any class of them above the rank of absolute serfs." They were the labourers employed not only in tilling their masters' fields but also in building their castles, and doubtless also their churches.[6]

We have found the Bishop of Aberdeen confirming Earl Gilchrist's gifts to our Priory. We now come to a higher confirmation in a Bull of Innocent III's between 1199 and 1216.

Innocent, etc. The Apostolic see is wont to agree to the pious wishes and honourable prayers of those who petition that a benevolent favour be granted them Wherefore beloved sons in the Lord, yielding to your just requests with pleased assent, we take under the protection of the Blessed Peter and ourselves, your place and the persons serving the Lord in it, with all the goods both ecclesiastical and secular which at present it rightly possesses or in future shall be

1 Ant. A. and B. IV. pp. 693, 694.
2 p. xvii.
3 p. xxxvi.
4 Archbishop of Canterbury, Fishers of Men, p. 81.
5 Abbeys, p. 9.
6 See also Mr. Cosmo Innes, Sketches, p. 98; Dr. Campbell, Balmerino, p. 28.

able to obtain by just means by the gift of the Lord—but specially the privileges and former liberties from the exactions of tithes and of the charges of Bishops and their officials And we confirm to you by Apostolic authority and secure to you by the title of this present writing all lands possessions and other goods granted by that noble man Gilchrist Earl of Mar as a charity to your house, and the Churches of St. Andrew of Alford, St. Marnoc of Leochel and St. Mary of Nemoth with all the lands and pertinents of the same as you rightly and peaceably possess them all And in testimony of this protection derived from the Apostolic see you shall pay to us and to our successors every year *two shillings* sterling Let no one therefore . . Given at Viterbium 20th June.[1]

It was this Pope who excommunicated John of England, and with whom John then, two years before Magna Charta was signed in 1215, agreed to hold England as a fief of the papacy, and to pay the Pope a thousand marks a year as an acknowledgment of his position. We see how universal the Roman rule had become by this time in our country, when a small Priory like ours places itself under the protection of the Pope.

Up to this time the Culdees here have been favoured with gifts and protected, but 'the storm soon after burst upon them.' In 1211 a complaint was laid before the Pope regarding them by the Bishop of St. Andrews, who was displeased at some efforts they were making of their own accord to bring themselves into harmony with advancing changes in the constitution of Monasteries.[2] Pope Innocent III issued a Commission dated from Rome, 23rd Mch., 1211, the Commissioners being Adam,

[1] Reg. St. And. Priory, p. 375, 376; Colln. A. and B. pp. 173, 174.
[2] Mr. Skene, Celtic Scotland, II. p. 390.

Abbot of Melrose, who afterwards became Bishop of Caithness, and was killed in 1222 owing to his too rigorous exaction of tithes,[1] William, Abbot of Dryburgh, and Robert, Archdeacon of Glasgow, who afterwards visited Rome, and dying in London on his return, was buried in St. Paul's.[2] "Two ancient copies of this valuable record are preserved, one in the Register of St. Andrews Priory, the other in the Register of the Bishopric of Aberdeen, the title of which is curious as showing the use of the word *Kildey* in the fourteenth century."[3] "This settlement also illustrates the much disputed constitution of the Culdees and incidentally evidences some ancient church dues, the nature of which, and the very etymology of whose names have been lost. The copy in the Register of St. Andrews Priory is much the older of the two."[4]

Adam Abbot of Melrose and William Abbot of Dryburgh and Robert Archdeacon of Glasgow to all who shall see or hear of this letter Eternal greeting in the Lord We have received a letter of our Lord Pope Innocent III to this effect INNOCENT Bishop servant of the servants of God to our beloved sons the Abbots of Melrose and Dryburgh of the diocese of St Andrews and that of Glasgow and to the Archdeacon of Glasgow greeting and apostolical benediction We have received a complaint from our venerable brother the Bishop of St Andrews that certain Keledei [Kildei *Reg. Abdn.*] who profess to be Canons and certain others of the diocese of Aberdeen in the village of Munimusc which pertains to him do not fear to establish a certain Regular Canonry [Canonicam *Reg. St. Andr.* canoniam *Reg. Abdn.*] contrary to justice in opposition to him to the prejudice and hurt of their Church Wherefore we entrust to your discretion

[1] Mr. Cosmo Innes, Sketches, p. 77; Mr. Stephen, History, p. 351.
[2] Mr. Walcott, Ancient Church, p. 191.
[3] Dr. Reeves, Culdees, p. 255.
[4] Reg. Episc. Abdn, I. p. lxxx.

by our Apostolical writing that parties being convoked and what is put forward on either side having been heard you determine what has been canonical an appeal being reserved [or (?) disallowed, appellacione postposita] causing what you have determined to be strictly observed under ecclesiastical censure and if the witnesses who have been named withdraw through favour hatred or fear that you compel them by this same force and without appeal to give testimony to truth no letter prejudicial to truth and justice having been procured from the Apostolic See But if you are not all able to take part in the execution of this that nevertheless two of you should execute the commission Given at the Lateran the 23rd March 1211 the thirteenth year of our pontificate By the authority of this letter parties being constituted in our presence It was thus amicably agreed between Lord William Bishop of St Andrews and the *Kildei* of Munimusc with the consent of their archdeacons and their chapter of St Andrews namely That the Lord Bishop of St Andrews granted that the same Culdees shall have in future one refectory and one dormitory in common and one oratory without a cemetery So that the bodies of Culdees and of Clerics or laymen who may die while staying with them shall receive ecclesiastical burial in the cemetery of the parish Church of Munimusc as freely as hitherto they are wont to be buried the right of mother church being preserved in all cases And there shall be twelve Culdees there and a thirteenth Bricius whom the Culdees themselves shall present to the Lord Bishop of St Andrews that he may be their *Master or Prior* And on his retiring or dying the Culdees shall by their common consent choose three out of their fellow-Culdees and present them to the Bishop of St Andrews whoever he may be that the Bishop of St

Andrews according to his own will and disposition may select one of the three to be *Prior or Master* who shall do fealty to him as the founder of the house of the Culdees And in the election of the Prior or Master of the Culdees this shall be observed for ever with the addition that it shall never be lawful for the same Culdees to profess the life or order of monks or Canonical brethren [Canonical Regulars, *Reg. Abdn.*] without the assent of the same Bishop or his successors there nor to exceed the number of Culdees before mentioned But when a Culdee retires or dies they shall be at liberty to substitute another up to the number before named So that every Culdee shall swear in the presence of the Bishop of St Andrews or the person deputed by him for the purpose to keep and observe faithfully and without guile or evil spirit as far as in him lies the terms of the foresaid agreement But the foresaid Culdees shall retain the half-ploughgate of land called Eglismenythok which they had by gift of Robert of good memory Bishop of St Andrews as freely &c They shall also have a fourth part of the revenues which are usually granted to Culdee Clerics persis and ferdys [spersis and ferdis *Reg. Abdn.*] by those who choose burial there and the part that concerns them of the common gift called sauchbarian and the part that concerns them of the grant called the thomneon tharmund [thonneom thraumund *Reg. Abdn.*] according as they have had this from ancient times up to the present times reserving in all cases the right of the person and of mother church The lands however which the same Culdees received by the grant of Gilchrist Earl of Mar without the assent of the said Bishop namely Dolbethok and Fornathy they have resigned in the hand of the same Bishop so that henceforth they shall maintain no right in them except by his concession or that of his successors They promised also strictly that they shall henceforth receive no lands that are known to pertain to the Bishop of St Andrews by gift of the Earl himself or of another without the consent of the Bishop of St Andrews himself nor do anything that is to the prejudice of his dignity or of the liberty of the Church of St Andrews or to the hurt of the parish Church of Munimusc That whenever the Bishop of St Andrews shall happen to come to Munimusc the foresaid Culdees shall receive him solemnly in procession Also William Lord Bishop of St Andrews promised for himself and his successors that they will help the said Culdees and maintain them as their own And in order that by the security of the present writing this agreement may always continue in future times ratified and unimpaired it has been confirmed by the attachment of our seal and the seals of the parties and by the interposition of the oath of the Culdees Bricius and Andrew for themselves and their fellow-Culdees (eleven witnesses being specified).[1]

Bishop Malvoisin thus brought the highest arm of the Church against the poor Culdees here by his appeal to the Pope. They are shorn of possessions that they have enjoyed for only a few years, and are to have only what the Bishop consents to give them. They are also brought under the more direct control of the Bishop of St. Andrews. They are reminded that the 'founder' of their house was a Bishop of St. Andrews, and they are assimilated to the state into which the Culdees of St. Andrews had been brought. Like them they are to consist of a Prior and twelve members, and like them they are excluded from all parochial functions.[2] Yet,

[1] Reg. St. And. Priory pp. 370-372 ; Collns. A. and B. pp. 174-176; Reg. Epis. Abd. II. pp. 264-266. [2] See Mr. Skene, Celt. Scot. II. p. 392.

notwithstanding the displeasure expressed by the Bishop at their wishing quietly, of their own accord, to become Canons, we shall find immediately in a grant that he makes to them that he drops the name Culdee altogether and calls them 'the Canons of Munimusc,' and that before the agreement is thirty-five years old the name of Culdee has disappeared altogether from Monymusk, and the Pope himself in a Bull recognises their home as a Priory of Canons Regular of the order of St. Augustine. 'This attempt at self-reformation shows the strength of the current which had set in for the new institutions,' and which had reached this distant part. If a Bishop of St. Andrews was the original founder of the Priory here, he may have sent some of the Culdees from St. Andrews itself to institute the home. Although by this agreement the Culdees here were precluded from taking any part in parish duties, the terms show that they received some share of the burial dues, etc., for certain dues and customs of the Church are evidently expressed in the words 'sauchbarian,' etc., "terms which await the explanation of some learned Gael."[1] In the preface to the Register of St. Andrews Priory[2] this agreement is called "a very curious transaction," and it is added, "It is probable that the Culdees most nearly resembled in their constitution the order of Canons Regular of St. Augustine, who may be considered as the 'reformed' Culdees of Scotland, since we find the Culdees sometimes styled simply Canons."

As we have so often to speak of them, it may be well here to say something about the Augustinian Canons. Bishop Stubbs of Oxford in his 'Constitutional History of England,'[3] says, "The institution of Augustinian Canons which resulted from

[1] Reg. St. And. Priory, p. xviii.
[2] Ibid. p. xv.
[3] Con. Hist. of Eng. Vol. I. p. 286.

. . projects of reform, was not adopted by any English Cathedral until the See of Carlisle was founded by Henry I." [in 1132; his wife was Maud, daughter of Malcolm III and Margaret] "and this continued the only Augustinian Cathedral until the Reformation. Many of the Scottish Cathedrals were, however, made Augustinian in the 12th and 13th Centuries." "In England, where the Augustinians were established early in the 12th Century, they had about 170 houses—the earliest, it would seem, being at St. Oswald's at Nosthill near Pontefract. In Scotland they had about 25 houses. The earliest at Scone was founded in 1114 and was filled by Canons from Nosthill. The others of most note were at Inchcolm in the Firth of Forth, St. Andrews, Holyrood, Cambuskenneth, and Inchaffray (the Island of Masses)."[1] There were also Loch Tay Priory, a cell of Scone—St. Serf's on Lochleven, Portmoak, the Isle of May transferred to Pittenweem, and Monymusk, all cells of St. Andrews—Inchmahome on the Lake of Menteith, Abernethy Abbey in Perthshire, and St. Mary's Isle in Galloway which was a cell of Holyrood.

Augustinians were not always restricted like other Regulars to the duties of their own house, but were sometimes engaged as parish clergy. They lived, slept, and took their food together under the same roof. They assumed their title as Canons after the Lateran Council in 1139. Their dress was of a coarse substance—the chief part consisting of woollen material manufactured often by themselves, while a cloak or hood of white or black indicated at sight their brotherhood. "They wore beards, a cassock, a linen rochet and black open cape, with square black caps on their heads instead of a cowl. The secular Canons had a surplice with a furred almuce, were without beards, and used a hat in travelling."[2]

[1] Chambers' Encyc.   [2] Mr. Walcott, Anc. Ch. of Scot. p. 299.

A bell summoned them seven times in the 24 hours to perform together their devotional services—at midnight, at 6 in the morning, at 9, at noon, when they dined in silence while one of them read aloud the Bible or other edifying books, at 2 or 3, about 4, and at 7 in the evening. They also assembled in the Chapter-house, if there was one, for discipline, and an instance of its severity will by and by come before us.

All monks were distinguished by a shaven crown, and on admission to the different orders took the three vows of poverty, celibacy, and obedience to their superiors. In course of time all the orders became possessed of great power and wealth, and being exempt in many cases from the jurisdiction of the Bishops, their ambition became excessive. The number of the various Abbeys and other Monasteries in our country exceeded 100.

There is also a letter, the words of which are of the most severe nature, from Bishop Malvoisin, regarding some Culdees here who had not been steadfast to their vows. Dr. Reeves says, "The same bishop, whose remonstrance led to the foregoing decision, soon after, at the request of the Prior and Keledei of Monymusk, forbade any person who had made a regular profession in this house to be received elsewhere without the Prior's license."[1]

William by the grace of God Bishop of St Andrews to the Abbots, Priors, Archdeacons, officials, and all rectors of Churches, and all their subordinates both clerical and lay, settled throughout his diocese, eternal greeting in the Lord It is certain that those who under cover of religion leaving the secular state, assume the habit of Regulars and take the vow of such profession . . deprive themselves of the freedom of returning to the common ways of men and of

[1] Culdees, p. 174.

regress, So that if any one [denying] the assumption of the habit of Regulars and the profession made in any place of Religion, should presume by his own rashness to retire from it—as a dog returning to its vomit or a sow that was washed to her wallowing in the mire—he is to be reckoned worthy of contempt and of abomination both of God and men Wherefore moved by the just supplications of our beloved sons the Prior and Culdees of Munimusc, we command you all, instructing you by these present writings that you presume to admit none of the Brethren of the aforesaid place, who may have assumed the habit of Religion there and made professsion, without leave and letter commendatory of the aforesaid Prior and Culdees, to stay among you or to hold communication, but rather that you reckon him as a heathen man and a publican until led by penitence he return the sooner to his own proper house and brethren, to give fuller satisfaction for his transgressions and to receive canonical discipline according to the institutes of their order.[1]

We have seen how this Bishop deprived the Culdees of some of their farms. He showed them however some kindness (as kindness then went) bestowing on the Priory another Church, that of Keig, which was dedicated under the name of S. Diaconianus—a confessor and martyr, but beyond this, an unknown Scottish Saint.

William by divine mercy the lowly minister of the Church of St. Andrews to all etc. . eternal greeting in the Lord We wish it to come to the knowledge of you all that with the assent and will of the Chapter of St. Andrews we have given . . to God and St. Mary and the Canons of Munimusc serving . . God there, for the soul of King William and

[1] Reg. St. And. Priory, pp. 368, 369 ; Colln. A. and B. pp. 176, 177

for the souls of our ancestors and successors and for the salvation of our own soul, the Church of Keig with all its just pertinents for free, pure, and perpetual charity. Wherefore we wish &c.[1]

This grant was confirmed by Gilbert de Stirling, Bishop of Aberdeen (1228-1239), and by Pope Innocent IV. in 1245.[2]

It is singular to find Bishop Malvoisin after his appeal to the Pope, in this writ of his own gift, making no mention of the name 'Culdees,' but speaking definitely of 'the Canons of Munimusc.'

William Malvoisin was a native of Normandy—"a Frenchman at least by education."[3] He was Chancellor of Scotland in 1199. "He was consecrated in France by the Archbishop of Lyons in 1200,"[4] and translated from the see of Glasgow to be 'Bishop of the Scots' at St. Andrews in 1202. In 1215 he, as Papal Legate, along with the Bishops of Glasgow and Moray and the Abbot of Kelso, attended the 4th Lateran Council, summoned by Pope Innocent III, when the doctrine of Transubstantiation was adopted, though not in its final form. The Cup however was not withdrawn from the laity till 1415—two hundred years after.[5] He also held a Council at Perth to promote the Crusades, but in 1217 a papal commission was appointed to enquire into a number of charges that were made against himself, and among other things he was accused "of having absolved the Culdees (of St. Andrews, doubtless) from the sentence of excommunication passed against them by the papal see on appeal."[6] The very next year, however, as shown by a Bull dated from the Lateran, 19th December, 1218, in answer to his petition,

---

[1] Reg. St. And. Priory, pp. 366; Colln. A. and B. pp. 619, 620.
[2] Ibid. pp. 367, 372; Ibid. pp. 177, 178.
[3] Mr. Walcott, Anc. Ch. p. 85.
[4] Mr. Cosmo Innes, Sketches. p. 38.
[5] Mr. Stephen, Hist. p. 345.
[6] Ibid. p. 346.

he and his successors in the bishopric are received under the protection of the Papal see by Pope Honorius III, the successor of Innocent III, along with all the possessions belonging to the Bishop of St. Andrews. In the Pope's Bull granting this protection about thirty places are mentioned by name, most of them within the diocese, but some of them far beyond it. Among them are the Island of Lohlevenoh with its appendages, MUNEMUSCH, Culsamuel, and Elon with the lands of their Churches and all their pertinents.[1]

This 'fiery Norman' was 'the most energetic bishop of his age,' and his episcopate extended to nearly forty years. It was he who, in 1230, introduced another order into Scotland—Vallis Caulium—reformed Cistercians, whose chief monastery of that name, Val des Choux, was in Burgundy. Their three monasteries were the beautiful Pluscardine near Elgin, Beauly in Ross, Ardchattan in Lorne—all of them Priories.[2] His charters, yet extant, attest how carefully he laboured to carry on the work of the new church of St. Andrews to its consummation. He was the first Bishop buried within the walls of his cathedral (1233). But it was not till eighty-five years after this, in 1318, four years after Bannockburn, that it was consecrated by Bishop Lamberton in the presence of King Robert Bruce, seven Bishops, fifteen Abbots, and almost all the Earls and Lords whom the wreck of war and revolution had spared to Scotland, the King endowing it with a hundred merks yearly from his own coffers as an oblation in gratitude for his victory.[3]

"Of fifteen prelates who were elected to the primatial see of St. Andrews during the twelfth and thirteenth centuries, and who wrote themselves in charter and on seal 'Episcopi

---

[1] Theiner's Vetera Monumenta, pp. 8, 9.
[2] Mr. Stephen, Hist. p. 293; see also Mr. Walcott, Anc. Church, p. 46.
[3] Dr. J. Robertson, Abbeys, pp. 46, 47.

Scottorum,' not one appears to have been a Celtic Scot; only a few sprung from the Anglo-Norman houses of Scotland; the great majority were Saxons and Normans from England. We see in the list a Prior of Durham, a monk of Canterbury, a Canon of St. Oswald's near Pontefract, a son of the Earl of Northampton, a son of the Earl of Leicester."[1] "Not till 1472 did it receive for the first time a native primate—the best of the mediæval prelates of Scotland—good Bishop Kennedy."[2] Of him it is said, " The spiritual interests of the people were at that time disregarded, and preaching was almost entirely neglected except by the Friars. Attempts were made to remedy this evil by some good men such as Bishop Kennedy of St. Andrews, who preached regularly throughout his diocese, and obliged the parochial clergy to remain at their Churches and attend to their duties. But such cases were rare."[3]

We now return to the gifts of the Earls of Mar. Gilchrist's brother, Duncan, was fifth Earl, 1214-1234, and he
executes a writ in which he names the clergy 'Culdees or Canons' and confirms to them the Church of Leochel with all its tithes, liberties, offerings, revenues, and with that whole half dauach of land in which the Church is situated in free charity for the soul of . . King William . . the soul of his father M Morgrund and his mother Agnes . . for the salvation . . of King Alexander . . and for his own salvation and prosperity as also of his wife and all his heirs.[4]
"The transition state of their discipline accounts for the peculiar way in which the clergy are spoken of in charters of this date as when Earl Duncan styles them *Keledei sive Canonici*."[5]
Even these repeated confirmations are not enough, for in

[1] Dr. J. Robertson, Abbeys, p. 31.
[2] Dean Stanley, Lectures, p. 40.
[3] Dr. Campbell, St. Giles, p. 96.
[4] Reg. St. And. Priory, p. 362; Colln. A. and B. p. 603.
[5] Dr. Reeves, Culdees, p. 174.

the time of Earl Duncan's son, a letter has to be written regarding this same Church by King Alexander II, 1214-1249. In it the name 'Culdee' is dropped, and the clergy are called simply 'Canons.'

Alexander by the grace of God King of Scotland to all greeting, let all . . know that when peace was made in our presence and before many honourable men in full council, between the son of Duncan Morgrun Earl of Mar on the one part and David son of the Earl on the other, about certain lands regarding which there had long been a controversy between them, both of them at our petition and that of our honourable men who were present, gave the Church of Leochel with its pertinents to God and the Church of S. Mary of Monymusk and to the 'Canons' serving God in the same, and each of them resigned in our hand all right that he had or could have in the said Church, for the use of the said 'Canons' And that the truth of this may not be hidden, we in testimony of this fact have caused this public letter to be written.'

The charter of another gift of Earl Duncan's is preserved and is of great interest, and in it the term *Canons* alone is used.

To all . . Duncan Earl of Mar . . we make it known that we have given to God and S. Mary of Munimusc and the *Canons* serving God there . . the Church of St Andrew of Kindrouch with . . all its other just pertinents and with one acre of land in Aucatendregen on the other side of the stream which is called Alien for pure and perpetual charity Wherefore we will that the said *Canons* may possess the said Church of St Andrew of Kindrouch as well as . . any charity . . is possessed, etc.[2]

[1] Reg. St. And. Priory, p. 363 ; Collns. A. and B. p. 604.
[2] Ibid. p. 367.   Ant. A. and B. II. p. 86.

"The inquirer," says Mr. Cosmo Innes,[1] "will have no difficulty in recognising in 'Aucatendregen,' the village of Auchendryne, now partly superseded by the modern appellation of Castleton of Braemar." Mar Castle, "the Castle of Kindrocht in Mar, a frequent residence and probably a hunting-place of our early Kings, seems to have given its name to a Church and parish . . forming part of the parish of Crathie." Dr. Reeves says—" It is said of S. Regulus and his company that leaving Monichi, now Monikie in Forfar, 'transierunt montana seu Moneth, et venerunt ad locum qui vocabatur Doldencha, nunc autem dictus Chondrochedalvan' (Pinkerton I. 460). This last name is the Kindrouch of the charter, with the name of the river, then called 'Alien,' attached to it, the compound signifying 'Bridge-end of Alien.' Kindrocht is the old parochial name of Braemar in the union of Crathie, and the Church stood near Castleton on the east side of the Clunie water, which enters the Dee from the south. 'Alien' or 'Alvan' is the ancient name of the Clunie, and Auchatendregen [*i.e.*, Achadh-an-draoighen, 'field of the thorn'] now Auchindrain is situated on its east bank."[2] Or, as is told us in "Under Lochnagar,"[3] "the ancient name of the parish of Braemar was St. Andrews, but after Malcolm Canmore, who had a hunting seat there, built a bridge across the Cluny, the name was changed to Can-drochet or Kindrochet—Bridge-end." The parishes were united probably about the beginning of the seventeenth century as " Crathie and Kindrochet "—afterwards "Crathie and Braemar."

But while giving the Church of Braemar to our Priory, Earl Duncan took from it the Church of Logie Ruthven (? Logie-Coldstone) "giving it to the Church of St. Mary, St. Machar's Cathedral, and the Canons of Aberdeen for the maintenance of

[1] Reg. St. And. Priory, p. xviii. [2] Culdees, p. 258. [3] Under Lochnagar, p. 20.

a chaplain to celebrate for his soul in that Church, where he vowed and bequeathed his body to be buried—ubi vovi et legavi corpus meum sepeliendum—among the venerable fathers, the bishops thereof."[1]

The Earls of Mar had a residence, Mar Castle, at Braemar as well as at Kildrummy,[2] and it was there that the Earl of Mar, John Erskine, in August 1715, gathered ten thousand clansmen round him, though his own people about Kildrummy were very reluctant to join him in rebellion, and raised the standard in favour of James, the Chevalier. It was his own parish minister at Kildrummy, Mr. Alexander, whether by compulsion or willingly, who offered the prayer, for which he was deposed by the presbytery of Alford in April 1717. The Earl's estates were all forfeited to the Crown, and he himself was driven abroad as a wanderer. His signature is given in fac-simile in the Cartulary of Cambuskenneth.[3]

The name of the Church, St. Andrew's of Kindrouch in our charter, connects it with the legend of the Greek St. Rule or St. Regulus, and Mr. Skene[4] sees a connection between the gift of the Church and the fact that our Priory was under the protection of the Bishop of St. Andrews. Bishop Dowden is "inclined to think it is a fruitless inquiry to ask who was the historic Regulus of St. Andrews."[5] According to the legend, St. Rule had come with his Greek brethren from Byzantium or Achaia, bringing with him in his sail-less and oar-less boat, what were believed to be some sacred relics of St. Andrew the Apostle, who became the patron saint of Scotland, in place of St. Peter, the popular saint of Pictland. They touched Scottish ground at St. Andrews, but were received at Braemar by

[1] Reg. Epis. Abdn. I. p. 16; Mr. Cosmo Innes, Sketches, p. 18.
[2] Colln. A. and B. p. 643.
[3] p. xiv.
[4] Celtic Scot. II. p. 390.
[5] Proceed. Soc. Antiq. April 10, 1893, p. 254.

Hungus or Angus, the Christian Pictish King, who with all his nobles, prostrated themselves before the relics, and gave the place to God and St. Andrew, and on it was built the first Church beyond the Mounth.[1] Then they returned to St. Andrews, where the King gave a large grant of land for the erection and maintenance of Churches, and where St. Rule chose a cave by the seaside for his oratory. This is thought to have happened about 736. Some have supposed that S. Rule was S. Raighall, an Irish saint. It is singular that the Church of Braemar so ancient in its associations, and so distant, with its pertinents and an acre of land so definitely named, should have come into the possession of our Priory. The original Church being built of stone and lime, was called "the white Church," as at Whithorn.

Gilbert, Bishop of Aberdeen, 1228-1239, confirms the gift of the Church of Braemar almost in the same words.[2]

Another family now appears with benefactions. The Earldom of Mar has been the subject of many disputes down to the present time.

Duncan's son, William, succeeded as sixth Earl in 1244, but his title was contested during the minority of Alexander III. The family of Malcolm of Lundy in Forfarshire laid claim to it through the maternal line. He was "Hostiarius" or "Doorward" to the King in David of Huntingdon's time, and from this came his family name 'Durward.' The principal claim was unsuccessful, but by a compromise this family obtained possession of large portions of the lands of the Earldom in the valley of the Dee and in other parts of Aberdeenshire. By the gift of Thomas de Lundyn, the Durward, the monks of the

[1] Dr. J. Robertson, Abbeys, p. 13; Dean Stanley, Lectures, p. 39.
[2] Reg. St. And. Priory, p. 368; Ant. A. and B. II. p. 86.

Abbey of Arbroath obtained the Church of Kinerny, now united to Cluny and Midmar, while his more celebrated son, Alan, founded the 'Hospital' at Kincardine O'Neil. Thomas was buried in 1231 at the door of the Abbey of Cupar Angus, as was also Alan in 1275.[1]

Thomas, Hostiarius of the Lord King, executes a charter before 1231—1207-1227 (Dr. Reeves)—to which William, Abbot of Holyrood, is witness,

> confirming the charity which his grandfather and his mother gave to the Culdees of Munimusc, namely ten bolls of barley and ten stones of cheese from Outhirheyclt [Upper Echt], and so that he who shall hold the land of the said charity shall forward the said bolls of barley and stones of cheese to the home of the said Culdees at the Feast of St. Martin.[2]

Thomas Hostiarius also gives anew to God and the Church of the blessed Virgin of Munimusc and the *Canons* there . . . the Church of Afford, with everything justly belonging to it, which Adam, Bishop of Aberdeen confirms, the dedication being in the same terms, and the word *Canons* being used.[3]

About 1240 Colin Hostiarius confirms by charter

> . . to God and the Church of the blessed Mary of Munimusc and the *Canons* serving God in the same and to serve in perpetuity, the whole half dauach of land in which the Church of Leochel is situated . . along with common pasture for forty cows and a hundred sheep 'cum sequela de duobus annis' (? with their calves and lambs until they are two years old) and for four horses, the land being free from all secular services . . for perpetual charity for the salva-

---

[1] See Mr. Cosmo Innes, Sketches, p. 148; Skene of Skene, p. 13; Dr. Campbell, Balmerino, p. 30; Ant. A. and B. IV. pp. 694, 695.

[2] Reg. St. And. Priory, p. 369; Collns. A. and B. p. 174.

[3] Reg. St. And. Priory, p. 365; Antiq. A. and B. IV. pp. 693, 694.

tion and prosperity of his own body and soul and of Ada his wife . . and for the souls of all his forefathers.[1] Colyn Ostiarius witnesses a charter of Alan Ostiarius, 1232-3.[2]

Another charter is dated 'at Leochel' probably about 1250, . . To all the faithful in Christ who may see or hear of the present writing Philip of Mount Fichette and Anna his wife, daughter and heiress of the deceased Lord Colin Hostiarius confirming for ever to God and St. Mary of Munimusc and the "canons" serving God in the same . . the whole rights . . in a certain half dauach of land in which the Church of Leochel is situated . . with the common pasture for the cows, sheep, calves, lambs, and horses as specified in the last charter.[3]

We have seen how Bishop Malvoisin gave the Church of Keig and all its pertinents to "the Canons" of Monymusk; this is now followed by a further grant by charter of David, Bishop of St. Andrews, 1240-1253,

. . to God and the Blessed Mary and 'the Canons' of Munimusc, of two acres of our land of Keig lying round the cemetery of the Church of Keig between two rivulets namely Conglassy and Puthachin, stretching on the south side as far as the great river which is called Don . .[4]

The Bishop calls this land his own, being part of Malcolm Canmore's great gift. Every one admires the beautiful view to the right hand as one stands on the Bridge of Keig and looks toward Castle Forbes. Close beside the bridge are seen the ruins of an old parish Church, and round it lies the original

---

[1] Reg. St. Andrew Priory, p. 363; Collns. A. and B. p. 604.
[2] Dr. Reeves, Culdees, p. 255.
[3] Reg. St. Andrews Priory, p. 364; Collns. A. and B. p. 605.
[4] Reg. St. Andrews Priory, p. 366; Colln. A. and B. p. 620.

churchyard here spoken of, in which the ancient church of St. Diaconianus had been. The two acres given to our Priory stretch toward the river and are within the Park of Castle Forbes, which used to be called " Putachie." Modern improvements have reduced the size of the brooks, but the one towards the bridge is very evident still.

The same Bishop by Charter restores to his lord brother . . the Prior of Monymusk and the " Canons " serving God there . . Dolbethoc with its just pertinents to be held by them and their successors . . in perpetual charity for sustaining poor persons and travellers meeting there. In witness A . . of Makerstoun (near Kelso).[1]
Dolbethoc was one of the farms of which the Priory had been deprived by Bishop Malvoisin. Hospitality was dispensed by the Clergy with generous hand. " It was the business of the almoner of the monastery to seek out both the sick and the poor of the district and to minister the charity of the house to them. None were better friends to the poor than the religious houses."[2]

Bishop David of Bernhame was raised to the Episcopate from being only a Sub-Deacon. At his election "two of the Culdees of the Church of St. Mary, Kilrymont (St. Andrews), who call themselves Canons," voted, but their votes were received under protest by the Chapter.[3] He became Chancellor of Scotland and died of fever at Nenthorn, when attending the marriage of Alexander III at York Minster to the daughter of Henry III. He had crowned Alexander at Scone in 1249 when quite a boy. He was buried at Kelso.[4]

A remarkable monument of the activity in Church-building which prevailed in the thirteenth century is found in the

[1] Reg. St. Andrews Priory, p. 369; Colln. A. and B. p. 177.
[2] Mr. Stephen, History, p. 301.
[3] Theiner's Monumenta, p. 67.
[4] Mr. Walcott, Ancient Church, p. 86.

list of Churches consecrated by him, which is written on a fly-leaf of his Pontificale, now in the Imperial Library at Paris. "His episcopate extended from 22nd Jan., 1240, to 26th Apr., 1253. He consecrated 3 Churches in 1240; 9 in 1241; 40 in 1242; 49 in 1243; 17 in 1244; 6 in 1245; 4 in 1246; 5 in 1247; 3 in 1248, and 3 in 1249"[1]—in all 139 in 10 years, within his own diocese, though there were not 300 in the whole of it, 234 according to one account. As became one who consecrated so many Churches, great stress is laid in his Constitutions of 1242 on the maintenance of the sacred buildings, on their proper furnishing, and on suitable vessels for the Sacraments. A non-resident parson or vicar is to be deprived upon three months' warning, and fugitive monks and canons are to be sent back to their monasteries or excommunicated as apostates.

Baldwin was "Parson of Monymusk" at this period, as in the St. Andrews Register[2] he is one of the witnesses to two deeds by Bishop William Malvoisin, and[3] to one by Bishop David Bernham, and[4] to two regarding the Churches of Cupar-Fife, Haddington, &c., "at Tinningham," near North Berwick, on the same day, 13th Jan. 1240, when there were also present Clergy from various quarters, St. Andrews, Edinburgh, Methven, &c.

We now reach two confirmations issued by Pope Innocent IV within ten days of each other, dated Lyons the 19th and 28th May, 1245. "The *style* in these Papal confirmations shows that the change from the ancient character of the Priory

---

1 Dr. J. Robertson, Stat. Ecc. Scot. pp. clxxxv-vi.
2 Reg. St. Andrews Priory, p. 157.
3 Reg. St. Andrew's Priory, p. 162.
4 Ibid., pp, 166, 167.

had now been formally completed,"[1] and that the "Culdees" of Monymusk have entirely and for ever disappeared.

The first refers to some of the lands of the Priory—

Innocent, Bishop, servant of the servants of God, to our beloved sons the Prior and Convent of Munimusc of the order of St. Augustin, in the diocese of Aberdeen, greeting and Apostolical benediction, It is right that we grant an easy assent to the just desires of petitioners and fulfil wishes that are not unreasonable by giving effect to them Wherefore beloved sons in the Lord granting your just petitions with ready assent we confirm the lands of Dolbethok, of Leochel, of Eglismeneyttok according as you rightly and peaceably possess them, to you and through you to your church by Apostolic authority and secure them by the protection of the present writ, Wherefore let no human being break this page of our confirmation or dare rashly to act contrary to it If any one however presume to attempt this, let him know that he shall incur the indignation of Almighty God and His blessed Apostles Peter and Paul Given at Lyons (date as above), in the second year of our pontificate.

The second refers to the Churches we have so often heard of—

Innocent (&c., as before) Wherefore beloved sons in the Lord . . We confirm the Churches of St Andrew of Afford, of St. Marnoc of Loychel, of St. Diaconianus of Kege, of St. Andrew of Kindrocht with their pertinents, to which you refer, acquired as you rightly and peaceably possess them—to you and through you to your Church by Apostolic authority and secure you by the title of the present writing Wherefore let no one, &c., If any one however, &c. Given at Lyons (date as above), in the second year, &c.[2]

[1] Book of Deer, p. cxx.
[2] Reg. St. Andrews Priory, pp. 372, 373; Collns. A. and B. pp. 177, 178.

Regarding this Dr. Reeves says [1]—" It would appear that the Keledei of the Church of Monymusk had from the commencement of the century been endeavouring to reform their discipline ; and their efforts eventuated in the abandonment of their ancient name, and the adoption of the rule of regular Canons of St. Augustin. The date of the present instrument proves that Robert Gordon is wrong in referring the change to the year 1300, as given in the 'View of the Diocese of Aberdeen,' printed by the Spalding Club.[2]"

One might picture the reverent satisfaction felt by the Prior that day in early summer six hundred and fifty years ago, when he received this answer from the Pope, and summoned his twelve brethren, the 'parson' of the parish, and the officials of the Priory, and with all the clergy in their vestments standing on his right hand and left in the chancel of our Church, read the two Bulls from his stall. We recall the efforts they had made to adapt themselves of their own accord to the advancing changes in the Church, and how strangely they had been checked by their distant Bishop, although eagerness had been shown to force their Culdee brethren beside his own Cathedral, who were of an opposite spirit to their own, to adopt the new system. Thus the Prior and his clergy would gratefully find security in the assurance of the Papal protection and benediction, and in this express recognition of them by the full title as now belonging to the order of St. Augustine. Their name of Culdees had come to be felt as an anachronism, and it was at last shown to be for ever passed away by authority that no one would gainsay, while the revenues from their four Churches, their tithes, offerings, and farms were also secured to them, so that their Convent could not be in want.

These letters were probably never read before in English

[1] Culdees, p. 259.   [2] Colins. A. and B. p. 169.

K

in this Church in which the Culdees so long worshipped. We have together revived the knowledge of their records and the gifts they received, and we will not forget to thank God for our own inestimable privileges, for the lessons of the past, and for the light that streams from the Gospel. We will remember Jesus' words that cannot pass away, and that do not admit of any modified interpretation, but apply to us as they never applied to any Christians before, breathing as we do the sacred influences and strengthened as we should be through the strugglings of all the past centuries, "Unto whomsoever much is given of him shall be much required;" and we will also ponder with deepening penitence what are almost the last words of the Apostle of the Gentiles, that the Gospel has this as one of the seals of the Covenant of Mercy,

"Let every one that nameth the name of Christ depart from iniquity."

CHAPTER VII.
RECORDS FROM 1268 TO 1500.
WRITS REGARDING THE BRECBANNOCH.
'THE MONYMUSKS.'

ONE other very interesting record is preserved to us in the St. Andrews Register. It is placed before the other writs, probably owing to its having to be often referred to and as embodying the essentials of the others. It is fully dated in 1268, and we are able to account for its being drawn up. It also contains names that we are familiar with.

Special returns of the Canons of Munnimusc on the arrival of Brother Alan the Prior, in the year of grace MCCLXVIII, in the Feast of the Nativity of the Blessed Virgin, both regarding lands and regarding churches.

The sum of the church of Afford, In fee of money x merks. In fee of meal xviii chalders [a chalder equals 16 bolls,]

The sum of the church of Loychel, without the half-dauach of land, xv chalders and xii bolls meal,

The sum of the church of Keg 100 shillings, of which there is nothing, as it was mortgaged by (our) predecessor,

The sum of the church of Kindrouch, by sheaves vi½ merks and vi shillings, of which there are the dues belonging to the altar ('cujus alteragium est'),

From the land of Loychel ii½ merks,
From Fedarg and Folayth iii merks [Earl Gartenach's gift],
From Tulibaglagh ½ merk,
From bracina (probably = brasina, the malt kiln), ½ merk,
From 'Thom Maro' x shillings,

From the cottars vi shillings,
From Eglismenigcott nothing because it is mortgaged [Bishop Robert's gift],
From the kain [rent in poultry, &c.] of Houctireyht [Upper Echt] x bolls barley and x stones cheese [Thomas Hostiarius' confirmation],
From the kain of Mukual [perhaps connected with the old name of Castle Fraser] ½ chalder of barley.[1]

Monymusk Church itself is not included in this return, no doubt because it was separate from the Priory. The cottars are here mentioned. They were the dependants of the Priory, and "their social scale was higher than in modern times; they lived in the hamlet, each family possessing a cottage and from one to nine acres of land."[2]

Popes Innocent III, Honorius III, and Gregory IX were zealous in preaching the sixth Crusade, and levied forces and money over all Europe. Scotland, richer in soldiers than in gold, sent at first her share of crusaders to the Holy Land. The Crusade failed, and the best blood of France and of all Europe was shed in Asia in vain. To promote the last Crusade greater exertions were made, and some of a nature which we should think not only objectionable but little likely to be productive. In 1254, when Alexander III was King of Scotland, Pope Innocent IV, whose letters to our Priory we have given, actually granted to Henry III of *England*, provided he joined the Crusade, a twentieth of the ecclesiastical revenues of *Scotland* during three years, and the grant was subsequently extended. In *1268* Clement IV renewed this grant and increased it to a tenth, but when Henry attempted to levy it, the Scotch clergy resisted, and appealed to Rome. It is not

---
[1] Reg. St. And. Priory, p. 361; Collns. A. and B. pp. 178, 179.
[2] Mr. Stephen, History, p. 299.

probable that Henry succeeded in raising much of the tenth in Scotland, though the expedition of his gallant son, afterwards Edward I, to the Holy Land both supported his claim and rendered the supply more necessary.[1]

Is it not singular that owing to this 'taxation' for the last Crusade, there should be preserved the valuation roll of our distant Priory for the very year in which this strange grant was renewed?

There is another similar record. "A provincial Council met at Perth in 1273. An encyclical letter was read from the Pope summoning the Bishops of Scotland to the General Council which was to assemble at Lyons in the following spring. The Bishops of Dunkeld and Moray were appointed to remain in Scotland to watch over the Church and serve the offices. One of the first acts of the Council of Lyons was to impose a tax of a tenth part of all Church revenues during the six following years for the relief of the Holy Land." [" It is remarkable that in all these devices for procuring funds for the Crusades, it was chiefly the stipends of the Clergy—prelates and priests—that were assessed."[2]] " Pope Gregory X. wrote, 17th September, 1274, to the Scottish Bishops . . exhorting them to preach the Crusade, and appointed Boiamund of Vicci, a canon of the Cathedral of Asti in Piedmont, to collect the subsidy in Scotland. Hitherto taxes had been levied in the Scottish Church according to an old conventional valuation called the 'Antiqua Taxatio.' But the new tax-gatherer proposed to assess the clergy according to the 'true value'—'the Verus Valor'—or actual yearly worth of their benefices as ascertained by their oaths. They reclaimed against the proposal, and at a Council held at Perth in August 1275, prevailed

[1] Mr. Cosmo Innes, Sketches, pp. 23, 24.   [2] Mr. Stephen, History, p. 387.

on Boiamund by large payments and larger promises to return to Rome and entreat the Pope to levy the subsidy according to the Ancient Valuation, and spread its payment over seven years. His journey was in vain, and he returned to complete a valuation roll that still retains his name, and served for the apportionment of Church taxes until the Reformation—a roll that was long known and hated among us. It evidently gives the valuation in round sums according to a roughly graduated scale, and there are entered in it—

The Priories of Fyvie and of MONYMUSK each at £133."[1]

"Churchmen were careful of their 'Old Valuation.' It is found engrossed in the Chartularies both of seculars and of regulars, and the parts preserved give us the state of Church livings as at the beginning of the thirteenth century, and but little altered probably since the period that followed immediately on the great ecclesiastical revolution under David I."[2]

The 'Antiqua taxatio' of four dioceses is preserved, and in the St. Andrews Register we have what refers to our churches. There begin the taxations of Churches and ecclesiastical benefices, divided separately by Deaneries, and first by

THE DEANERY OF MAR.

The Church of Kyndroucht	iij ꝏa ½
The Church of Keg	x ꝏa
The Church of Afford	xviij ꝏa
The Church of Loychel	x ꝏa (of which the vicar receives iiij mar.[3])

GARUIACH.

Munimusc	xxx ꝏa [4]

The sum collected in the diocese of Aberdeen in the first year was £298, being the tenth part of £2980.

[1] Dr. J. Robertson, Stat. Eccles. Scot. pp. lxiv-lxx.
[2] Mr. Cosmo Innes, Sketches, p. 24-26.
[3] Collns. A. and B. p. 219. Reg. Epis. Abdn. II. p. 52.
[4] Reg. St. And. Priory, p. 355, etc. Reg. Epis. Abdn. II. p. 52.

"Of the great valuation of the benefices of the Scotch Church that took place about 1275 under Baiamund, fragments applicable to particular districts are scattered through most of the Chartularies of Scotland. As generally the oldest materials of parochial history, these valuations, constructed for assessing in due proportion the taxes to be raised from the Clergy, whether for Rome or for domestic claims, are of considerable importance."[1]

The record of the taxation given in the Register of the Bishopric of Aberdeen, is followed immediately by a statement of the "Procurations due to the Lord Bishop of Aberdeen" from the various parishes in the diocese.

IN THE DEANERY OF MAR.

Kyndrocht paid	- - -	vj sh.
Keyge ,,	- - -	xx sh.
Afford ,,	- - -	xxvj sh. viij d.
Lochell ,,	- - -	xx sh.
Munimousk ,,	- - -	xl sh.[2]

"These 'Procurations' were dues paid to the Bishop, in lieu of the ancient burden borne by the rural clergy, of entertaining him and his suite during his visitations. They seem to have been put upon the footing which they finally maintained all over Scotland, by the legate, Cardinal Ottobon, or by the Council which assembled soon after his unsuccessful interference in Scotch affairs in *1268*."[3]

As showing the difference in the value of money about this period, Dr. Joseph Robertson says that in 1326 King Robert

1 Reg. Epis. Abdn. I. p. lxxvii. 3 Reg. Epis. Abdn. I. p. lxxvii.
2 Ibid. II, p. 55.

Bruce granted to Melrose Abbey "for the fabric of its new Church, all the feudal casualties and crown issues of Teviotdale, until they should amount to £2000 sterling, a sum equal to more than £50,000 in the present day."[1] "It is reckoned that a merk at the time of the Old Valuation would purchase fourteen bolls of oatmeal."[2] Dr. Davidson says[3] "The merk may be rendered into ten times the number of pounds sterling," while for its value about 1740 we may refer to Rev. Dr. Walker's Life of Bishop John Skinner.[4]

In 1286, on the evening of March 16th, the stumble of a horse on the crags of Kinghorn in Fife, brought to an end the direct line of the ancient dynasty of our Celtic Kings, for this untimely death of Alexander III left his grand-daughter, the Maid of Norway, heir to the throne, and she died in 1290 in Orkney on her voyage to Scotland. It was followed by forty years of anarchy or war, from about 1286 to 1328. "The tide of civilisation which for two centuries had flowed northwards without check, was now to be stayed—was even to be rolled back. Regarding the country only in a material point of view, it may safely be affirmed that Scotland at the death of Alexander III was more civilised and more prosperous than at any period of her existence, down to the time when she ceased to be a separate kingdom in 1707."[5]

We now reach a date to which we referred when we mentioned the Brecbannoch—18th January, 1315, seven months after the Battle of Bannockburn, at which Bernard, Abbot of Arbroath, had himself been present. On that day he executed a charter making over the lands of Forglen, which the Abbey

1 Abbeys, p. 72.
2 Dr. Campbell, Balmerino, p. 23.
3 Inverurie, p. 35.
4 p. 5.
5 See Dr. Joseph Robertson, Abbeys, pp. 67, 68.

had enjoyed for a hundred years as Custodian of the Brecbannoch, to 'Malcolm of Monymusk.' Before giving the Abbot's deed, we may give that of William the Lion (1178-1211), by which the Abbey itself received the guardianship, a deed that also contains a name with which we are familiar.

William by the grace of God King of Scots to all honourable men of his whole land whether clergy or laity greeting Know all men present and to come that I have granted and by this my charter confirmed to the monks of Abyrbrothok the custody of the Bracbenoch, and to the same monks I have given and granted and by this my charter confirmed along with the said Bracbenoch the land of Forglen, given to God and to St. Columba and to the Bracbenach Wherefore I will and ordain that they have the said land and the custody of the Bracbenach freely and quietly Doing henceforth the service which is due to me in the army in respect of that land with the said Bracbenoch Witnesses G. Earl of Mar, Oliver my chaplain, Wm. de Bosco my scribe, Herbert de Camera at Aberdeen 28th June.[1]

Gilchrist, Earl of Mar, is the benefactor of our Priory. William de Bosco and Herbert de Camera [doubtless Herbert Chamberlain, or Herbert the Chamberlain] are mentioned in the Cartulary of Cambuskenneth[2] about the year 1201.

We now give the Abbot's deed, which is embodied in a writ by Malcolm of Monymusk. In it we meet with a designation that we shall frequently find in our records, the title 'dominus,' which has to be translated variously according to the context. With 'miles' which is equivalent to 'knight,' it is 'Sir.' With priests who had not the University degree it is also ' Sir.' 'Magister,' Master was in mediæval times very rigorously confined to those who had actually taken their degree at a University.

[1] Colln. A. and B. p. 510.   [2] pp. 92, 93.

'Dominus' or 'Sir' was singularly enough a lower title of honour, given to bachelors and to priests generally who had not taken the higher or any degree. 'Dominus Bernard' in this deed may be translated 'the lord Bernard, Abbot of . .' or 'Bernard the lord Abbot of . .' In the case of Benedictines the word would be rendered 'Dom,' a title which they still keep up.

To all who shall see the present letter Malcolm of Monimusk son of the late Sir (dominus) Thomas of Monymusk, knight (miles) greeting in the Lord Know that I have been infeft by my superiors (dominos) the lord (dominum) Bernard by the grace of God Abbot of Abbyrbrothok and the convent of the same place with the land of Forglen in these words Let all both present and to come know that we Brother Bernard, by Divine permission Abbot of Abbyrbrothok, and the Convent of the same place, with the express consent and approval of our whole Chapter, after diligent consideration given to this matter and having regard to the advantage of our Monastery, have given, granted, and by our present charter confirmed to Malcolm of Monymusk the whole of our land of Forglen which pertains to the Bracbenniach, with all its pertinents along with the right of patronage of the Church of the same land, to be held and possessed by the same Malcolm and his heirs, of us and our successors for ever freely &c. We have also granted to the same and to his heirs ('curiam suam,' probably) to hold his own court over the people living on the said land in respect of all manner of decisions and complaints that can happen within the said land along with the penalties and forfeits thence justly accruing, reserving to ourselves and our successors the moving of decisions in respect of four complaints that pertain to the crown of the Lord King in all cases But the said Malcolm and his heirs shall perform in the army of the Lord King in our name the service for the said land that pertains to the Bracbennach, as often as there is need, Rendering nevertheless thereafter for every other secular service and claim to us and our successors, himself and his heirs, at Abbyrbrothok yearly forty shillings sterling in name of fee &c And to us and our successors and our Monastery both he and his heirs successively shall render the oath of fidelity In testimony of which the common seal of our Chapter has been cordially appended to our present charter our said Chapter being witness In testimony of which I have affixed my own seal to these presents Given at Abbyrbrothok the Thursday immediately preceding the feast of the Chair of St Peter the Apostle in the year of grace 1314.[1]

Who "Malcolm of Monymusk" was is a matter one can hardly venture to speak of. "It was already the thirteenth century before fixed surnames became prevalent north of the Tweed. The larger number of Scottish family names, though by no means all, were taken from lands which the family possessed."[2] Some of the lands of Monymusk, given originally to the Church, may have come to be held under the Church by a manorial tenant, who may thus have adopted the name "de Monymusk." By a charter the original of which is preserved at Buchanan Castle, Malcolm's father 'Thomas of Monymusk,' who is mentioned in our writ as deceased, granted to Sir Patrick Graham the lands of Cuyl in the Earldom of Strathern. The charter is without date, but was granted about the year 1285, the first witness being "domino Johanne Abbate de Cambuskenneth";[3] and also in 1299, fifteen years before our

1 Collns. A. and B. p. 511.
2 Principal Shairp, Sketches, p. 88.
3 Cartulary of Cambuskenneth p. li.

writ, Malcolm's father, 'Thomas de Monymusk miles,' is mentioned in the Chartulary of Arbroath.[1]

King Robert Bruce died in 1329, leaving his son David II, only eight years old. David II was taken prisoner at Nevil's Cross by Philippa, Queen of Edward III, in October 1346, two months after Crecy, and was ransomed in 1357 (after Poictiers), in the eleventh year of his imprisonment.

'Henry of Monymusk,' probably Malcolm's son, fell under royal displeasure, and forfeited the lands of 'Petfethik and Balnerosk in the barony of Monymusk,' thus leading one to think that 'Pitfichie' had been the family residence, for David II granted a charter of these lands to David Chalmer, as shown in Robertson's Index of Missing Charters.[2] By the following deed however the attainder was reversed, and Henry of Monymusk got a new gift of all his lands in the sheriffdom of Aberdeen and Banff, 3rd June, 1357, the very year in which David II was ransomed:—

David by the grace of God King of Scots to all honourable men of his whole land greeting, Know that since we of our special grace stayed all our Royal action and prosecution against Henry of Monymusk which we had adopted toward him on account of his protracted delay in England while adhering to our enemies We have given and by this our present charter have confirmed to the said Henry all his own lands belonging to him by hereditary right within the viscounty of Banff and Aberdeen to be held by the said Henry and his heirs with all liberties and their just pertinents whatsoever on his performing the due and customary services thereupon In testimony of which we have made our seal be attached to this present charter Witnesses the venerable fathers in Christ William Bishop of St Andrews

[1] Chartulary of Arbroath, p. 20.   [2] p. 48. n. 8.

Patrick Bishop of Brechin Robert our Marischal of Scotland Earl of Strathearn Patrick Earl of March and Moray Thomas Earl of Mar William of Livingstone and Robert of Erskine Knights (milites) and many others at Edinburgh 3rd June the twenty-eigth year of our reign.[1]

Two years after this David II must have come on a visit to Monymusk, for in the Exchequer Rolls[2] there is the following entry :—

Account of Robert Bullok burgess of Aberd. with the Chamberlain 21st April 1360, Aberdeen

. . and to William of Coryne, burgess of Abyrden, for one large jar (or cask) of wine bought for the use of the Lord King and carried (usque) all the way to Monymousk vi Lib. xiiis. and iiiid. And to Laurence of Garvok for fodder bought from the same for the use of the Lord King and carried all the way to Monymousk £ iii*s*. iiii*d*.

A charter of this period is preserved,[3] in which ' Andrew de Berclay, dominus (owner) de Garntuly,' in the parish of Gartly, near Huntly, gives and confirms to Janet de Berclay, widow of the late Sir (dominus) John de Monymous knight (miles) his " whole land of Melros with its pertinents, &c. within the viscounty of Banff, as concerns his rights to all the lands which had been acquired by his father, to be held by the said Janet, and Mariot and Elizabeth daughters of the deceased Sir John of Monimous aforesaid," and by whichever of them survives, and by their heirs. Mr. Macdonald in his " Place Names in Strathbogie,"[4] gives an account of the Barons of Garntuly and Berclay, the first being John de Barclay, whose charters range from about 1351 to 1357 and the second, his son Andrew,

1 Ant. A. and B. III. p. 573.   3 Reg. Epis. Abdn. II. pp. 281, 282.
2 II. p. 32.   4 pp 82 94.

whom we have just mentioned, and whose charters run from 1360 to 1385.

The unworthy David II. died in 1371, and was succeeded by his nephew, Robert II, the first sovereign of the Stuart line, being the son of Walter the Steward of Scotland and Marjory the eldest daughter of King Robert Bruce. In 1355 Robert had married as his second wife, Euphemia Ross, Countess of Moray, daughter of Hugh, Earl of Ross (1320-1333). It is mentioned that Queen Euphemia's sister, Lady Jannet, married first, Sir John of Monymusk, and secondly Sir Alexander de Moravia (Moray) of Abercairney, but our information is too meagre to allow of our understanding about her marriage with Sir John of Monymusk.[1] Sir John had gone to the Continent, for in February 7th, 1369, he signs as a witness to a deed and seals it at Königsberg in Prussia, along with others from this country.[2]

The family 'de Moravia' (of Moray) was rising into great power. In 1196 Hugh de Moravia, the chief of the family, had acquired that vast territory—the 'Southern Land' of Caithness—which now gives the title of Duke to their lineal descendant. Gilbert de Moravia, archdeacon of Moray was in 1223 appointed Bishop of Caithness and then built the Cathedral at Dornoch, as we mentioned before, and it was his kinsman, probably his nephew, Bishop Andrew de Moravia, who about 1224 laid the foundations of the grandest of all the northern minsters, 'the lantern of Moray' at Elgin, on the opposite shore of the firth.[3]

Michael of Monymusk—whose relationship to Sir John we do not know, but they may have been brothers—was canon of Brechin in 1349.[4] On the 10th February, 1362, he subscribes

[1] See Mr. Monday, From the Tone to the Don, pp. 33-35.
[2] Ibid p. 31.
[3] Dr. Joseph Robertson, Abbeys, pp. 48, 50.
[4] Mr. Walcott, Ancient Church, p. 396

himself on a charter at Aberdeen, as 'Michael de Monimusk Dean,' another subscriber being 'Richard de Moravia Subdean.'[1] We shall find immediately that he was Dean of Glasgow in 1366. He was Bishop of Dunkeld from about 1367 to March 1376, and was buried in the choir of the Cathedral there.[2] He held the office of Great Chamberlain of Scotland for a short time about 1364, and he sat in the Parliament at Scone 3rd April, 1373.[3] The Scottish Parliament consisted of only one house, as all the representatives—prelates, peers, and commissioners—sat and voted together as a single house, while its grand committee was styled 'the Lords of the Articles.'

Two interesting notices of him are preserved in the Public Records of the reign of Edward III. In the thirty-seventh year of his reign, in a paragraph with the title 'Safe conduct for the Earl of Mar and others,' there is given the letter of Safe conduct to England for "Magister Michael Monemusk of Scotland coming peaceably with one companion and two servants of his retinue and four horses and other things—such to continue for one year. Given at Westminster, 20th day of February, 1362." Four years after, under date, Westminster, 2nd July, 1366, another entry occurs—" Magister Michael de Monymusk, Dean of Glasgow, has a letter from the King of safe conduct, permitting him to come whether by land or sea into the kingdom of the King of England for the sake of studying in the University of Oxford or elsewhere as he wished, with six horsemen and two footmen, to stay there and study and thence return to Scotland—this protection to last for one year."[4] It must have been very unusual for a Dean, travelling in such state, to go to the University of Oxford for the sake of studying.

1 Reg. Epis: Abdn. I. p. 93.
2 Mr. Walcott, Ancient Church, pp. 191, 213.
3 Bishop Keith's Cata. of Scot. Bishops, p. 84.
4 Rotuli Scotiæ, I. pp. 870, 871, 904.

Yet what a spirit was stirring Oxford at that very time, when "Wycliffe was the champion of a great party in the University and in the Church, and honours, dignities crowded upon him!"[1]

For three generations the family of the 'Monymusks' owned the 'fair barony' of Forglen, and when a female became heiress, her husband, John Fraser, received the lands by charter in 1388.

To all who shall see or hear of this charter John by the divine permission Abbot of the Monastery of Aberbrothok and the convent of the same place eternal greeting in the Lord, Know that we by consent of our whole Chapter after a diligent consideration of the matter, have given to John Fraser and the heirs of his body to be lawfully begotten, our whole land of Forglen which pertains to the Barchbennach along with the right of patronage of the Church of the same land for homage and service to us and our successors and for doing in the army of the Lord King in our name for the said land what pertains to the Bracbennach as often as there may be need Which land indeed Gilbert Urry and Johanna his spouse, heir of the late Marjory spouse of John Fraser, daughter and heiress of the late Sir John of Monimusk knight, at Forglen the third day of the month of August in the year of our Lord 1387 before very many men worthy of faith viz. Sir Robert of Dunbar, John son of Nicholas, John Boners, monks, Alexander Skyrnich of Aberbrothoc our marischal, Thomas Fraser of Kornton, William of Dissynton son and heir of Sir William of Dissynton knight, Andrew Melvyn, John Seton, burgesses of Aberbrothoc, John Conan of Conansythe and many others, restored and resigned &c to us by

---

[1] Dean Milman, Latin Christianity, VIII. pp. 161, 162:

staff and baton To be held and possessed by the same John and his lawful heirs of us and our successors for ever freely &c And if it happen that the said John and his lawful heirs fail of lawful heirs Andrew son of the said John for himself and his lawful heirs shall possess freely in the same manner the aforesaid land And if it happen that the said Andrew or his lawfully begotten heirs depart into the fates no heir surviving as is set forth William Fraser his brother and the heirs of his body lawfully begotten shall possess well and peacefully the said land of Forglen in the way in which it is expressed above, Preserving always to us and our successors the Regality in the same land Preserving also the right of every one Rendering thereupon to us and our successors yearly xl shillings sterling at two terms of the year &c But the said John and his heirs and also Andrew and William and their sons and heirs as is set forth before shall none the less do homage to us and our successors The said John also and his heirs &c shall in no manner sell or mortgage the said land or in any ways alienate it without our special leave or that of our successors sought at the same time and obtained In testimony of which transaction we have affixed our common seal to our present charter drawn up in form of manuscript while to another part of this charter the seal of the said John has been openly affixed our said Chapter being witness at Aberbrothoc 2nd of March, the year above stated.[1]

Pitfichie seems thus to have gone to the Urry family through Joanna Fraser, the daughter of Marjory of Monymusk and John Fraser. We never hear again of 'the Monymusks.'

After being only twenty-three years in the Fraser family the

[1] Colln. A. and B. pp. 511-513.

lands of Forglen were restored to the Abbey of Arbroath in 1411. It seems very singular self-denial.

> To the venerable father in Christ and his lord Superior in this part lord Walter by the grace of God Abbot of the Monastery of Aberbrothok and to the Convent of the same place John Fraser lord of Forglen, due reverence with honour, I John Fraser aforesaid, not compelled by force or fear nor fallen in error nor seduced by deceit or fraud but moved by my own mere and spontaneous will, restore into your hands and for myself and my heirs by staff and baton absolutely and 'simpliciter' resign all and singly my lands of Forglen with all their pertinents which I hold of you 'in capite' along with the whole right and claim of right which I or my heirs have, had, or shall be able to have in the said lands with their pertinents in whatever way so that you my Lord Superior in this part may be able freely to dispone the said lands with their pertinents, according to the good pleasure of your own will so that neither I nor my heirs nor any man nor any woman in our name shall be able to claim or in any way defend any right or claim of right possession or property in the same lands with their pertinents or in any part of them In testimony of which thing I have placed my seal to these presents At Aberdeen 11th December, 1411.[1]

As was mentioned, the kindly intercourse between England and Scotland was fatally interrupted by the War of Independence, which was also injurious to religion. Owing to the long Civil War few gifts were bestowed on the Church, but it was some time before 1357 that the famous 'Chapel' at Chapel of Garioch was founded by Christian Bruce, Lady of the Garioch, the sister of King Robert,[2] who was married to Sir Andrew

[1] Colln. A. and B. p. 513.   [2] Dr. Davidson, Inverurie, p. 80.

Murray of Bothwell, a brave and valiant soldier, afterwards Regent of Scotland.[1]

In 1333 an inquisition was made at Aberdeen in regard to the 'second tithes' from all returns and forfeits falling to the King of Scotland, and among others there is a memorandum to the effect that from the lands of the Bishop and Church of St. Andrews, lying within the vicecounty of Aberdeen and of Banff when that See of St. Andrews is vacant, the second tithes are due to the Bishop and Church of Aberdeen, namely from Monymuske, Kynkel, &c.[2] In regard to this we find in 1385 a letter from Robert King of Scots directing his chaplain, Walter Bell, rector of Dumberny, to give satisfaction to Adam, Bishop of Aberdeen, respecting the second tithes due to him from the lands of Monymusk and others on account of a vacancy in the See of St. Andrews.[3]

In 1365 Andrew was Prior of Monymusk and witnesses a deed by Thomas, Earl of Mar, who is mentioned in David II's deed reversing the attainder of Henry of Monymusk. He was the tenth and last earl of the Celtic line, succeeding in 1332 and dying before 1377. St. Machar's Cathedral, Old Aberdeen, was begun in 1366.

In 1373-4 Symon de Katness was rector of the Church of Menymous, also spelled by him Monimous, witnessing two deeds at Edinburgh, January 14th and 15th.

In the Exchequer Rolls[4] there is the following record,— Account of Sir (dominus) Walter of Byger, rector of the Church of Erole [Errol in the Carse of Gowrie] Chamberlain of Scotland, rendered at Perth, Feb. 17, 1374.

Contributions of the Clergy . . And of xxx Lib. of the contribution of the bishopric of Aberdeen. And of

---

1 Cartulary of Cambuskenneth, p. xlv.
2 Reg. Epis. Abdn. I. pp. 54, 58.
3 Reg. Epis, Abdn. I. p 171.
4 Exchequer Rolls, ii. p. 457.

vs viii*d* of the lands of Monymousk which belong to the Bishop of St. Andrews, in the Bishopric of Aberdeen.

Alexander Stewart by murder and enforced marriage seized on the Earldom of Mar. He was leader at the battle of Harlaw near Inverurie, in 1411. He was a son of Alexander Stewart, Earl of Buchan, the Wolf of Badenoch (a son of Robert II.) who burned Elgin and its cathedral in 1390. Dr. Joseph Robertson[1] gives an account of the lawlessness of the time, while the Register of the Bishopric of Moray speaking of the burning of the cathedral says, "There was no law in Scotland, but the great man oppressed the poor man, and the whole kingdom was one den of thieves; slaughters, robberies, fire-raisings, and other crimes passed unpunished, and outlawed justice was banished from the realm." Mr. J. R. Green says[2] "the victory of Harlaw saved the Lowlands from the rule of the Celt," and Mr. Hill Burton[3] estimates it as "a more memorable deliverance than even that of Bannockburn."

We now come to a 'remarkable' letter that would be read by the Prior with due solemnity in the Chancel of our Church to the canons and clergy. In 1424-5, March 17th, James I, 'the flower of the Scottish kings,' 'the ablest and most accomplished sovereign of all the Stuart line,' the year after his release from captivity in England, having summoned his second Parliament to meet at Perth, wrote the following letter to the Benedictine and Augustinian Abbots and Priors in Scotland, being 'evidently bent on the reformation of the Church as well as the State.'

James by the grace of God King of Scots to the venerable fathers in Christ the Abbots and Priors of the orders and

---

[1] Stat. Ecc. Scot. p. lxxvii.   [2] History II. p. 752.   [3] History II. p. 394.

rules of SS. Benedict and Augustine, greeting, with prayer for
your advancing to greater heights of perfection. The somewhat precipitate fall and threatening ruin of our sacred
religion, declining daily from the primitive basis of its
institution, urge us to attempt to stir up rather sharply your
torpid spirits and their sleepy slothfulness. Wherefore it is
fitting that you should awake and take to heart how in our
kingdom the perfection of monastic religion has been as far
as possible relaxed, how prelacy tends to extinction, everywhere defamed and reduced to disgrace; just as formerly our
mother Jerusalem contemned by her degenerate sons and
repudiated by their ignoble fathers, herself, doubtless, as we
painfully recall, repressing her bitterness, prostrates herself
flat on the ground as defamed. Against her piteous—nay
pitiable fall, the holy Church of Zion, His daughter, cries
into the ears of the Lord of Sabaoth, because her regular
discipline, formerly shining with angelic brightness, terrible
as an army drawn up for battle, deprives us of her likeness
owing to her dissolute fathers and untamed sons, so that by
your pernicious doing and example she, most squalid and
worthy of compassion, is left covered with reproaches and in
affliction. On this account and owing to the matters aforesaid, our inmost mind being wounded unto death, and we
being affected with pain of heart, desiring that the foresaid
matters should be thoroughly reformed as soon as possible,
require and admonish you, Religious Fathers, exhorting you
in the bowels of Jesus Christ, to put away all excuses for sins
and neglects, and to be zealous to meet, at a suitable place
and time, for the reformation in this manner of your sacred
religion, degraded too deeply as we stated, and using diligent
consideration and matured thought, to strive to resume
fitting ways in accordance with God, especially in celebrations

of the Chapters General, in order that the fervour of
religion may be able more easily to breathe in accordance
with its pristine state ; lest on account of your careless sloth,
the munificence of the King 'which formerly notably
endowed, and nobly enriched your monasteries in former
times, for the preservation of himself and the salvation of
his subjects, may repent of having erected marble walls, when
he has considered how you have so shamelessly lost the
morals of religion. Therefore rise up with manliness and
holy severity against this ignominious plague—and with
greater fervour of spirit cut off by a rigorous discipline
all such occasions of dissolution, considering that, when the
helm of discipline is despised, nothing is to be looked for
but that religion shall suffer shipwreck. We therefore
wishing to make you attentive intend, while you are zealous
to give effect to the matters aforesaid, to direct and defend
you and your deeds according to God in all things with our
Royal protection ; if perchance there have been any
contradictors, to restrain and beat them back as far as we
are bound ; we shall rejoice also that you have such
petitioners as may intercede for our Royal State, by whom
certainly the honour and advancement of our kingdom shall
prosper. May the Most High inspire you, Fathers, for the
service of your religion and for prosperous and wished-for
successes according to God. Given under the testimony of
our private seal in our Parliament at Perth the 17th March,
in the 19th year of our reign.[1]

With what chastened feelings must the Prior have read
such a letter from the recently released King, to the clergy
assembled in our Church, its "exhortation showing that the

[1] For the Latin see Dr. J. Robertson, Stat. Ecc. Scot. p. xc.

corruption of the religious orders throughout the country was already general in the year 1425."[1]

In 1437 Monymusk is entered in the Cathedral Body, Old Aberdeen, as among the twelve "Ebdomadarii," the sum assigned to it being iiij Lib., Kynkell and Rethven alone having other sums,[2] and in 1445, with the consent of the Bishop of St. Andrews, it was added to the 'College of Canons' by Bishop Lindsay.[3] In 1448, when a tax had to be levied by the Bishop for providing vestments, the sum of 40 Lib. is stated as the value to be assessed upon the prebend,[4] and in a deed of 1468 we find a reference made to the town 'Manse of Monymusk,' in the Chanonry beside the Cathedral, 'as one goes by the high-way to the hill of Tillydrone.'[5] It is singular :hat 40 Lib. is also the sum given as the value of the beneice of the parish for 1445 in the rent-roll at Castle Forbes, *hich we shall afterwards mention.

From 1466 to 1478 Patrick Graham was Bishop of St. Adrews, succeeding Bishop Kennedy who was "the greatest arl best man of his age." He confirmed by deed to John Dvidson, the lands of Cornabo, with its pertinents, in the ba)ny of Monymusk. This is the oldest deed in Monymusk Hase relating to property on the estate.[6]

[o all who shall see or hear this deed Patricius by the grace f God and of the Apostolic see Bishop of St. Andrews ternal greeting in the Lord Know that we have given and ganted and by this our present charter confirmed to John Lvidson as heir of the late Helen of Cornabo—Cornabo

1 Dr., Robertson, Stat. Ecc. Scot. p. xc.
2 RegEpis. Abdn. II. p. 65.
3 Ibiop. 152, 253.
4 Reg. Epis. Abdn. II. p. 71.
5 Ibid. I. pp. 302, 303.
6 Mr. Monday, From the Tone to the Don, pp. 79, etc.

with its pertinents lying in the barony of Monymusk within the County of Aberdeen which land belongs to the heir of the said deceased Helen and which land the late John of Cornabo with staff and baton surrendered and resigned in the hands of our late predecessor of blessed memory and all right and claim which was in him and his heirs in perpetual peace in all time to come To be held and had the said whole land with its pertinents of us and our successors Bishops of St. Andrews in fee and heritage by all their boundaries and marches of the same with woods plains meadows pastures moors passages bye-ways waters springs and fishings and with all other and sundry liberties commodities easements and righteous pertinents as well under ground as above looking towards the said land or whatever way one is able to look as freely quietly and honourably as the said late John of Cornabo held or possessed the aforesaid land of our predecessors before resignation of the same afterwards made quite freely quietly and honourably Paying to us and our successors the said John Davidson and his heirs six shillings and eight pence usual money of Scotland at the term of Pentecost and feast of St Martin by eqal portions in name of Kain and the fruits of the said lad due to us and customary and that for every other buren which shall be able or requires to be exacted In witess whereof our seal is appended to the aforesaid presnts A.D. 14— there being present Master Hugh Douglas rctor of the .. St Andrews, and James Stry.. our .. with vaous other witnesses to the foregoing specially called and ased.

This Bishop was the Hon. Patrick Graham, son of Lord Graham, and the second of the two grandsons of King Robert III who in succession held the Bishopric of St. Andres, the other being Bishop Kennedy—Mary, Robert III's daghter, being three times married. Bishop Patrick when at Rome in 1472 prevailed on Pope Sixtus IV to erect St. Andrews into an Archbishopric, making him Papal Legate, with all Scotland for a province and the other twelve bishops as suffragans. "He also received a commission as Apostolic Nuncio to Scotland that he might more effectually levy subsidies and soldiers for a crusade against the Turks, who under the victorious standard of Mahomet the Second were spreading grief and terror through Europe. But as this had been done without the knowledge or consent of the King or of the Bishops, it was vigorously resisted by both. The Bishops considered themselves specially aggrieved. They were subjected as suffragans to a prelate whose equals they had so long been; and as if the character and powers of a Metropolitan were not sufficiently offensive, he came among them with the odious commission of an Apostolic Nuncio to extort a tithe of their benefices for a year against the Turks. In their indignation they taxed themselves in 12,000 merks, and making common cause with the King and the Court, precipitated a conflict which proved fatal to the Archbishop. Obstructed and assailed on every side, impoverished, imprisoned, excommunicated, his reason at last gave way. The Pope deposed him 9th January 1478 from his Archbishopric, degraded him from all holy orders and office, and condemned him to captivity for life within the walls of a monastery. His first prison was Inchcolm in the Firth of Forth, then Dunfermline, and then he was carried to Lochleven, to find a grave in the ancient Priory of St. Serf's Inch."[1]

In 1473, 1475, and 1483, John Myrton of Monymusk, one of the Prebendaries and Canons of Aberdeen Cathedral is present as a witness to various writs,[2] and in the Register[3] there is the following entry, such as we have not met with before:—

[1] Dr. J. Robertson, Stat. Ecc. Scot. pp. cix.-cxvi.
[2] Reg. Epis. Abdn. I. pp. 309, 311, 315.
[3] Ibid. II. p. 219.

4th October, the anniversary for the soul of Master John Myrtoun formerly rector of Monymusk—xiij*sh*. iiij*d*. from land formerly belonging to David Kyntor now belonging to Alexander Kyntor in Castle-street (in vico castri) Aberdeen, on the north side of the same, who died A.D. 1489.

In 1479 Richard Strathaquhyn was vicar of the parish, perhaps the same person who became Prior in 1500, twenty-one years after.

In 1496-7 Gavin of Douglas was Prior, or more probably Rector. The teinds were in danger, and Lord Forbes who afterwards obtained the Church lands in Keig, had something to do with them. Here we see the lay-element appearing for the first time, as far as we know, which we shall find in our next chapter to be so disastrous. There must, however, be some mistake in the date given for this letter, for we shall find that both Duncan Forbes and his wife died in 1584, so that they could not have had to do with the teinds in 1496.

A letter was directed from the Lords of Council to the Sheriffs in that part to charge them to command in the King's name the Lord Forbes Duncan Forbes and Duncan's wife to have no intermeddling with the teinds of Monymusk pertaining to Master Gavin of Douglas and to charge the parishioners to obey the said Master Gavin in the paying to him and his factors of the same teinds according to the Prior's letters and to summon the said persons for the 12th October next.[1]

[1] Ant. A. and B. III. p. 483.

CHAPTER VIII.

RECORDS FROM 1500 TO THE REFORMATION IN 1560.
THE DECADENCE OF THE OLD ORDER.
THE SPOLIATION OF THE LANDS.

KING'S College, Aberdeen, was founded by James IV. in 1494, and was constituted in 1505 by Bishop Elphinstone, 'the most distinguished of all the bishops of Aberdeen.'[1] He was the son of the Archdeacon of Teviotdale, and to him was largely due the introduction of printing into our country, under the auspices of James IV and his queen, Margaret, the sister of Henry VIII, in 1507, thirty years after it was common in England.

In 1500 Richard Strachan was presented as Prior by James IV. Here again we see the lay-element appearing. "In the reign of James III. the Monasteries lost the right of the election of their superiors, and thus a new element of disorder, state-interference and secular influence, was introduced."[2] "From that reign the Monks were seldom, if ever, allowed to exercise their canonical right of electing their abbots, or Cathedral-chapters their bishops; and the sovereigns, adopting the papal practice, disposed of these offices for pecuniary or other considerations to persons who, in too many cases, were unworthy of them, and unable to perform the duties they involved."[3]

Probably before he became Prior (if we compare the dates), Strachan, like Bishop Elphinstone's father, believed in the

[1] Mr. Cosmo Innes, Reg. Epis. Abdn. I. p. xlii.
[2] Mr. Walcott, Ancient Church, p. 8.
[3] Dr. Campbell, St. Giles, p. 95.

ancient privilege of marriage, although it could not be celebrated. His daughter, who bore his own name, being called Strauchine, thus showing that there was no concealment in the matter, married William Forbes in Abersnithock, now Braehead, one of the farms belonging to the Priory. He was a grandson of Sir John Forbes, first laird of Tolquhon in Tarves, of whom Dr. Temple[1] and Mr. Jervise[2] speak. Dr. Davidson[3] calls him a son, but he does not seem to have had a son called William. Mr. Forbes-Leith now represents the family.

"Without under-rating the effects of the Reformation of religion, it may be safely said that no revolution in politics or opinions can have produced such a change in the structure of society as the emancipation of the clergy from celibacy and the sudden destruction of the monastic societies. It was an age of general immorality which peculiarly disgraced the Church."[4] "The monastic orders were becoming more and more degenerate, and the nobles were beginning to hanker after their immense possessions. Thus the Church, which in the twelfth century had been assimilated to the Roman model, had at the commencement of the sixteenth (the time we have now reached) sunk even more than its Celtic predecessor from a state of purity and energy into one of corruption and decay,"[5] and just as the possessions of the Celtic Church had been seized by laymen in the days of its decay, so did the Church come to be plundered again at the Reformation.

In 1500 a 'visitation of the Jewels of the Cathedral,' Aberdeen, was made in the presence, among others, of the rector of Monymusk, as had been done on 10th March, 1497.[6]

[1] Fermartyn, p. 379.
[2] Epitaphs, II. p. 350.
[3] Inverurie, p. 127.
[4] Mr. Cosmo Innes, Sketches, pp. 117, 87.
[5] Dr. Campbell, St. Giles, p. 96.
[6] Reg. Epis. Abdn. II. pp. 170, 169.

In Bishop Elphinstone's constitutions of the Cathedral-Chapter in 1506, Monymusk is mentioned among the twenty-three prebendaries, the sum stated as payable by it for the sustenance of the vicars in the choir being vj Lib., while among the twenty choral-vicars the nineteenth is—
dominus John Litstar at the stall of Monimusk
from the same . . . . . . iij lib. vj shil. viijd.
and from the chaplainry of Fyvy . . vj lib. xiij shil. iiijd.
and of the sum distributed at 'le Mydlettroun' there is given domino John Litster of Monimusk . . . xxvij shil. viijd.[1]

On September 9th, 1513, James IV fell at Flodden, aged forty-one. He had a stall in the choir and a vote in the chapter of Glasgow Cathedral, and in penance for his complicity in his father's murder, he went to the end of his life with an iron girdle round his waist. Bishop Elphinstone died the next year, 25th October, and lies beneath his tomb of black marble in King's College Chapel.

At this time Alexander Symson was rector of Monymusk, and Thomas Scherar was vicar or curate, the rector being evidently much occupied with his duties in the Cathedral. In the list of the Cathedral Jewels drawn up in 1549 by Master Alexander Galloway, rector of Kynkel, of which we shall speak afterwards, there is mentioned—

The tenth Communion Cup with a Plate, of silver-gilt, the gift of the venerable man Master Alexander Symsoun formerly rector of Monymusk, of date 1516, weighing one pound fifteen ounces and a half-ounce;

and in the list of ornaments for the High Altar of the Cathedral drawn up by Bishop Gavin Dunbar there is the entry—

one pall or hood of red colour, of gold, with gold fringes for the same, the gift of Master Alexander Simsoun rector of Monymusk.[2]

[1] Reg. Epis. Abdn. II. pp. 93, 94, 97, 98. [2] II. pp. 180, 194.

While he was himself of so generous and cultured a nature, others tried to take advantage of him.

On the 10th December, 1518, which day appeared in person the discreet man Master Thomas Scherar curate or vicar of Monimusk and had a personal interview with Duncan Elmisle living in Petfeche, and humbly and with due persistency required him and asked from him in name of procurator, as he asserted, for the venerable and excellent man Master Alexander Symsone rector of Monimusk, if the tithes of corn of the town of Petfeche were collected in the yard of the said Duncan with the leave and power of the same, and if the said Duncan hindered the servants of the foresaid Rector in the correction and emending and raising of the said tithes. The same Duncan confessed that he had given leave so that the said tithes could be collected in his yard and likewise confessed that he had hindered and interrupted the said rector's servants on account of the breaking and destroying of his fences (or ditches). On which replies and confessions the said Master Thomas with his authority as procurator as above, imposed in addition to the said tithes of corn the sum of twenty-four merks Scots money to be paid by the said Duncan at the usual terms for the reasons aforesaid And protested for remedy at law On which the said Master Thomas by authority as procurator as above took instruments Done within the parish Church aforesaid nine o'c. a.m. present in the same David Farquhar, Dik clerk-depute, Alexander Robertson, Findlay Quisne, with diverse others summoned for the foresaid matters and questioned.[1]

On the 14th November, 1519, 'the venerable and discreet

[1] Ant. A. and B. III. pp. 499, 500.

man Master Alexander Sympson, rector of Monimusk,' presented to the Cathedral Chapter an inventory of all the goods left by Bishop Alexander Gordon, in the Bishop's palace, and in the same year, Gavin Dunbar being now Bishop, in the list of the Cathedral body, Monymusk is entered at viij Lib. (two pounds more than in 1506) in the account of the funds 'for the sustentation of the vicars-choral and others ministering in the Cathedral.'[1] Alexander Symsoun of Monymusk was present when a charter was signed in the Chanonry on the 8th June, 1521. There are also two entries of peculiar interest regarding him. In the list of " Masses founded by deceased venerable men " there is given[2]—

Daily Mass for the soul of Master Alexander Symsone formerly Rector of Monymusk.

From the croft of Andrew Brabnar xiij sh. iiijd. but now belonging to Gilbert Molysone. And from our croft in the hands of Master John Gordoun lying beyond the gate of the street of the gallows (*i.e.* the Gallowgate) on the west side of the late Alexander Bynne xlv sh. And in the village of Kyntor (Kintore) of the lands occupied by Fergus Hendersone xxxiij sh. And of the lands in the same place occupied by James Duff xiij sh. And by John Byssait xxiij sh. And by William Kelle xx sh. And from the lands and roods of the owner of Vatirtoun (Waterton) lying in the Newburgh iij Lib.

In all . . . x Lib. viijs. iiijd.

Besides this endowment for the daily Mass in the Cathedral, there was also another for a special yearly Commemoration on the day of his death.

On the 14th November the anniversary for the soul of Master Alexander Symson formerly Rector of Monymusk

[1] Reg. Epis. Abdn. II. pp. 174-178, 107.   [2] Reg. Epis. Abdn. II. p. 226.

xxvj sh. viijd. from the village of Auchinstiuk in the hands of the proprietor of Stralocht—who died A.D. [   ][1]

In an addition made to a memorandum of 1511 it is stated that Bishop Dunbar "received in whole for two years from the lands of Kege and Monemusk, 'the second tithes,' owing to the decease of the late reverend father, Andrew Forman, Archbishop of St. Andrews."[2] Archbishop Forman died in December, 1521, and Archbishop James Beaton was translated from Glasgow to St. Andrews in 1522. 'The second tithes,' which formed a fruitful subject of dispute, "flowed undoubtedly from a very ancient royal grant, and consisted of a tenth of the rents and dues payable by the thanes and tenants of the King's demesne lands; a tenth of the revenue levied from Crown vassals for ward, relief, marriage, and non-entry; and of the escheats, fines, and whole issues of the King's Courts—as well in burgh as *to land*, within that district."[3]

The next Prior that we know of was John Akenhead. David Farlie was appointed his colleague, and we have now an account of the ceremony at the installation of a Prior.

15th December, 1522—the eleventh indiction [a period of fifteen years, instituted by Constantine in 312]—in the first year of the pontificate of Pope Adrian VI. appeared in person the venerable and religious father dompnus (= dominus) David Farlie, Prior of the place and convent of Monymusk in the diocese of Aberdeen, of the order of St. Augustine, having and holding in his hands a certain process of the reverend father and lord in Christ John Baptist by the grace of God and the Apostolic See Bishop

[1] Reg. Epis. Abdn. II. p. 220.
[2] Ibid. I. p. 359.
[3] Reg. Epis. Abdn. I. p. xxxiv.

of Caserta—of date Rome 3rd October A.D. 1522, the bull of the most holy father and lord in Christ lord Adrian VI by divine providence Pope, in the first year of his pontificate, containing in itself about and concerning the provision of the said Priorship of Monymusk—which bull had been graciously granted to the same dompnus David Farlie— which process he delivered to be read, published and intimated and duly committed for execution to the venerable man Master Robert Elphinstone treasurer of Aberdeen— humbly requiring him to deliver and conclusively to convey to him really and with effect the real, actual, and corporal possession of the said Priory by virtue of the said Apostolic letter and process lately fulminated and under the penalties contained in the same. The said treasurer as a son of obedience and willing in all things to obey the Apostolic commands reverently took into his hands the foresaid process and the bull contained in the same letter, and the same being read *viva voce* and publicly, successively came to the Chapter-house of the said Priory and Monastery of the same, the Canons of the same being assembled at the touch of the bell as is the custom, and to the Choir of the said Church—and then to the said dompnus David the Prior, principally named in the said Apostolic letter and process, assigned the usual and accustomed place in the chapter and stall in the Choir and inducted and invested him in the said Priory with all his rights and pertinents . . for real actual and corporal possession, admonishing all and single Canons of this place and Priory and others having interest that they should obey and submit to him and no other promptly and readily in such Priorship. The said Canons took the oath of obedience successively to the said dominus Prior with joined hands as is the custom and received the

M

same as their Prior with all reverence and honour On which the said Prior took instruments Done at the said Monastery 10 a.m., present Master Duncan Udny dompnus *John Hay* dompnus John Jaffray Thomas Udny and Thomas Autan and different other persons.

The same day in the Indiction and Pontificate as above, appeared in person the Venerable and Religious Father dompnus John (Akynheid) lately Prior of the Monastery of Monymusk and Convent of the same of the order of St. Augustine in the diocese of Aberdeen, having and holding in his hands a certain process of an Apostolic letter of the most Reverend father and lord in Christ lord John Baptist by the grace of God and the Apostolic see Bishop of Caserta, Cardinal, Judge and Executor specially deputed by the said Apostolic see, along with his colleagues in this part . . namely a bull of the foresaid most Holy father and lord in Christ, lord Adrian VI by divine providence Pope, the contents of which had regard to the reservation of all and single fruits of the foresaid Priory to the same dompnus John as long as he lives, to be received taken and lifted by his own authority, and also had regard to his return to the same Priory if the said dominus David (Farlie) die or retire or in any way demit the said Priorship, as is said to be contained more fully and at length in the same Apostolic letter and process lately fulminated of date 13th October A.D. as above Which process he delivered to me the undersigned notary public to be read published intimated Which with all reverence as was becoming I took into my hands and I read through and published the same from beginning to end with a loud and intelligible voice On which the said dompnus John (Akynheid) took instruments of me the notary Done within the said Monastery 10 a.m. present witnesses as above.

The same day appeared in person dompnus David (Farlie) Prior of the Monastery of Monymusk and asserted that he from reasonable causes influencing his mind could by no means continue in the rule and charge of the said place and canons, and owing to the foresaid considerations made, constituted, and solemnly ordained and substituted the religious father dompnus John Akynheid as usufructuary of the said place and Monastery to whom by Apostolical authority the whole and single fruits of the same are reserved, and committed to the same his entire power and jurisdiction over the same place and the Canons of the same in absence of himself dompnus David (Farlie) yet without prejudice to his provision from the Priorship and to his bull granted him by the Roman Curia . . On which the said dompnus David prior aforesaid took instruments Done within the said Monastery 11 a.m. present in the same Master Duncan Udny, Thomas Autan, Thomas Udny and the Canons above mentioned.[1]

8th April 1524 which day personally appeared dompnus *John Hay, Canon-regular* of the Monastery of Monymusk and asserted that an arrest was laid with due notice by Master Thomas Scherar Dean of Christianity of Strathdon, upon his yearly pension of Echt sequestrated in the hands of John the Prior of the said Monastery in proportion to the excesses reached by it in the present year and he denies that the same would be a true arrest and that it should be by no means to his prejudice in the future and protested for remedy at law On which he took instruments Done in the village of Monymusk 4 p.m. present Patrick Huyd and Helen Tullacht.[2]

[1] Ant. A. and B. III. pp. 484, 485, 486.   [2] p. 486.

This is the second time we have heard of Canon John Hay. We shall afterwards refer very specially to him. We before found that revenue was got from 'Upper Echt;' this may refer to the same farm.

> 10th December 1524 Same day appeared in person Thomas Davidson of Auchinhamperis in name of procurator for the Venerable Religious Father dompnus John Akenheid usufructuary of Monymusk and had audience of the most powerful Lord, *the Lord of Forbes*, and he, in name as procurator as above, asserted that the said Lord had certain benefits from the said usufructuary and the said Monastery by reason of which he is held to defend and maintain the said usufructuary and the said monastery The said Lord aforesaid acquiescing in the said inquiries confessed that all and each of the foresaid things were true and consonant to reason and promised faithfully to maintain and defend the same usufructuary or Prior and the foresaid Monastery in all their just causes and actions as far as he could by right On which the said Thomas in his name as procurator as above took instruments Done at the Church of Tough 3 p.m. present at the same *William Forbes of Corsindae* Alexander Gordon of Strathdon John Baxter John Makky and George Maver.[1]

This is a most interesting record. Lord Forbes here comes under obligation to defend the Priory in all causes, but one of the witnesses to his deed is his own relative, William Forbes of Corsindae, who, we shall find, is ready on other occasions to be a witness in respect of the Priory lands, and whose son, Duncan, by and by takes possession of the whole of its property in this parish! This record is 35 years before the Reformation, so that Corsindae was preparing for it in good time!

[1] Ant. A. and B. III. pp. 486, 487.

13th December 1524, On the same day in the thirteenth indiction appeared in person Thomas Ronnald son of the late William Ronnald in Craig and acknowledged that he had received in his hands from the discreet man Master Thomas Scherar vicar or curate of Monymusk [who was spoken of in the deed of 10th December, 1518] the sum of six pounds nineteen shillings in money as reckoned, and one silver girdle with equipment of the same, one velvet falling collar, one silver cross with certain jewels, two small sleeves of velvet, in a casket previously given in custody by the said Thomas, the said Thomas exonerated the said Master Thomas in respect of the foresaid sum and the above-mentioned goods and gave him a perpetual discharge On which the said Master Thomas took instruments Done within the parish Church of Monymusk 9 a.m. in presence of Alexander Maver, John Tough, Thomas Brown and ' Alexander Cornabo.'[1]

13th October 1525, On the same day appeared in person the Venerable father dompnus John Akinheid usufructuary of the monastery of Monymusk and asserted that the Venerable and Religious father dompnus David Farlie Prior of the foresaid monastery had made a certain common seal of the said monastery anew with the consent of dompnus *John Hay canon-regular* of the same but without the consent and advice of the said usufructuary And broke and annulled the said seal as far as lies in him And protested that the said seal in future should by no means be to the prejudice of himself the said usufructuary and of the said monastery On which all and singly the said usufructuary took instruments of me as notary public These things

[1] Ant. A. and B. III. pp. 483, 484.

were done in the cemetery of the said Monastery as at 10 o'c. a.m. or thereabout, present there a venerable man and honourable men dominus John Carlyle Vicar of Glenbuchat, Peter Carlyle his relative, and William Russel with diverse others &c.[1]

Here mention is made a third time of Canon John Hay.

In 1526 Patrick Dunbar, Monymusk, and Alexander Elphinstone, Invernochty, were prebendaries of the Cathedral, Old Aberdeen,[2] the latter being instituted in October, 1520.[3]

The proper order of the Cathedral Body in the stalls, chapter, and procession, arranged according to the time of institution, is given for 1526, Monymusk closing the list, the names of "the venerable and eminent men, *magistri et domini*," who held the five offices of dignity (the dean, precentor, chancellor, treasurer, and archdeacon) and the twenty-three prebends, being also recorded.

3rd November 1527 On the same day appeared in person Robert Hart alias Master Buyt one of the Couriers of our supreme Lord King James V and produced and presented to the Venerable father in Christ John usufructuary of Monymusk a letter of the said supreme Lord our King the content of which related to a sum of twelve pounds taxed by the Lords of Council After the presenting of which letter the said usufructuary offered to the said Courier in name of the said Lord our King in part payment of the said sum eight pounds usual money of the Kingdom of Scotland that he might be able to pay more easily the remainder of the said sum, which sum of eight pounds the same Courier

[1] Ant. A. and B. III. p. 487.
[2] Reg. Epis. Abdn. II. pp. 254, 255.
[3] Reg. Epis. Abdn. I. p. 386

refused On which the said usufructuary took instruments This was done within the said Monastery 9 o'c. a.m. or thereabout, present *William Forbes of Corsindae*, Master Andrew Leslie, William Russel, William Straquhyn, and John Cuyk with various others.[1]

Though it is November, Forbes of Corsindae is able to be at the Priory by 9 o'c. in the morning.

In 1528 Patrick Hamilton, Luther's disciple and friend, suffered at St. Andrews, the proto-martyr of the Reformation. A spirit of madness seems to have possessed the rulers of the Church. Persecution, the burning of Hamilton, and by and by the burning of Wishart of Pitarrow provoked the fears and increased the hatred of the people—in the end making them fierce and enraged.

8th December 1533 On the same day there appeared in person James Allanson living in Ardniedly within the parish of Monymusk and gave his consent to Thomas Allanson his son to appear before the Archbishop of St. Andrews or his chamberlain to enter himself for his 4-oxen-gangs of the holding of Ardniedly and to place and enter the same Thomas in the rental of the said Reverend Father reserving however the said James's rights in the holding during his life-time—which the said Thomas promised faithfully to fulfil On which the said Thomas took instruments Done within the churchyard of Monymusk 7 a.m. present dominus John Carlyle Vicar of Glenbichat dominus *John Reid* [Vicar of the parish] and Allan Couts and several others.[2]

Two hours after this there is an assembly within the Chapter-house of the Priory.

[1] Ant. A. and B. III. p. 488.   [2] Ant. A. and B. III. p. 499.

8th December 1533 On the same day there stood in full canonicals the venerable religious father dompnus David Farlie Prior of the place and convent of the monastery of Monymusk in the diocese of Aberdeen of the order of St. Augustine, within the Chapter-house of the said monastery after ringing of the bells according to custom, holding in his hands a process of the reverend father and lord in Christ lord John Baptist by the grace of God and the Apostolic see Bishop of Caserta . . of date Rome 3rd October A.D. &c—xxij—containing a bull of the late most holy father and lord in Christ Lord Adrian VI by divine providence Pope, in the first year of his pontificate, concerning and about the provision of the said Priorship of Monymusk such bull being graciously granted to the said dominus David Which process he handed to me as notary to be read. I then as notary went to the Chapter-house of the said priory and the canons of the same being assembled at the sound of the bell as is the custom I read it with a loud and clear voice and brought the said process to their notice After the reading of which process the said dompnus David Prior aforesaid required dompni William Wilson, Andrew Mason, Patrick Anderson, James Child, and Allan Galt, canons of the said monastery, humbly and immediately to render obedience to himself as Prior aforesaid and that each of them should do so according to the custom of religion as if to his Prior . . The said Canons all replied with one consent and each of them replied and said that they and each of them advised with the said Prior and afterwards gave him a suitable and due reply regarding the said obedience and that they did to him what they are bound of right to do and what each of them is bound to do On which the said Prior took instruments Done within the

Chapter-house of the said monastery as at 9 a.m. in presence of dominus [applied to a notary, but we afterwards find him called a chaplain] Andrew Skeoucht notary and dominus John Reid with various others.[1]

Two months after, we come to the beginning of a great strife within the Priory, the records of which are preserved in the Register House, Edinburgh.[2] The Prior must have been acting in an oppressive way toward the other clergy, and it seems strange that after being almost hid for three hundred and sixty years in Latin, the records should now be translated, and read in the Church where the strife raged so fiercely. It would be interesting to know whether there remains as full a report of any such strife in another monastery.

6th February 1534 On the same day . . appears in person the religious father dompnus Allan Galt, canon regular of the monastery of Monymusk and gave to me as a notary public a paper schedule to be read . . of which the tenor follows and is to this effect :—I dompnus Allan Gault canon aforesaid with the mind and intention of appealing and bringing forward my case and entrusting the undermentioned business to you as a Notary Public and trustworthy person, Say and state with grave complaint, feeling and considering that in time past I have been gravely injured and damaged by you dompnus David Farlie, prior of the said monastery, and because the said Prior, contrary to the laws and rule of our religion, not having investigated the charges, if there were any, has acted with malice against me, as he acts now, as I intend to prove And also I offer to stand by the commands of the Chapter in whatever charges have been alleged against me according to the rule of our

[1] Ant. A. and B. III. pp. 488, 489.   [2] Ant. A. and B. III. pp. 490-496.

religion (or order) where it is said *If however he should deny &c* And if I should be convicted I offer myself for correction as is fitting, but if perchance it should turn out that the said dompnus David when the charges have been in no way investigated by the Chapter, is proceeding against me cruelly by whatever troubles and injuries have been inflicted on me as aforesaid or by any of them I further appeal from every future injustice to my dispensation granted me by the Apostolic see and I appeal under tenor of the same, leave being sought though not granted, as appears by the same, which leave I beg on bended knees from the said dompnus David and demand, as I shall be able to produce the same dispensation to the said dompnus David if necessary, So whatever shall have been done by the same against me I demand that it should by no means be prejudicial to me and my dispensation in future but that the said dispensation should remain entire and uninjured So I invoke you the said Notary and all bye-standers as witnesses On which he took instruments Done within the Nave of the Church of the said monastery 9 o'c. a.m. or thereabout, there being present dominus *John Reid Vicar of Monymusk*, Andrew Skeocht notary, *William Hurry of Petfeche*, John Makkie and John Baxter with various others.

(2) On the same day appeared in person dompnus Allan Galt, canon aforesaid, before the venerable father dompnus David Fairlie Prior of Monymusk and assembled all his brother canons of the same Monastery and begged them with lamentations, and humbly required of them that, laying aside all favour and hatred, looking to charity and the love of God out of a true conscience as they themselves would wish to answer to God on the day of judgment, they confess and declare before the said Prior and all bye-standers if they

knew him guilty of any charge or transgression against God
and religion Who all as with one voice acquitted him and
declared him to be free from all notorious crime, but a good
religious man imbued with good morals and given over to
virtues and a godly life On which he took instruments Done
as above before witnesses as in the other document &c.

(3) On the same day appeared in person the venerable and
religious father dompnus David Fairlie prior of the Monastery of Monymusk, having heard and seen the publications
and appeals of dompnus Allan Galt Canon-regular of the
said Monastery from the same to the supreme Pontiff as to
the correction of certain backslidings of dompnus Allan
himself, committed as is asserted by the same . . The
said Prior asserted that dompnus Allan himself had been
frequently admonished and encouraged by himself to
complete certain penances enjoined on him . . Yet he
dompnus Allan by no means wished to complete penances
of this kind but persistently and openly despised them to the
great injury and scandal of religion, Wherefore lest crimes
should remain unpunished, and wishing, as he asserted, to
proceed against him according to the order of law, he
delivered over for execution to be served a certain paper
schedule containing in itself a form of precept subscribed
with his own hand as appeared, to dompnus William Wilson
Canon of the said Monastery, of which the tenor follows—
We Dene Dauid Farlie priour of Monimvsk be the
tenour of this present wryt chargis and commandis vndir
the forme of precept in the virtu of the Holy Spirit and
of obedience you Dene Wilyem Wilsone suppriour (*i.e.*,
sub-prior) of the forsaid abbaye that ye pass to Dene
Allane Galt channon of the saymen and command hyme

to keip his chalmer in the dormitour and pass nocht furtht of it bot *ad necessaria* and that he be in continuale scilence with all maner of man except hyme that mackis hyme ministratioun and that he be all this tyme in breid and aill and twa dais in the ovik *videlicet* Uednisda and Friday at his disciplyne and that na bonnet cum one his heid the tyme of his pennence except his nycht bonnet vnto the tyme that he be fundyne penitent and throch his patience humilite and satisfaction and recompensatione done to God and religioun and to ws his laudable conuersatioun guid exampil he serwe be our jugment to be deliuerit or relaxit of the said pennence This we command you to do 'in virtue of your obedience' as ye will ansuer to God religioun and ws heirapoune and youre executione in thir premissis be you deuly execut and indorsit present the samen agane to ws be this oure precept gevyne and writyne with oure hand at Monimvsk the fyft day of Februar the yere of God xv$^{c.}$ and xxxiiij. yeris.

(Signed) Dene Dauid Farlie prioure of Monimvsk. On which he took instruments Done as above in presence of domini John Reid Andrew Skeocht chaplains William Hurry and John Macky with several others.

(4) On the same day appeared in person dompnus David, prior aforesaid, the before-mentioned purgations and depositions of the Canons-regular of Monymusk having been heard by him, which say and allege that the said Allan Galt is a good religious man, imbued with good morals and devoted to the worship of God—dompnus David said and alleged that the depositions of the same had resulted from the persuasions of dompnus Allan himself, from the fact that of their own proper initiative they purged him and were not compelled or called to this by the Prior himself;

therefore no faith was to be put in those aforesaid themselves, but they were to be regarded as prejudiced and participators in the crime of dompnus Allan himself On which the said Prior took instruments Done in the Nave of the said Church of Monymusk 9 o'c. a.m. in presence of domini John Reid and Andrew Skeocht chaplains, William Hurry of Petfeche and John Macky with various others.

(5) On the same day appeared in person dompnus David Prior of the aforesaid Monastery of Monymusk after the execution completed by dompnus William Wilson by the letter or precept of the said dompnus Prior admonishing dompnus Allan Gault to remain in his own cell within the dormitory of the said Monastery and to observe silence with all men except the servant waiting on him and not to have a cap on his head except his night-cap And because the said dompnus Allan after the warning given him by the said dompnus William Wilson deliverer of the same letter, owing to the same dompnus Allan, like a son of disobedience, having entered the Church and taken part in divine service with his brethren, and likewise shared at breakfast at 9 o'c. in eating and drinking, and because he was unwilling to obey his commands—he protested for remedy at law At all which the said Prior took instruments Done within the hall of the said monastery 2 o'c. p.m. in presence of domini John Reid Vicar of Monymusk and Andrew Skeocht notary, both chaplains, and John Makky with various others.

The strife goes on, and now actually there comes, nearly eighteen months after, an appeal by the Canons to the Pope himself, written at great length, and with extraordinary vigour.

22nd June A.D. 1535 On which day appeared in person

the religious men dompni William Wilson Andrew Mason Patrick Anderson and James Murray Canons regular of the Monastery of Monymusk of the order of St. Augustine in the diocese of Aberdeen and with one consent and assent handed a certain paper schedule to me the notary public underwritten to be read, whose tenor follows and is to this effect:—We dompni William Wilson Andrew Mason Patrick Anderson and James Murray canons-regular for the time being of the convent and monastery of Monymusk in the diocese of Aberdeen, thinking ourselves hurt, weighed down, and oppressed by you Venerable father in Christ dompnus David Farlie prior of the said monastery and fearing that we may be more hurt, weighed down, and oppressed in future—FIRST whereas you, domine Prior, proceeding in your fashion have issued and fulminated your plain letter of admonition against us without any investigation of the case, admonishing us on the 14th June of the present year to cease from Divine things and from celebrating Divine service to which we are bound and from which we seek and obtain food and clothes and other necessaries When therefore we offered ourselves like sons of obedience to comply with your wish and orders and to cease from celebrating Divine things of this kind, whether justly or unjustly, at all events with a good conscience, if you should be willing to provide us with necessaries of this kind, or through any other person, as you are bound to provide—you proceed unjustly against us, from the fact that we have no other means or mode by which we are able to seek the said necessaries. THEN SECONDLY Whereas in the past year on the 3rd day of November before noon we ceased from Divine things, you our father approving, favouring, and consenting, whence no little damage not less in money and expenditure than also in reputation had resulted, and also we are falling under and incurring the anger and indignation of the Reverend father in Christ William Bishop of Aberdeen our ordinary [William Stewart, son of Sir Thomas Stewart of Minto][1] and of the venerable father dompnus John Aikinhead usufructuary of the said monastery and of many others. THEN THIRDLY Whereas to our own exceeding great infamy and that of the said monastery you allege unjustly in your letter that we have been guilty of irregularity by participating and taking part, as you assert, with dompnus Allan Gault as one excommunicated and stigmatised again and again by the processes raised by you When therefore a process of this nature was presented in the gracious Synod of Aberdeen and there not proved, and after the presentation of a process of this nature—the said dompnus Allan was present in the Cathedral Church of Aberdeen during divine service along with yourself, our father, and was not shut out or expelled from it as an excommunicated person ought to have been and deserves. THEN FOURTHLY whereas since we have no intercourse with the said dompnus Allan or favour him in other respects or give him advice, you unjustly blame us, &c. hence we shall by no means be able nor have we now the power to serve God with a quiet and loving mind as men dedicated to God and professing religion, but you compel us to mix in secular and troublesome matters to the no little scandal of all religion and specially of our foresaid monastery, and for other reasons to be laid by us before the judge in due place and time Protesting that it was no part of our intention by word, deed, or act to appeal from you our father on account of the favour shown by us to the said Allan Gault or on

[1] Reg. Epis. Abdn. I. p. lvi.

account of the favour or hatred of any others whoever they be, but only that our monastery may suffer no loss or injury in its welfare WHEREFORE on account of the foresaid troubles brought upon us and our monastery, and others perhaps more serious to be brought in future by you WE APPEAL from you our venerable father and from all your power and jurisdiction and privilege and faculty as well ordinary as extraordinary if perchance you have such . . . and from your warnings, citations, and commands and those of your procurators, factors, executors, and others deputed or to be deputed by you our father, of suspension, excommunication, aggravation and reaggravation (either) by censures of interdict or penalties borne or to be borne, fulminated or to be fulminated—to the Reverend father in Christ William Bishop of Aberdeen and to our most holy Lord Pope Paul III and his sacred Apostolic See alternatively in these writings : We APPEAL and every one of us singly and in succession appeals And we beseech the Apostles and every one of us by himself urgently, more urgently, most urgently beseeches the Apostles . . . Submitting also ourselves, the said monastery and the convent of the same, all our goods, &c., our Churches, parish servitors, and domestics, clergy and laity, all and singly adhering to us in this part, or wishing to adhere, to the protection and defence of the said our most holy Lord Pope and the sacred authority of the Apostolic See Whereupon the said Canons . . took instruments Done within the hall or refectory of the said monastery 1 p.m. present Master David Scot vicar-perpetual of Colsalmont, domini John Reid vicar of Monymusk Andrew Skeocht notary and chaplain Thomas Paterson, &c.

The Decay of the Old Order. 177

Nearly another year passes by and the storm is not laid—and now things seem to go hard for the Prior's veracity.

19th April 1536 On the same day appears in person the religious father James Murray canon of the monastery of Monymusk in presence of the Reverend father dompnus David Fairlie Prior of Monymusk, saying and alleging that it reached his ears that the said Prior took instruments in the hands of dominus Andrew Skeocht notary that he (Murray) ought to have asked license from the said Prior and absolution to allow of his receiving orders and that he did really ask absolution of him, as he (the Prior) alleged that he (Murray) had incurred excommunication by participating with dompnus Allan Galt;—when the same dompnus James further alleged (before the notary) that he was under appeal from the censures of the foresaid Prior and imploringly besought the said notary to declare now before the said Prior if such things had been true. The said notary on hearing the questions of the same, said and alleged that he had never heard such things nor had given a document in such things against him : And that he never heard that he had asked absolution or license or relief from excommunication of this kind, if he had incurred any And that such things were *false* and *worthless* On which the said dompnus James took instruments Done within the refectory or hall of Monymusk as at 1 o'c. p.m. in presence of dompnus John Akynheid usufructuary of Monymusk, dominus Henry Whitewells chaplain Robert Maver and John Makky laymen with various others.

Such a strife as this shows how sadly our first thoughts would be mistaken when impressed with the sense of peace and devotion that should have been looked for amid the quiet chambers of such a secluded monastery as ours—and when such a mass of documents has been preserved regarding it, we are sorry not to know how it ended.

5th July 1538 On which day appeared in person the venerable fathers in Christ John Hepburn Prior of St Andrews and David Fairlie Prior of the monastery of Monymusk and mutually exonerated each other and each of them exonerated the other and satisfied the other of all and single debts due by them to each other and specially in respect of an intromission by the same dompnus David of all accounts and receipts dealt with by the same at any time as regards the fruits of the Priory of St Andrews in the time of his predecessor and regarding receipts for the same during the vacancy of the See of St Andrews And for receipts and intromissions by the said Prior of St Andrews as regards the goods of the said dompnus David Prior aforesaid in whatever places and this 'in foro fori seu litigioso sed non in foro poli' (? in the court of law but not in the court of heaven) On which they together took and each of them took instruments Done at St Andrews in the chamber of the said Prior of St Andrews as at 3 o'c. p.m. or thereabout in the presence of Patrick Kinnaird James Lamb and Master John Gairdner notary.[1]

Prior John Hepburn was the joint-founder in 1512 of St. Leonard's College, St. Andrews, along with Archbishop Alexander Stuart, son of James IV, who when only twenty-one marched at his father's desire to Flodden, where he fell by his side. Prior John Hepburn drew up the statutes of the college which were afterwards approved by Regent Murray, and are very curious and interesting. A monument of him still survives in the towered wall with which he surrounded the whole

[1] Ant. A. and B. III., pp. 496, 497.

precinct of the Cathedral and the Priory and the grounds of St. Leonard's College.[1] For the archbishopric thus rendered vacant, there was a fierce contest, in which Prior John Hepburn was supported by the turbulent and aspiring house of Bothwell, and got himself elected by the chapter—while the house of Angus was on the side of Gavin Douglas, provost of St. Giles, (afterwards Bishop of Dunkeld). Both had to give way to Andrew Forman, bishop of Moray, who had procured a papal Bull nominating him to the see. 'When the adherents of Douglas seized on the Castle at St. Andrews, Hepburn collected his followers, and attacked them, and having carried the fortress by storm, he strongly garrisoned it, which made Douglas retire from the contest. Then when Forman's supporters came to proclaim the Bull in his favour, Hepburn again rallied his adherents, manned both the Cathedral and the Castle, and planted artillery round them,' but in vain. 'The Duke of Albany confirmed Forman in the chair, but bestowed on Hepburn enough of beneficiary spoil to allay his disappointment.'[2] What strange doings!

We have now a record regarding some of the Priory lands in Leochel.

13th April 1534 On the same day there personally appeared the venerable religious father dompnus David Farlie Prior of the monastery of Monymusk, and holding in his hands according to justice, in the consistorial court of Aberdeen, a written paper schedule, he presented the same to the Commissary General at Aberdeen sitting on the bench, of which the tenor follows and is to this effect 'We Dean David Farlie Prior of the monastery and abbacy of Monymusk of the Order of St Augustine within the diocese

[1] Principal Shairp, Sketches, pp. 153-160.
[2] Principal Cunningham, History I., p. 160; Dr. J. Robertson Stat. Ecc. Scot., p. cxxvi.

of Aberdeen with consent and assent of one reverend father Dean John Akynhead usufructuary of the same and convent of the foresaid place, revoke, cause annul, and make of none effect or force charters, precepts of sasine, instruments, long assedations, and all other documents whatever made sealed or subscribed by Dean Alexander Spens, Richard Strachan sometime priors of the foresaid place and all other priors both before and since, and subscriptions of canons, made to Duncan Davidson alias Thomson and to Thomas Davidson his son or to any other person . . of the lands of Easter Leochel and Wester Fowlis with the mill and their pertinents, except one contract in form of obligation made by one Reverend father Dean John Akynhead foresaid to Thomas Davidson sometime of Auchinhamperis of the lands aforesaid—of the date the 8th day of July in the year of God 1522 years.' On which the said Prior took instruments Done in the consistorial court of Aberdeen 11 o'c. a.m.— present in the same Master John Galloway Commissary p.t., &c., &c.[1]

In the "Gordon Papers" printed in the Spalding Club Miscellany there are two 'bands of service' connected with this family—one in 1511, the other in 1537.

(1) Be it kend till all men be thir present lettres, me Thomas Dunccansone, sone and apperand air to Dunccan Thomsone of Achinhampris, to be bundin and oblist, and be the tenor of thir present lettres bindis and oblissis me, be the fatht in any body, lelile and trewly, in the stratast style of obligatione, to ane noble and mychty lord, Alexander erle of Huntle, and lord of Badzenach, that forsamekle as my said lord hes geven to me his letter of mantenance, that

[1] Ant. A. and B. III., 489, 490.

tharfor, I bindis and oblissis me to be cumin, and be the tenour of thir presentis, becumis leile trew man and seruand to my said lord for all the dayis of my lif, myn allegeance to our souerane lord the King alanerlie excepit, &c. In witnes herof I haf affixit my seele to this my letter of manrent, at Huntle, the xxv day of Junii 1511 years, befor thir vitnes Robert Innes of Inuermarky, James Gordon of Cabrach, and Schir Nicol Patersone, vicar of Kynnor, witht otheris diuerss.

(2) Be it kend . . me Duncan Dauesone of Auchinhamperis to be cumin man and servand to ane nobil and mychty lord George erl of Huntle, that is to say, that I the said Duncan, with my kyn, frendis and servandis depending one me, sal serue my said lord lelely and trewle in al and sindry his actiones and querelis movit or to be movit in al tymes to cum &c; this my band of serviss to enduir to my said lord for al the dayis of my lif, the Kingis grace alanerly beand exceppit; in witness . . at Lenturk the 25th June 1537, witnes Walter Berklay of Grantulle . . &c. &c.[1]

19th August 1538 On which day appeared in person the religious father David prior of Monymusk and came to a certain bounding ditch dug anew by Robert Lumsden and his tenants of Easter Fowlis between Easter Fowlis and the town of Wester Fowlis And asserted that the same ditch was upon the ground and common pasture of Wester Fowlis belonging to the monastery of Monymusk On which account lest in future the said ditch should be held for a boundary or march between the said lands, the said Prior by way of interruption threw down to the ground two or three turfs of the same On which he took instruments Done

[1] Miscel. Vol. IV. pp. 196, 202.

at the same ditch 2 o'c. p.m. present *Master John Elphinstone Rector of Invernochty*, dominus Alexander Shand, Duncan Davidson and Patrick Crom.[1]

25th September 1542 On the same day appeared in person David Prior of Monymusk and leased to an honourable man Robert Lumsden of Madlar, Isobel Forbes his wife, and Master Matthew Lumsden, and the longest liver of them, all and whole the teind sheaves of the towns of Easter Fowlis and mill and Carnaveran for the whole space of three years after the date of these presents Paying yearly to the said Prior on the feast of St. Bartholomew for the tithes of Easter Fowlis and its mill the sum of nineteen merks and for Carnaveran the sum of six merks, Scots money, And under this condition that the said persons shall be faithful to the said Prior and his monastery And that they shall inform him about any disadvantages and losses affecting him and the said monastery, when known to them And when they come to the village of Monymusk that they shall enter the said monastery and if they have not implemented the foresaid requirements, the lease shall be of no value On which they took instruments Done in the churchyard of Leochel 2 o'c. p.m. in the presence of *James Forbes of Corsindae*, Patrick Forbes of Corse, *Lord William Forbes* and me the notary.[2]

This is a very remarkable gathering of witnesses in 1542, preparing one for the appropriations that were soon to follow. Forbes of Corsindae is seen following the Prior as far as Leochel, and watching like a vulture; and, further, in ten years' time, according to his own rent-roll, which is still preserved, Wester Fowlis, Easter Fowlis, and Carnaveran are all taken possession of by Lord Forbes, as shall be afterwards detailed.

[1] Ant. A. and B. III. p. 497.   [2] Ibid., pp. 498, 499.

Farlie had still further to defend the property of the Priory. The scope of the first deed that follows is not clear, and the translation of it is doubtful, but the second is very perspicuous.

30th October 1540, On the same day John Forbes in Eglismatock required the venerable and religious father David, Prior of Monymusk, to give him the reply to a certain form of petition addressed to our supreme Lord the King and delivered by him to the said Prior, as he asserted, in order that he might be able to make reply to our supreme Lord the King Done in the court house at Aberdeen, 11 o'c. a.m. in presence of William Rolland &c.[1]

Not two years after we have the following record, given in English, only the spelling of which we change :—

18th July 1542. Concerning our sovereign Lord's letters obtained at the instance of David Prior of the Abbey of Monymusk and convent of the same against John Forbes *alias* Bousteous John. That where they obtained an enrolment of court before the sheriff of Aberdeen and his deputies finding that the said John wrongly occupied and laboured four oxen-gang of the said Prior and Convent's lands of Eglismenethok with the pertinents pertaining to them as patrimony and property of their said place lying within the sheriffdom of Aberdeen by a certain space byegone And therefore decerning the said John to desist and cease from all further occupation of the same in time to come and to remove therefrom . . nevertheless the said John as yet violently occupies and withholds from them their foresaid lands and will not remove therefrom without being compelled . . The said Prior and convent compeared by Master Andrew Leslie their procurator, and the said John Forbes being personally present The Lords of Council

[1] Ant. A. and B. III. p. 497.

decern and ordain letters to be directed in all the four forms . . charging the said John Forbes to desist and cease from all further occupation of the said lands of Eglismenathok with the pertinents in time to come and to remove himself his servants and goods therefrom.[1]

The following genealogy shows a remarkable relationship:—

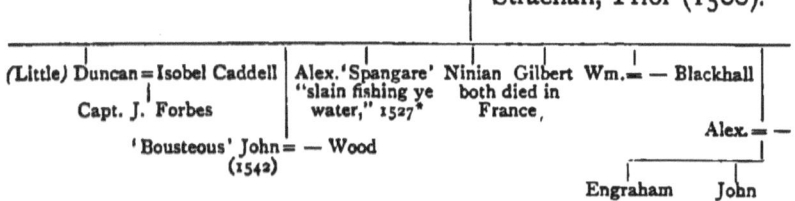

'Bousteous' John is thus the grandson of the Prior Strachan, and in Prior Fairlie's time tries to lay hold on some of the Priory lands.

The oldest monument in the Church is inserted in the wall beside the Chancel Arch. It is in beautiful preservation, and the inscription is in raised letters. It has the Leslie and Forbes arms on the top, with their mottoes and the letters J. L. and A. F.

The monuments of Johne Forbes of Abersnithak. Elspet his dochter ye first vyf of John Lesly, Balcarne who depted. 1583 Heir also lyis in one graif Agnis Forbes dochter to John Forbes of Finyach secvnd vyf to ye said John Lesly. George Lesly thair young sone who depted. ye 4 of April 1590 And in ys same bvriall lyis ye said John Lesly who depted. Anno 1.

John Leslie thus evidently died in the first year of the century, 1601. (A John Leslie, Balcairn is mentioned by

[1] Ant. A. and B. III. p. 498
[2] Dr. Davidson, Inverurie, p. 139; Ant. A. and B. III. p. 377.

Dr. Davidson,[1] 13th May, 1609, who may be a son.) His first wife, Elspet, was daughter of John Forbes, Abersnithack, and she died in 1583. It is singular that though it is her father who erects the monument, he does not put her initials at the top of the stone, but those of Leslie's second wife, another Forbes of Finziach, now Harthill, in Keig. One William Forbes there, is mentioned as married to a daughter of William Johnston of Caskieben, who fell at Flodden.[2]

If "Bousteous" John, after having to leave Eglismethok, succeeded his father in Abersnithack (Braehead), this is his monument, and his daughter, in whose memory it is placed, was a great-grand-daughter of Prior Strachan!

In 1535 we have seen that John Reid was Vicar of the parish, and that William Hurry of Pitfichie was a witness along with him in Gauld's protest against Prior Fairlie's oppression. We also met with the Hurry family in the Charter of 1388 regarding the Brecbanach. This William Hurry is mentioned in a Crown Charter of confirmation 20th May, 1546, in connection with the lands of Wester Corse, in the parish of Coull, which they possessed under the superiority of Skene.[3]

In 1537 Henry Forsyth was Rector of Monymusk, his name appearing in the list of the Chapter when constitutions were drawn up for receiving persons among the Canons of the Cathedral, and for dispensations and leases.[4] His name also appears in 1540. It was in this year that the performance of Sir David Lyndsay's satire of "The Three Estates" contributed so powerfully to the Reformation of the country which was growing impatient of the corruptions of the Church.[5]

1 Inverurie, p. 193.
2 Ibid, p. 448.
3 Skene of Skene, New Spal. Club, pp: 90, 101.
4 Reg. Epis. Abdn. II. pp. 110, 112.
5 Dr. J. Robertson, Stat. Ecc. Scot. p. cxxxix; Mr. Walcott, Ant. Ch. p. 9.

In the deed of 19th August, 1538, John Elphinstone, Rector of Invernochty (Strathdon, a Church that had once been given to our Priory, although the gift had not been carried out) is mentioned as a witness. In 1542 he was presented by the Earl of Arran, Governor of Scotland in Queen Mary's minority, as Prior-coadjutor to David Farlie.[1] He was the Honourable John Elphinstone, son of Alexander, second Lord Elphinstone, and Catherine, daughter of John, Lord Erskine. John Elphinstone of Elphinstone received from James IV part of the lands of the Earldom of Mar, including Invernochty and Kildrummy in 1507-1509. His son Alexander succeeded in 1510, becoming Lord Elphinstone. Sir James Elphinstone, parson of Invernochty, the third son of the third Lord Elphinstone, was in 1598 made Secretary of State, and in 1603-1604 the Abbacy of Balmerino was erected into a temporal lordship in his favour.[2]

It is stated that the Bishop of St. Andrews, possessing as he did the Church lands of Keig and Monymusk, and the other properties bestowed by Malcolm III, sat as Lord Keig and Monymusk in the Scottish Parliament.[3]

We come now to a charter of much importance, preserved at Gordon Castle, in the hands of the Duke of Gordon and Richmond. It gives rise to great strife afterwards.

In the Name of God Amen By this present public instrument let it be plainly apparent to all . . that in the year 1543 A.D. 23rd April . . in the presence of our fellow notaries-public and underwritten witnesses, the noble and powerful Lord George Earl of Huntlie Lord of Gordon and Badenoch being personally present, having and holding in his hands a certain sasine order written on parchment . . of which order the following . . is the

[1] Colln. A. and B. p. 170.
[2] Dr. Campbell, Balmerino, pp. 283, 284.
[3] Mr. Low, Proc. Soc. Antiq. VI. p. 227.

tenor . . DAVID by Divine mercy of the title of St. Stephen in the Celian Hill of the Holy Roman Church Presbyter Cardinal, Archbishop of St. Andrews Primate of the whole kingdom of Scotland and legate natus of the Apostolic see, and Administrator of the Church of Mirepoix in France, and perpetual Commendator of the Monastery of St. Thomas the Martyr of Arbroath, to our beloved Alexander Gordon of Strathdon and John Leslie of 'ly Syde' and James Gordon of Haddoch and to each of them jointly and separately our bailiffs . . Greeting with divine blessing Whereas we . . with consent of our chapter of our metropolitan and primatial Church of St. Andrews . . for the yearly augmentation of the rental of the same up to the sum of 14 pounds 6 pence and 1 obolus more than the lands, mill, and malt-kiln underwritten have ever previously brought in to us or our predecessors . . and for the grace and public policy of the kingdom . . and in return for great and diverse . . aids . . frequently rendered by the noble and powerful Lord George Earl of Huntlie Lord Gordon and Badenoch to us and our Church aforesaid, and for defence of . . ecclesiastical liberty at this present time of danger while Lutheran heresies are sprouting on every side and striving to subvert . . ecclesiastical liberty, (we) Have demitted all and single the lands . . with the several pertinents of the same Brinie, Armagattin, Ballingowin, Outhirkeig, Southoulyie, Pettindreich, mill of Keig with the malt-kiln and croft of the same, Pyttochy, Glenton, Uppertollache, Nethertollach, Fyndacht, with the mill, Little-Abercaultye, Mickle-Abercaultye, Edindourno, *Tillyfourie, Todlochy, Pitmuny, Ardniedly, Delab, Coullie, Enzean, Mill of Monymusk with the malt-kiln and croft of the same, Inver(y)* [all these being in this parish] the towns of Cottilstane and the Church lands of Kynkell and the lands of Dyiss [? Dyce] with each of the same and their pertinents . . lying respectively in the lordships and baronies of Keig and Monymusk within the regality of St Andrews and vicecounty of Aberdeen, along with the bailiffship of the said baronies of Keig and Monymusk . . to the said . . Earl in fee . . Therefore . . we order you . . to . . hand over . . the sasine . . of the foresaid lands . . and bailiffship . . to the foresaid . . Earl . . or to his certified attorney . . In testimony of which, these presents being signed by our hand, our authentic seal along with the common seal of our said Chapter of St Andrews was appended to the foregoing . . in sign . . of agreement at our said metropolitan and primatial Church of St Andrews on the 7th Apr. 1543 A.D. and the fifth year of our consecration After the reading . of the which order . . the foresaid bailiff . . delivered . . the sasine . . of the foresaid lands and of the office of bailiffship . . to the attorney . . of the said . . Earl . .

This was done on the soil of the said lands . . at the hours of 10, 11, 12, 1 p.m., 2, 3, 4, 5, 6—between 9 a.m. and 7 p.m. or thereabout owing to the distance of the places . . there being present there the noble Lord John Earl Sutherland, the honourable and circumspect men Alexander Gordon of Strathdon, John Leslie of 'Varderris' James Gordon of Coldstone, Nicholas Ross of Auchlossan, Robert Duguid of Auchinhuif (Auchinhove), John Vass of Mayne, John Drummond of Inverpeffray, John Strachan of Linturk and Alexander Leslie of 'Tulche' (? Tough) with various other witnesses . .

Also I William Gordon, professor of arts, cleric of the Diocese of Moray, public notary by sacred Apostolic authority &c Also I Andrew Robertson, presbyter of the Diocese of Moray, notary public by sacred Apostolic authority &c Also I John Gordon, presbyter of the Diocese of Moray notary public &c.[1]

David Beaton succeeded his uncle Archbishop James Beaton. He had been Abbot of Arbroath, and was Bishop of Mirepoix in France, was Lord Privy Seal in 1528, and was appointed a Cardinal in 1538, "the first and only Scottish Prelate on whom that dignity was bestowed by the undivided Latin Church." In January, 1544, the Regent Arran and Beaton executed four persons at Perth as heretics, and when they burned Wishart of Pitarrow, they so provoked the fears and increased the hatred of the people that two months afterwards Beaton was surprised in his castle at St. Andrews, and murdered 28th May, 1546. His private life was very lamentable.[2]

In 1542, 13th December, James V died at Falkland Palace, aged thirty, leaving Mary, Queen of Scots, when only eight days old.

Canon John Hay has been mentioned in the writs of 15th December, 1522, 8th April, 1524, and 13th October, 1525. In the "View of the Diocese of Aberdeen,"[3] from which much of our information is drawn, he is spoken of as being sent by Queen Mary as an envoy to Queen Elizabeth in MDXLV. It is a misprint for MDLXV, the X being put before the L instead of after it. Mary returned from France to Scotland in 1561 on the death of the Dauphin, and Elizabeth succeeded to the throne of England in 1558.

Dr. Campbell in his "Balmerino and its Abbey," mentions that Hay was appointed Commendatory Abbot of that monastery, probably in 1561. This entitled him to two-thirds of its

1 Ant. A. and B. IV. pp. 480-482.   3 Colln. A. and B. p. 170.
2 Dr. J. Robertson. Stat. Ecc. Scot. I. p. cxxx; II. p. 302.

revenues, subject to the maintenance of the surviving monks, the other third being reserved for the use of the Protestant minister and the Crown. He says that he was also Prior of Monymusk, Principal Master of Requests to Queen Mary, and a Privy Councillor.[1] He was employed by his Royal mistress on various missions of a confidential nature. He was a prudent and able man, a favourer of Moray, and a friend of Randolf, the English Ambassador. On one occasion he was sent by Queen Mary as Legate to Christian III, King of the Danes, &c. He entertained the Queen at Balmerino in January, 1564-65, when she had completed her twenty-second year, and in June, 1565, she entrusted him with a mission to Queen Elizabeth to induce her to consent to Mary's marriage with Lord Darnley, and to intercede for the liberation of Darnley's mother, the Countess of Lennox. He died at Edinburgh, December 3rd, 1573.[2] His wife, Agnes Leitch, survived him; as did also his son Archibald, and other children.[3] He appears to have belonged to the family of Hay of Naughton in Balmerino parish, and one wonders how he was led to become a Canon in our Priory. Its connection with St. Andrews must have been to the last well recognised in Fifeshire families.

It was in April, 1542-43 that Cardinal Beaton, as Archbishop of St. Andrews, gave over the church lands of Inver, Delab, &c., to the Earl of Huntly. The very next notice that we have, shows that the Forbeses of Corsindae have dealings with him immediately in regard to the lands he now possessed in our parish.

Be it kend till all men be thir present lettres, me James Forbes of Corsindawe to be bunden and obleist, and be the

---

[1] See Knox's Works, Laing's Ed. II. p. 482. [3] Dr. Campbell, Balmerino, p. 384.
[2] Dr. Campbell, Balmerino, pp. 130, 133-137.

faith and treuth in my body bindis and obleissis me in the strataist forme and styill of obligatioun to ane nobill and mychty lord George erll of Huntlie, lord Gordoun and Bauzenocht &c and to his airis ; that forsamekill as my said lord hes gevyn to me in lifrent the landis of Inuer with thar pertinens, liand within the paroche of Monimusk and sherifdoum of Abirdeine, lik as in his lordschipis letter of assedatioun maid to me thairapone mair fullelie is contenit, and uther certane gratitudis done to me by said lord diuerss tymmes, tharfor I the said James Forbes grantis and obleissis me to becumin leill trew anefald man and seruand, and be the tennour heirof becumis leill trew anefald man and seruand to my said lord and his airis, and sall keip his counsall &c aganis all lewand or de ma, my allegiens to the Quenis grace and my service of law for infeftouris alanerlie exceptit &c in witness . . at Huntlie 19th June 1544 before . . Johnn erll Sutherland, William maisteris Forbes . . Robert Forbes of Eicht &c.

James Forbes, witht my hand.[1]

It was quite worth riding over to Huntly to make more secure the possession of Inver in life-rent, for it then included the whole of that part of the parish as far as the Don—Upper and Nether Inver, and Bridge-foot. When the old house at Nether Inver was taken down in 1888, parts of a still older house were discovered.

We shall see what spoliators of Church lands and goods the Forbeses were, showing how the landowners and their sons understood the meaning of the Reformation. " Nor can we understand," says Dr. Rankin of Muthill,[2] "the working of one of the secret and most potent motives that led to the

[1] Gordon Papers, Spalding Club Mis. IV. p. 214.
[2] Ch. of Scot. Past and Present, II. p. 401.

Church's overthrow with a sudden crash in 1560, unless we have seen in detail the nature, extent, and growth of the old ecclesiastical endowments which were so strong a temptation to greedy, turbulent, and unscrupulous barons and landowners, who shrewdly foresaw in an ecclesiastical revolution a rich chance of plunder, besides the crippling of a rival or superior power in the State."

In the same year, 1544, in which James Forbes thus made secure his possession of Inver in life-rent, two years after the defeat of the Scottish army at the Solway Moss, and the consequent death of James V, Bishop Stuart of Aberdeen, on account of the English war that was then raging, and in fear of the advance of the forces, sent under care of men on horseback and on foot, all the Cathedral plate and ornaments, except six Communion Cups for daily use, into the country, hoping that they might be safe. A little beyond the Bridge of Balgownie this same "James Forbes of Corsindae with his companions and satellites, sons of Satan," fell upon those who were carrying them, and robbed them of them all, and refused to return them until they were ransomed, imperfect and mutilated, by the Bishop for six hundred merks. The Bishop and Chapter actually agreed to give this robber four ploughgates of land in lieu of that sum, at Montgarry in Tullynessle—the writs connected with this being preserved.[1]

In 1559 an inventory of the silver-work, vestments, &c., was drawn up, when these were delivered by Bishop William Gordon for safety to the custody of the Canons, the Earl of Huntly, who was Chancellor of Scotland, and others. This inventory is preserved, and is very interesting, and among those who attested it, strange to say, appears the name of James

[1] Reg. Epis. Abdn. I. pp. lvii, 427, 428; II. pp. 195, 196.

The Spoliation of the Lands.

Forbes' brother, who signs himself "Mr. Duncan Forbes of Monymusk."[1]

Duncan Forbes had evidently advanced some money to the Priory here, and we shall now find how amply he repaid himself, and with what apparent credit to himself the restitution was made. David Farlie and the Hon. John Elphinstone were joint-priors, while the sub-prior was Robert Elphinstone, who had been Archdeacon of Aberdeen in 1499 and Treasurer in 1512.

To all who shall see or hear of this charter David by divine permission Prior of the priory—the monastery of Monymusk with consent and assent of Master John Elphinstone Rector of Invernochty, canon of Aberdeen and our coadjutor at the said place and monastery of Monymusk, to the which Master John has been given all power by decree of the Bishop of Aberdeen and of the canons of the same chapter and by letters ordinary of the said Bishop of Aberdeen, conforming to the appointment of the same Master John to the said coadjutorship to rule, locate, assess, and demit in fee the fruits and lands of the same, with the consent and assent of the convent of the foresaid place And we the said Master John for ourselves and our successors, eternal greeting in the Lord, Know that we— assembled for this purpose as a Chapter with unanimous consent, the foregoing public edict being affixed on the doors of the Church of the priory of Monymusk for the space of 21 days, citing all who have an interest for the purpose written below, Consulting with regard to our advantage and that of our said monastery and that of our successors, and with a view to the augmentation of our

[1] Reg. Epis. Abdn. I. pp. lxxxvi-xci.

rental as is written below, in furtherance of the policy of the kingdom and in view of the statutes of Parliament And in return for the great and arduous services, aids, counsels, and merits rendered in other respects by the honourable man Master Duncan Forbes in our arduous affairs, to us and to our said monastery And for the large sum of money paid into our hands by the said Master Duncan and Agnes Gray his spouse in our urgent necessity to us and the said Master John Elphinstone, coadjutor aforesaid, and to our said convent And to be turned to the advantage of our said place and monastery now in ruins, and otherwise actually spent for the upbuilding and restoration of the same regarding which sum we hold ourselves thankfully and completely paid &c And owing to other reasonable causes moving our minds to this effect—HAVE GIVEN, granted, sold, and demitted in fee or for perpetual occupation in heritage, and by this present charter &c to the foresaid Master Duncan Forbes and Agnes Gray his wife along with him, in joint fee and to the one of them who longer lives and to the heirs lawfully begotten or to be begotten by them, failing whom to the nearest lawful male heirs of the said Master Duncan and to their assignees whatsoever, All and single our *lands of our manor* of Monymusk with mills multures mill-lands tofts crofts and their pertinents lying within the parish of Monymusk and vicecounty of Aberdeen To be held and possessed &c by the foresaid Master Duncan and Agnes his spouse &c of us and our successors in fee or hereditary occupation for ever throughout all their correct marches &c They rendering thence annually &c to us and our successors the priors of Monymusk the sum of *twenty-four pounds* usual money of the kingdom of Scotland in fee of the said manor &c And the sum of *thirteen shillings and four pence* of the same money for the annual augmentation more than ever before of our rental of this land Reserving also to ourselves and our successors the place of our monastery with the garden called 'the Prior's yard,' with the pasture for 4 saddle horses for the use of the Prior and his domestic servants and pasture for 30 sheep for support of the family of the said Prior when he shall happen to reside personally in Monymusk—where the said feudatory and his heirs pasture their horses and sheep We will also that each heir or assignee entering newly into these lands shall on his first entry double to us and our successors the Priors of this said place the annual feu-duty &c In testimony of which there are appended to our present charter subscribed with our own hands the common seal of the said Priory and the seal of the office of coadjutorship of the said Master John Elphinstone the foresaid coadjutor, at Monymusk and Aberdeen respectively the 17th March 1548 years In presence of witnesses David Kyntor Alexander Gray burgesses of Aberdeen &c.

David Prior of Monymusk
Master John Elphinston coadjutor of the Monastery of Monymusk
dominus James Chyld, canon of Monimusk with my own hand at this   James Murray, canon of Monimusk, with my own hand at this.[1]

It was rather early, however, for Duncan Forbes' ownership to be fully recognised. On the 3rd January of the next year, 1549, Mary Queen of Scots, the Earl of Arran being Protector and Governor of the realm, "understanding that our old enemies of England intend the spring of this year to invade our realm

[1] Colln. A. and B. pp. 179, 180.

with all their force and power," orders a general tax over the Kingdom, according to the value and extent of all lands; and in the list for Aberdeenshire occur these notices—

The Queen's grace feu lands within the said shire: Patrick Forbes . . .
for his lands of Pefechei and roods of Monymusk iij libs
The spiritual and kirk lands and patrimony after following : . . .
The Archbishop of St Andrews for his baronies and lands of Keig and Monymusk &c . . .   xl libs
The Pryour of Monemusk with the Manes . .   v libs
The Persone of Monemusk for the toune of Bovak [Balvack] . . .   xx sh[r]

In the record of the Provincial Synod at Edinburgh the same year, 1549, among the Abbots, Priors, and Commendators is named "Joannes, prior de Muny"[musk] *i.e.*, John Elphinstone.[2]

In "the list of Barons and Freeholders that were or are obliged to give suit and presence to the three head courts held yearly by the sheriff of Aberdeen" are—

Spiritual Barons :—
Archbishop of St. Andrews.
Prior of Monimusk.[3]

Thus, in the beginning of 1549, the Prior was still accountable for the Mains or Manor, but next year the same two canons who had signed the first Charter, subscribe a confirmation of it which is in English, as written then, but which we may put into a more usual form.

Be it known to all men by these present writings We Deyn James Chyld and Deyn James Murraye canons of the Abbey and Priory of Monymusk have seen, visited, and

[1] Colln. A. and B. pp. 113, 119, 120, 121.
[2] Dr. J. Robertson, Stat. Ecc. Scot. II. p. 83.
[3] Colln. A. and B. p. 109.

considered an infeftment by charter and precept given by
our supreme head of the said Abbey to Mr. Duncan Forbes
and his heirs, of all and sundry our lands of the Mains of
of Monymusk with their pendicles and pertinents which
infeftment we ripely advised and we have found that the
same was set to the great utility and weal of our said Abbey
for restoration of the same and also for augmentation of
our rental as is contained at greater length in the same
infeftment Wherefore we the said canons and convent for
the time of the said Abbey subscribed the said charter and
precept given thereon to the said Mr. Duncan and his heirs
in feu-farm and heritage Which subscription we by these
presents ratify and approve in all time coming And by these
presents testify and make it known that we, not one of us,
in no time byegone have given our consent or subscriptions
to any other person of the lands of the Mains of Monymusk,
except to the said Mr. Duncan and his heirs And herefor
bind and oblige us and every one of us lealy and truly, the
Holy Gospel touched with our hands, thereto of our own
free will never to come in the contrary nor to give our
consent to nor subscribe any charter, precept, or infeftment
whatsoever on the said lands in any time coming to any
others whatever And this because we have received the
said Mr. Duncan our tenant thereto and his oath of fidelity
thereon, for payment and fulfilling of all and sundry the
points contained in the said infeftment And in case our
Prior, ordinary, or administrator, having jurisdiction over us,
not having God or good conscience before them or respect
of the foregoing done by them and us to the said Mr.
Duncan, have given their consent and subscription to any
others, on the said lands in prejudice of the said Mr.
Duncan's title and in betrayal of their fame and truth We

by these presents renounce and revoke all consents and subscriptions given or to be given in any time coming by our said ordinary on the said lands to any other person or persons whatsoever except to the said Mr. Duncan and his heirs alone And further if it happens, which God forbid, that by our foresaid ordinary's warrant and disposition of the said lands to any others, by the same there be raised letters on the said Mr. Duncan or his heirs for reduction of our said infeftment given to the said Mr. Duncan and his heirs on the said lands, then in this case we the said Canons renounce and revoke the said letters and instance thereof now as then and then as now And herefor make constitute and ordain honourable men Masters Robert Lumsden Thomas Davidson and Gilbert Johnston our lawful and undoubted procurators executors factors and special errand-bearers to pass in our name before any judge or judge's day or place that the said Mr. Duncan or his heirs be called for the same and there in our name renounce and revoke the said letters and instance thereof as we ourselves might do if we were there present in our own person And for the faithful observing and keeping of all and sundry the foresaid we the said Canons and Convent for the time leally and truly bind and oblige ourselves by the faith in our body, the Holy Gospel touched of our own free will, never to come in the contrary, by these our subscriptions and under penalty of infamy and perjury In presence of John Forbes in Kylbethok Alexander Lumsden William Merser and Alexander Youngson notary public whom we have constituted to put these presents in more ample form as need be under form of instrument at Monimusk 10th July 1550 years.

Den James Chyld cannone of Mvnymwsk vith my hand

The Spoliation of the Lands. 199

Jacobus Murray cannone of Mvnymwsk vith my hand
So it is Alexander Youngsoun notary public and witness
in the foregoing.[1]

But it would seem that something more than all this was
reckoned necessary for security, for in the same year (1550) the
highest spiritual power is invoked for permitting the indisputable
disposal of some of the lands by way of having the building
repaired—and authority to do so is granted from Rome to
Prior Elphinstone.

RAYNUTIUS by divine pity &c Presbyter Cardinal of S. Angelus
to the discreet men the treasurer and archdeacon and Arthur
Talliefer canon of the church of Aberdeen Greeting in the
Lord A petition presented to us on the part of John Elphinstone Canon of Aberdeen was as follows That whereas the
house and buildings of the Monastery or Priory of Monymusk
of the order of St. Augustine of the diocese of Aberdeen
which David Farlie holds either in some title or Commenda
or otherwise by concession or Apostolic dispensation, are
found to be ruinous and almost levelled to the ground so that
the said David being so old and infirm that he cannot provide
for their repair, and unless this is speedily provided for, it is
feared that the Monastery or Priory aforesaid must come
down Wherefore if to the said Petitioner,—who was deputed
under certain authorities in due mode and form as coadjutor
of the said David with the future Apostolic succession first
and thereafter for the rule and government of the same
Monastery or Priory so that he may be able to receive, exact,
and raise the fruits, returns, and incomes of it and to do
other things relating to the rule and government of it and to
carry out the ordinary intentions of the said David in his old

[1] Colln. A. and B. pp. 181, 182.

age and infirmity,—power should be granted by the Apostolic see to dispose and grant certain possessions or pieces of land situated and placed near his marches and rightfully belonging and pertaining to the said Monastery or Priory or its sustenance and not exceeding the annual value of six pounds sterling, for perpetual occupation or else for a certain long time to one or more persons under a fixed annual rule, return, or census to be agreed on, and also with certain stipulations and conditions of occupation for the manifest advantage of the same Monastery or Priory, and (power) to spend the money coming in from the disposition and concession of the same for the restoration and repair of the houses and buildings aforesaid—assuredly the security of the same Monastery or Priory would be abundantly provided for. Wherefore the said Petitioner humbly caused supplication to be made that merciful provision might be afforded him in these matters by the foresaid See by way of timely remedy. WE THEREFORE holding the situations, confines, denominations, values, qualities, quantities, and circumstances of the said lands and whatever titles might be inserted in these presents for full and sufficient expression And considering that we ought to be favourable and kind in these things which are marked out to be set aside for the use of monasteries and places under Rule By the authority of our Lord Pope whose charge we primarily bear and by his special mandate committed to us in reference to these things by his viva voce utterance, (We) LEAVE to your discretion or to two of you jointly to see how far by diligent information to be gained by you regarding the foresaid matters, with the necessary reservations, you shall find the foresaid disposition and concession, if made, are for the evident advantage of the said Monastery or Priory, as to which things we burden your conscience, That you should grant liberty or power by Apostolic authority to the same petitioner with consent of the said David to dispose of and grant pieces of land aforesaid for occupation as said before, and to spend the moneys thence coming in, for the restoration and repair of the houses and buildings aforesaid and to do other things all and single in the foresaid matters —the foresaid considerations not being opposed to the constitutions and ordinances, general or special, of Prebendary Paul of happy memory as to the inalienable character of ecclesiastical property, or to any other Apostolic deliverances and such as have been given out in Provincial and Synodical Councils, or to the statutes and customs of the Monastery or Priory and order of the aforesaid, even though supported by oath, by Apostolic confirmation, or any other security and whatever else may be contrary—Given at Rome at S. Peter's under the seal of office with supreme authority the 9th December in the first year of the Pontificate of Pope Julius III.[1]

It was easy to declare even from Rome "the inalienable character of ecclesiastical property." We shall now learn in a wider way than before, how far this held good in the minds of our nobles and landlords at this era.

In a "rental-book," ranging from 1552 to 1678, preserved at Castle Forbes, we gain our widest information as to the possessions of our Priory beyond our own parish, and learn, he himself being witness, how these were appropriated by Lord Forbes. It is singular that it is after the seizure has been made that we are able to look back on the lands from which the Priory drew a large part of its revenue. The record shows with what an unsparing hand the work was done by those who had power, just that they might add land to land.

[1] Colln. A. and B., pp. 182-184.

There is no effort made to conceal the matter, but the tale of appropriation is told with the greatest clearness. The farms still retain the old names, although the spelling is slightly changed. This roll, we think, is of great historical value.

We have repeatedly learned that the teinds of Alford were bestowed on the Priory. We now learn what they consisted of, at least as far as they were taken possession of by Lord Forbes.

RENTALE OF THE TEYNDIS OF ALFURD.

Cobilseitt of Alfurde pais zeirlie to my Lord for ye teind of ye samin iiij bollis victuale, tua pairt mele and third pt. malt, with ane weddir [sheep].

Smedy of Alfurde pais zeirlie to my Lord for ye teind yrof four bollis victuale in maner forsaid.

Argathin pais zeirlie xxix bollis victuale in maner above written, wt. four wedderis.

Kirktown, Dauid Moris croft, pais for ye teind zeirlie three bollis victuale, ane weddir.

Mill of Alfurde pais zeirlie for ye teind thre bollis victuale, ane weddir.

Wolhows pais zeirlie v bollis victuale, in maner forsaid, wt. ane weddir.

Sum of ye Teindis forsaid, Tua pairts mele and third pt. malt—fourte aucht bollis victuale.

Sum of wedderis viij.

THE RENTELL OFF YE PRYORIE OFF MONYMOUSK.

ALFURD.

Argathyne in my Lordis hand which ues xl mks.

Aslong . . .	xviij Libs. with the pertinents.
Achintowill . .	xx Libs. with ye pertinents.
Carnaverane . .	xiiij merkis.
Archballoch . .	xvij Libs. xij geis (geese).
Kynstare . .	xxj Libs. vjs. viijd.
Lytilledindive . .	iiij Libs. xiijs. iiijd.

Tullichetlie . . iiij Libs. xiijs. iiijd.
Braidgauch of Kynstare
wt. ye myll . . x Libs. xiijs. iiijd.
Mekilledindovie . xiij Libs. vjs. viijd.
Pofluge . . . iiij Libs.
Bandly . . . iiij Libs. xiijs. iiijd.
Baddivine

The Rentall of ye teind silver off KEIG *1623 zeres, peyit off auld to ye priory of Monymusk.*

Sevidlie . . . xix Libs. 6s. 8d.
Westerkeig . . xvj Libs.
Ballgowan . . x Libs.
Brvnye . . . iiij Libs.
Puttachy . . . viij Libs.
Auchnagathill . . vj Libs. xiijs. iiijd.
Pittindreich . . vj Libs. xiijs. iiijd.
Glentowne . . vij Libs. vjs. viijd.
Mylln of Keige, pertaining to bruchlie, ij£.

Sum off ye teind silver off Keige extends to zeirlie to fourscoir punds money, and sax shillingis, and aucht pennies augmentation.

LOCHALLE.

Craigyvare, wt. ye pertinentis . . xl Libs.
Lenturkis, wt. ye ptinentis. . . xvj Libs.
Esterfoullis, wt. ye myll . . . xij Libs. xiijs. iiijd.
Westerfoullis . . . . . viij Lib.
Craigmyll . . . . . iij Lib. vjs. viijd.
Ouer Lochall ·. . . . . x Lib. tua wedders.

KYNDROCHT, XLV LIBS.

The temporall Landis (*i.e.* the Church lands) in Mr. George Gordone his handis extending zeirlie till xxxij Lib. of LOCHALLE.

Item, vij dissoun pultre, tua weddirs, tua bollis aitts, with ye fodder.

THOMEBEIG, xl s.

ABERSMYTHOK, xj Libs. vjs. viijd., iij dissoun of capones, tua wedders.

The MAINS OF MONYMOUSK, xxvj Lib. xiijs. iiijd.
The Vicarage of Alfurd, ye auld rentell yairof, L merkis (50).
The Vicarage of Lochell, . . . xx Libs.
The Vicarage of Keig of auld, . . xx Libs.

bot Jon Straquhen hes it off me for xij Lib., and to ——
—ye kirkis ye tyme of peace, and to prech yairat quarterlye.
There is also added a note :—

The benefice of the parish of Forbes in 1325 was worth £13 6s. 8d., that of Tullynessle in 1366 £20, and that of Monymusk in 1445 £40—all Scots money.[1]

It is singular that, according to this rent-roll, Lord Forbes somehow for a time got the dues from Tombeg, Braehead, and Mains of Monymusk, farms that have been often mentioned as belonging to the Priory and that are in this parish, but doubtless he and his kinsman, Duncan Forbes, came to an understanding about this.

With regard to John Strachan's allowance, this is an instance of what Mr. Cosmo Innes writes[2] about "the stipendiary vicars being ground down to the lowest stipend that would support life," only here this is done not by the monastery, but by the Baron who, without having the smallest right to them, had appropriated the teinds and the lands to himself. It rather anticipates our narrative, but this mention of Strachan makes it most suitable to say here that in "The Register of Ministers

---

[1] Mr. Rait, Castle Forbes, in "Banffshire Journal," 1876.
[2] Mr. Cosmo Innes, Sketches, p. 19.

The Spoliation of the Lands. 205

and their Stipends since 1567" a John Straithauchin is mentioned as "translated from Forvie, Slains, and Logy Buchane in 1569 to Tullinessel, Kyg, and Towch, the stipend being jc merks and xl merks mair" (*i.e.*, a hundred and forty merks), while in the list of 'Reidars' there is another record "Clat, Forbes, Kirne, John Strauchin, minister, jc merks."[1] In Dr. Hew Scott's "Fasti,"[2] under Leochel occurs the entry "1588, John Strathauchin of Seveidlie, removed from Alford, having Kemnay, Alford, Leslie, and Keig also in charge; continued in 1594, and removed to Keig"; while under Keig[3] is this entry—

1576 John Strathauchin translated from Cushnie, having Alfurde, Loquhill, and Kindrocht likewise under his charge; continued in 1580. He returned previous to 1595; and continued in 1597.

This last is of importance. The Forbeses were among the leading Protestants of our district. Yet here we learn that after the Reformation, one minister, living at Keig, had actually "under his charge" all the four parishes whose teinds &c., had been payable to our Priory—Keig, Alford, Leochel, and far-distant Braemar! and in this rent-roll that tells how Lord Forbes had appropriated its lands as well as its teinds, he himself, using the first person—"hes it off me"—hands down what was the magnificent allowance for which he farmed out the vicarage or lesser teinds to the poor minister! One wonders that the minister was able to travel even once a quarter to Braemar, and we are able to judge how dependent the parishes were upon 'readers.' We find that "at Kyg Robert Raitt was reader, at Alfurde John Patersoun, and at Kyndroch in Braymar James Hanye, each with xx lib."[4]

In regard to the "preaching quarterly," there is a record of

[1] Collns. A. and B. pp. 226, 227, 230.
[2] Dr. Hew Scott, Fasti, III. part II. p. 560.
[3] Ibid. pp. 555, 556.
[4] Collns. A. and B. pp. 228, 229

great interest. In January, 1559, at the instance of the Queen Regent, Mary of Guise, the mother of Mary Queen of Scots, a General Provincial Council was summoned to assemble at Edinburgh on the 1st of March. It was called mainly for the consideration of the remarkable articles of amendment that had been submitted to the Queen Regent by certain laymen, nobles, and barons, not disaffected to the Church of Rome, but anxious for the correction of its abuses. One article asked that there should be sermon in every parish Church on every Sunday and other holiday, or at least on Christmas day, Easter, Whitsunday, and every third or fourth Sunday. "The Council enacted that there was to be sermon not only *four times in every year, as had already been enjoined*, but as much oftener as the Ordinary should see fit."[1] This was the last Council of the Roman Church in our country. Whatever might have been the effect of such rules of amendment at an earlier stage, they were too late now, for in a few months the Roman Church was overthrown, ending the supremacy of the Pope in our land, which had lasted for about four hundred years.

Duncan Forbes, who succeeded in getting possession of the Church lands here, belonging both to the Archbishop of St. Andrews and to the Priory, which in the end embraced the whole parish, was the son of William Forbes of Corsindae in Midmar, whom we years before met with as looking after the lands, and who was himself the second son of the second Lord Forbes. Corsindae itself was held of Lord Forbes, for in the 'rent-roll' of 1552 the entry runs :—"Corsindavy pays zeirlie to my Lord of few male x£.[2]

We now come to a very important record, for from it we

[1] Dr. J. Robertson, Stat. Ecc. Scot. pp. clv.-clxiii.
[2] Mr. Rait's Pamphlet, p. 16.

The Spoliation of the Lands. 207

learn that there had been a fire in the Priory, which was the cause of the buildings' becoming ruinous.

Decree of the Lords of Council and Session in the cause between the Parson of Invernochty and the Prior of Monymusk, 11th July 1554.

Regarding our Sovereign Lord's letters procured at the instance of Master John Elphinstone Parson of Invernochty against one Venerable father in God David Prior of Monymusk making mention That whereas at the last Justiciary (Court) of Aberdeen the said Prior, Master Duncan Forbes feuar thereof, and the said Master John submitted themselves to the Lords Compositors then present for the time regarding certain debates and controversies among them Who decerned thereupon that the said Master Duncan, feuar foresaid, should refund, satisfy, and pay to the said Prior the sum of 100 merks, money of this realm, in complete payment of all the bye-past fruits And for the more sure payment to the said Prior of the sum of 12 score merks yearly to be paid to him conformably to his lease made by the said Prior to the said Master Duncan   The said Lord Compositors ordained the said Master John Elphinstone yearly to make payment to the said Prior during his life time, notwithstanding that the said Master Duncan had six years' occupation thereof to run for yearly payment of the foresaid sum only And the said Master John took security of the said Master Duncan for payment of the same to him And because the said Master John was successor to the said Prior they ordained him that he should cause to be upheld the Divine service which of verity is better done and more account is put thereto than has been these ten years past And also ordained that the said Master John should cause to be repaired and built *the Place of*

Monymusk which is entirely burned except one part thereof, also destroyed with fire through negligence of the Prior and his servants which the whole fruits of the said Abbey during the space of three years will not do the same And the said Master Duncan has the whole fruits aforesaid for 3 years to run except the payment of the said 12 score merks contained in the said Prior's lease made to him thereof And the mind of the said Lord Compositors was that the said Master John as soon as he entered on the fruits and profits of the said benefice should cause to be upheld the divine service and build the said Place which he is ready at all times to do Which deliverance was given by the foresaid Lords Compositors by an instrument taken in the hands of Master· Robert Lumsden shown before the said Lords of Council Because the said Master John has caused make diligence to know if the same be registered under form of decree and cannot apprehend the same which in no way is registered And although the said Prior has obtained letters in all the four forms for not fulfilling the same and by that through general clauses contained in the same, namely to cause to be upheld the divine service which is more sufficiently done than has been these diverse years past And also to have built and repaired the Place thereof while the said Master John has none of the fruits and it cannot be built in the space of three years because the same is utterly destroyed he has charged the said Master John thereto on three days and from three days to three days And . intends to denounce him as a rebel wrongfully . The said Master John Elphinstone compeared by Master John Spens his procurator and the said Prior compeared by Master David Borthwick his procurator THE LORDS OF COUNCIL RELIEVE the said Prior from the petition of the said

Master John and from all the points and articles contained in the said letters at this time as it is now set forth and decern him free therefrom in time to come And therefore ordain the said Prior's letters to have effect and to be put into execution for aught that they have yet seen . .[1]

One is grieved to have to tell what Dr. Joseph Robertson says regarding Elphinstone's character, taking from us, as it does, all sympathy with him in regard to his claims in this deed. 'The scandalous immorality which prevailed among all classes of the priesthood might surpass belief, were it not too clearly avouched. . . In 1550 John Elphinstone, Rector of Invernouchtie, and one of the cathedral dignitaries was brought to trial for the following offences :—"That, under silence of night, he murdered Thomas Cult in Old Aberdeen ; that he theftuously wasted and destroyed the goods of William Lowsoune burgess of Aberdeen, for the space of ten years," during which he sinned against him with the deepest family-wrong possible ; "that he assaulted and several times felled to the earth Mr. Duncan Burnet, Rector of Methlic, "with roungis [cudgels] and battounis," *within the Cathedral Church of Aberdeen, when he was celebrating matins and divine service.*"'[2] The italics are Dr. Robertson's and the passage shows a very different spirit from what Elphinstone claims for himself regarding the services conducted in our Priory during this very time !

We saw James Forbes, Duncan's elder brother, becoming in 1542 the true man to Lord Huntly, for the life-rent of Inver. Now we find Duncan in 1559 taking the same course and getting his first hold on another beautiful possession, in addition to what he already held of the Prior.

[1] Ant. A. and B. IV. pp. 778, 779.
[2] The Reformation in Aberdeen, pp. 19, 20, quoting Pitcairn's Criminal Trials, I. p. 356.

P

Be it kend till all men be thir presentis, that for samekle as ane noble and potent lord George erll of Huntly, Lord Gordoun and Badzenocht &c hes set to me Maister Duncan Forbes of Monymusk the toun and landis of Dullab, the outseitt of Monymusk callit Kemboig (? Tombeg) witht thar pendicles and pertinentis for all the dayis and terms of 19 years, and the said erle has gewin the proffitis of the said tounis and landis to the said master Duncan, fre during the said space for his service done and to be done to the said erll and his airis ; for the quhilkis takkis and profits I the said master Duncan Forbes oblessis me faythtfully and trewly to keip trew pairt and kyndnes to the said erle and his airis and to be ane trew frend and seruand to thaim &c. In witnes at Aberdeen 2nd Feby. 1559 before &c.

        Duncan Forbes wytht my hand.[1]

Soon after the Gordons and the Forbeses were constantly at feud, as we shall see in our next chapter.

"We learn from Wingate that in the spring of the same year, 1559, large numbers of the Clergy joined the ranks of the Reformed, and there is no reason to doubt that the Reformation was effected with 'the consent of the greater part both of pastors and people.' They asked among other things that the Church should be reformed in accordance with the precepts of the New Testament, that the Sacraments should be administered in English, that the bishops should be appointed with the consent of the gentry of the diocese, and parish ministers with the consent of the parishioners. It was not a secession—but a movement *en masse*."[2]

"The appointments to the Scottish bishoprics at this time

---

[1] Gordon Papers, Spalding Club Misc. IV. p. 224.
[2] Dr. Sprott, Church Society Conference, pp. 161, 162.

throw a lurid light upon the condition of the Church. The good and the bad were strangely intermingled, but unhappily the bad predominated. Worse men than the bishops of the falling hierarchy never wore a mitre. It has been often said in Scotland that the strongest argument against episcopacy was the episcopate. The bishops of this age give point to the remark."[1] As Mr. S. R. Gardiner says, " Episcopacy had been retained in England because the bishops had taken part in the English Reformation. *Episcopacy had ceased in Scotland because the bishops had not taken part in the Scottish Reformation.*"[2] Another great difference in the two countries was, that in Scotland the Reformation was the work of the Clergy and the people, that is of the nation, and was carried through in spite of the opposition of the Crown and of the bishops.

By his rent-roll of 1552, William, seventh Baron Forbes, who succeeded his father five years before, possessed estates in Auchindoir, Tullynessle and Forbes, Alford, Glenmuick, Tough, Cluny, Kincardine O'Neil, Midmar, Birse, Foveran, and King-Edward.[3] His elder brother had been beheaded by James V. in 1537, on his visit to Aberdeen, for conspiracy, but afterwards the King was convinced that the execution had not been warranted, and restored his father to his title and estates, and made William a gentleman of the bed-chamber. William married Elizabeth, daughter and co-heiress of Sir William Keith of Inverugie, the sister of the Countess Marischal. They had sixteen children, and their fourth son, the Hon. Robert Forbes became the last so-called Prior of Monymusk, thus making everything absolutely secure to the Forbes family.

In 1560, August 24th, the Reformation was consummated by the enactments of the Scottish Parliament. The revenues

[1] Mr. Stephen, History, p. 530.
[2] The Puritan Revolution, p. 102.
[3] Mr. Rait's Pamphlet, p. 1.

of the Priory at the time it came into Duncan Forbes' hands, amounted to £400.[1] The part of the lordship of Keig and Monymusk that lies in Keig parish, came afterwards into Lord Forbes' hands and the greater part of it is still possessed by this family.

The Prior, Robert Forbes, who was 'Commendator,' receiving two-thirds of the revenues, the rest being allotted to the maintenance of the surviving monks, was or became a Protestant and married Agnes, daughter of William Forbes of Corse,[2] and had four sons, one of whom, Captain John, was killed at the battle of Stirling, James (of Fowell) became a Lieutenant-Colonel, Robert died abroad,—and two daughters, one of whom was married to the Laird of Auchinhove, and the other to William Fraser of Boghead. In December 4th, 1612, among the scholars attending the grammar school, song school, and writing school at Aberdeen, is mentioned "John Forbes, son to the pryoir of Monymusk."[3]

In 1562, September 9th, Queen Mary visited Balquhain, the seat of the Leslies, and attended service at 'the Chapel' of Garioch.

In 1563 Duncan Forbes granted a reversion of the lands of Abersnithock and Mill of Ramstone, both of which had long belonged to the Priory, in favour of William Leslie of Balquhain.[4]

"In 1567, of the five superintendents, two hundred and eighty-seven ministers, and seven hundred and fifteen readers who were officiating, the great majority must have been old priests, and in that year Parliament declared the Reformed

---

[1] Mr. Walcott, Anc. Ch. p. 322; Dr. Campbell, Balmerino, p. 133.
[2] Collns. A. and B. p. 170.
[3] Burgh Records, Spalding Club, II. p. 310.
[4] The Leslie Family Papers.

Church to be the only true Church in the realm, and entitled to the teinds as its proper inheritance."[1]

In 1570 James Johnston, who will be spoken of afterwards, was Parson of Monymusk, and one of the Chapter of Aberdeen. "He was possibly the last Roman Catholic Incumbent."[2] In this year the Bishop of Aberdeen executes a charter by way of feu, disposing of the property of the Loch-lands, which is subscribed by "James Johnston at Monymusk."[3]

In this year only about twenty ministers were obtainable for all Aberdeenshire. There were but few in the Garioch, as the Reformation spread slowly in this county,[4] owing in a great measure to the immense influence of the Earl of Huntly and his family connections.

On 26th July of this year, "Master Duncan Forbes of Monymusk" signs as a witness at Aberdeen to a contract "betwixt Lord Huntly and Lord Lovat."[5]

In 1584, as we shall state more fully afterwards, Duncan Forbes died. He was succeeded by his son William, and NOW WE REACH THE END, for only one other deed remains, but without a date, and by it the Prior, Robert Forbes, hands over the whole place, which we have found they had been allowing to go to ruin, to his kinsman, William Forbes of Monymusk.

To all who shall see or hear of this Charter Robert by divine permission Prior of the Priory of Monymusk eternal, everlasting greeting in the Lord Know that we having on all sides forethought to the utility and advantage of ourselves and our successors Commendators of Monymusk, and of that locality &c And in special considering that the place and monastery of the said Priory of Monymusk is now almost ruined and waste And that all convents of the

[1] Dr. Sprott, Ch. Soc. Conf. p. 162.
[2] Dr. Davidson, Inverurie, p. 128.
[3] Ibid., p. 148.
[4] Dr. Davidson, Inverurie, p. 152.
[5] Gordon Papers, Spalding Club Mis. IV. pp. 227, 228.

same are extinct So that there is no residence or house fit for habitation for the present at the said monastery In order that the ruinous houses and buildings of the said place may be restored and that a literary institution ('gymnasium') may be established within them for instructing boys in honourable studies and literature And for the augmentation of our rental and for certain sums of money paid to us by the honourable man William Forbes of Monymusk feudatory of the lands of the Manor of Monymusk &c Have given, granted &c to the said William Forbes of Monymusk his heirs male and assignees whatsoever All and whole the ruinous houses and buildings of the said Monastery of Monymusk and one croft or part of croft lying behind the garden that stretches towards the north of the said place for the sowing of 4 bolls of barley yearly along with all and each of the houses, buildings, gardens, formed and to be formed lying on the north of the stream running near the said place and monastery, close by the cemetery of the parish Church of Monymusk, with all and single parts &c along with the common *pasture for 6 horses and 50 rams*, lye wedders, to be pastured on the lands of the Manor of Monymusk (which are specially and expressly reserved for us and our successors by the charter and infeftment of fee granted by our predecessors to the late Master Duncan Forbes, father of the foresaid William) all as lying within the parish of Monymusk and vicecounty of Aberdeen To be held and possessed &c by the foresaid William Forbes, his heirs male and assignees of us and our successors the Priors of the said Priory in fee and heritage for ever throughout all their proper marches &c They paying thence yearly &c for the said croft or part of croft twenty-six shillings and eight pence And for the said *pasture of 6 horses and*

50 wedders ten shillings And for the houses, buildings, and pertinents of the said place the sum of thirteen shillings and fourpence for the augmentation of our rental &c They also maintaining, building, and repairing at all future times one suitable house or building for a literary institution or school for the instruction of youth, with the necessaries referring to the said school—only instead of all other burden &c.

    Robert Commendator off Monymosk.
    Alexander Gray witness to the foregoing.[1]

It may be most convenient to mention here what seems to be the only remaining link with the Priory in respect of the lands of Monymusk. It is seen in the feu-duties. When Sir William Forbes was served heir to his father Sir John Forbes, October 5th, 1702, details are given regarding the superiorities. It is simpler for us to call the farms by their present names, some of the smaller ones that are mentioned being now included in the larger, and it is to be observed that here we speak of the position in 1702. The sums of money paid in respect of the feu-duties are also mentioned, but there is no need for our detailing them.

Inver, Ardniedly, Overmill of Monymusk, the multures of Enzean, the old town and the outhouse of Monymusk, Tornagloyes (Damhead, beside Swinton), Cornabo &c were held of the *Archbishops of St. Andrews*, and now (1702) of the *King* in feu-farm.

Coullie, Enzean, Braehead, Tombeg, Delab, Tillyfourie, Todlachy &c and part of the moss of Craigearn (in the parish of Kemnay) were held of the *Duke of Gordon*.

  1 Colls. A. and B. pp. 184, 185.

Pitfichie with the castle-fort, manor-place, mill, mill-lands, and salmon-fishing, Ordmill, Mildourie, Overton, Netherton, Rowrandle &c were held of *the Queen* according to the Charter of Charles II in favour of the said Sir John Forbes, 22nd July 1661.[1]

With regard to the feu-duties stated as held by the Duke of Gordon, these were sold by the last Duke to the late Mr. Robert Grant of Tillyfour about 1820, so that the Duke's representatives have no longer any interest in the lands in our parish that were given over to the Earl of Huntly by Cardinal Beaton, but these feu-duties are now heritable in the late Mr. Robert Grant's family.

As regards the feu-duties payable to the Crown for the other farms mentioned, these are shown (being repeated from old charters) in a precept from Chancery in favour of the late Sir James Grant in 1821. Some particulars in it are of much interest as carrying us directly back to what was specified in the agreements made between the Prior and the Commendator and the two Forbeses; and when we think of this, is it not singular to learn that, for instance, the value of the pasturage for the six horses and fifty sheep, as specified in the charter we have just given, is actually paid to this very day by our proprietor who holds the place of the Forbeses? Out of curiosity we shall mention one or two particulars to show how this ancient bargain is still binding and being implemented. It is to be noted that it is all Scots money that is mentioned, and though the relative value is so different at the present time, it is to be remembered that one shilling Scots is equal to one penny sterling, and one Lib. Scots to twenty pennies (one shilling and eightpence) sterling.

[1] Ant. A. and B. III. pp. 504, 505.

Feu-duties payable to the Crown for the estate of Monymusk:—

Lands and Dominical lands of Monymusk	£26 13 4	(Scots)
Croft adjoining	1 6 8	
Pasturage for six horses	0 6 0	
Pasturage for fifty sheep	0 4 0	
Balvack	7 10 0	
Cornabo	0 13 4	
Feu-duty for Pitfichie	2 0 0	
In all including all the places named	£42 11 4	(Scots)
Equal in money sterling to £3 10 11.		

This sum is still payable yearly from the estate to the *Deans of the Chapel Royal*, the revenues of which form part of the salaries of certain of the Professors of Divinity in the Universities. This is the sole amount now received for Church purposes from the lands of this parish that were included in Malcolm III's great gift, the rents of which were paid in olden times to the Bishops of St. Andrews or to the Priory.

Up to 1878 a rather larger feu-duty was payable by the estate, but in that year the late Sir Archibald Grant paid to the Crown redemption money for the feu-duties payable to the Crown and for the casualties of the whole Crown lands. This applied to Inver, Ardniedly, Pitmuny, Overmill of Monymusk &c., and came to a little more than the other sum—being £49 13s. 4d. Scots. It is amusing to read the particulars, of which we may give as samples, the sums named being of course Scots money—

Ardniedly,	£6 13 4
for 12 pultreis	0 4 0
,, 2 bolls oats	0 8 0
,, half a mart [ox]	0 12 0
,, sheep or wether	0 4 0

		£	s.	d.
Pitmuny		6	13	4
for 12 pultreis		0	4	0
„ 2 bolls corn		0	8	0
„ half a mart		0	12	0
„ sheep or wether		0	4	0
„ grassum of Ardniedly and Pitmuny		5	6	8
„ augmentation of rental		1	1	8
Inver		13	6	8
for 24 pultreis		0	8	0
„ 4 bolls oats		0	12	0
„ 1 mart		1	4	0
„ 2 sheep or wethers		0	8	0
„ grassum		5	6	8
„ augmentation		0	1	8

We are not aware of there being any other records or notices connected with our Priory. We shall meet on two occasions with the gift by the Crown of the small feu-duties that we have just spoken of as payable to it, but with these exceptions we have now traced its history to the end, and have always let the records speak for themselves. Step by step we learned the gifts that were bestowed on it, and now we have seen the passing away of the old order and have been witnesses of the appropriation of its tithes, its home, and of every acre of its lands. The mere reading of many of the records must have been wearisome, and their translation from the mediæval Latin has been often hazardous to an inexperienced translator, but they give us an insight into the process of decay and consequent spoliation that no general statements can approach in clearness, and as we consider their particulars they throw side-lights on several points connected with the internal government of the ancient church and with the conditions of society, of considerable value from an historical point of view. We have also learned something of the inner life and circumstances of a secluded Northern monastery. The spirit that pervaded those far-off times has opened out in a little way before us. By contact with the details of actual records and rent-rolls we become acquainted with particulars that must be otherwise unknown to us, and we see what an unsparing hand was laid upon the Church's possessions; and when we think of the wide-spread needs of our land, we rejoice that when the Church had passed through the ordeal, the Gospel came to be ministered to all in the simplicity, and richness, and freeness of the Word of Christ.

CHAPTER IX.

THE STRIFE BETWEEN THE FORBESES AND THE GORDONS.

THE FICTION OF ARCHANGEL LESLIE.

To avoid interrupting our account of the parish since the Reformation, it may be well to take by themselves two narratives that fall in order of time at early periods embraced in the next chapter. The second of them may perhaps be reckoned in one sense as an amusing interlude, and as they touch on few points that come before us afterwards, neither of them will make us materially anticipate our history.

We have drawn much information from the 'rent-roll' of William, seventh Lord Forbes, which begins in 1552. His eldest son John, Master of Forbes, married first Lady Margaret Gordon, daughter of George, fourth Earl of Huntly, who, we saw, received in 1542 from Cardinal Beaton the gift of the lands and barony of Keig and Monymusk. She continued a Roman Catholic, and the marriage was a most unhappy one. They had a son, John, who became a Friar, and whose "career gives a curious interest to his biography. His mother died in January 1606, at Antwerp, and John died in August of the same year near Tremonde." A biography of both mother and son was published at Cologne in 1620, and other editions of it were published in Modena, Naples, Valentia, and Douay down to 1675, while a second English translation was printed in London as recently as 1872.[1] This marriage being so unfortunate, taken in connection with the gift of the lands of Keig and Monymusk

[1] Mr. T. G. Law, Edinburgh Bibliogr. Society, 1890-91, No. III.

by Cardinal Beaton to Lady Margaret's father, led to the breaking out anew of the old family quarrel between the Forbeses and the Gordons, who were the most powerful families in Aberdeenshire at the time. During this period the power of the Earl of Huntly was enormous, and the influence of his house had attained an unlimited height. He was zealously devoted to the Romish faith, so that while in other districts it was tottering to its overthrow, its authority was maintained by the strong hand of Huntly throughout the provinces from the Dee to the Ness. In 1572 the Gordons attacked and defeated the Forbeses at Druminnor, a very ancient seat of the family, when Arthur, Lord Forbes' brother, was killed. Several very long writs are preserved[1] referring to Cardinal Beaton's gift of these lands to the Earl of Huntly, in connection with this strife between the two clans; and as Duncan Forbes of Monymusk and his brother James of Corsindae are among the parties to the legal appeals, we shall give an abstract of them, as far as they relate to our narrative.

In June, 1573, before the Lords of Council and Session, William Lord Forbes and his kin complain against George [fifth] Earl of Huntly that although they had hoped for relief from the late troubles, many of their kinsmen were slain and their houses ruined by the Earl. Their wrongs had not been redressed, they had still to be on their guard, and they were liable to be arrested, for the Earl was Sheriff-principal of the county. The Lords of Council having examined Lord Forbes and his friends, among whom are named William Forbes of Barnes, John Forbes of Abersnithock, James Forbes of Corsindae, and Master Duncan Forbes of Monymusk, ordain all actions to be tried before themselves.

Five years elapse, and in July, 1578, in the action raised by

[1] Ant. A. and B. IV. pp. 760-770.

Lord Forbes, Master Duncan Forbes of Monymusk, and others of their kin, specially "the old native possessors" of the lands and barony of Keig and Monymusk, against the Earl of Huntly [the sixth Earl, his father having died in May, 1576], they make the following complaint and assertions. They say that they possessed and occupied these lands by themselves and their dependents, as principal and old native possessors and tenants under the Archbishops of St. Andrews, to whom the lands and barony belonged as part of their patrimony in all byegone times, past memory of man, before '*the pretended infeftment*' thereof made to the late George Earl of Huntly, grandfather of the present Earl, by the late David, Cardinal Archbishop of St. Andrews, who, they allege, had formed a new familiarity with the Earl of Huntly owing to some great affairs between themselves. [The news of the disaster of Solway Moss had a fatal effect on James V. Huntly and other three persons were named as Regents in the King's will produced by Cardinal Beaton, but asserted by the Earl of Arran to have been forged. When the Cardinal was arrested, *January* 20, 1542-43, Huntly with others offered themselves as his surety and demanded that he should be set at liberty. After the escape of Beaton, Huntly organised with him the conspiracy by which the infant Queen Mary and her mother were seized at Linlithgow and carried to Stirling. On a reconciliation taking place between Arran and Beaton, Huntly attended the coronation of the infant princess at Stirling.[1] It is to be noted that it was in *April*, 1542-43, that the deed making over the lands was signed by Beaton.] They also allege that Cardinal Beaton had most unkindly given their native possessions over their heads to the Earl and his heirs, never intending, however, that they should be removed or made pay more than the old dues paid to him and the former

[1] Dict. of Nat. Biogr. xxii. p. 179.

bishops of St. Andrews, but wishing simply to show his favour for the Earl. They were the old native possessors and holders of the lands, and these being Church lands the Archbishop had no rights over them except according to the old and laudable customs applicable to such lands. The Earl had 'for worthy considerations' bestowed on some of the principal of the complainers in 'heritage' and on others of them by 'lease,' their own native possessions which they had continued to hold without molestation, no question being raised against them as to removing until lately, and this being now done simply on account of their loyalty to the Crown. They have now received warnings to remove, and the present Earl has raised actions against them, intending to displace them, owing to their services to the King and to 'his dearest mother in the time of her authority,' such services being specially rendered when Earl George himself [the fourth Earl] rebelled in 1562, and died with his banner displayed against her. [In August, 1562, Mary set out on her northern progress, and on account of the flagrant defiance of her authority by the Earl of Huntly's son, Sir John Gordon of Findlater, she declined while at Balquhain to visit the Earl in Strathbogie, and passed on to Inverness. On her return journey an attempt was made to surprise some of her followers at Cullen, and Huntly was summoned to appear before the Council, and, failing to do so, was denounced as a rebel. When the Queen approached Aberdeen, he marched toward it with about 800 men, and on November 5th, at the skirmish at Corrichie, on the Hill of Fare, about fifteen miles from Aberdeen, being hopelessly outnumbered by Moray's troops, his men were at once overpowered, and he was either crushed to death or died suddenly from excitement.[1]] They had also, they say, rendered similar services when the present Earl's father rebelled

[1] Dict. of Nat. Biogr. xxii. p. 181.

against the King, in whose defence many of the complainers' kindred laid down their lives in the battles of Tillyangus and Craibstone. Their houses and goods were then destroyed or burned and the rents of their lands interfered with, in contempt of the King's authority and of the truce concluded in 1572; and although the Earl's forces had so failed that he had to accept the conditions of peace made at Perth in *February* of that year, he and his kindred had been able to delay the hearing of the causes and were frustrating the administration of justice. [The fifth Earl of Huntly commanded the expedition to Stirling, when the Regent Lennox was captured and afterwards mortally wounded. Morton, on being chosen Regent, made use of Argyll to enter into communication with Huntly and the Hamiltons for a reconciliation, and at a convention at Perth, where Huntly and the Lord of Arbroath acted as the representatives of those with whom the treaty was made, articles were finally agreed upon on the 3rd *February*, 1572. The secession of Huntly and the Hamiltons from the Queen's cause virtually ended the Civil War, and from this time Huntly lived chiefly in his own dominions, scarcely taking any further part in public affairs, and died very suddenly in 1576.[1]]

This complaint being considered, the King and Parliament appoint Commissioners, whose names are recorded, to decide the cause within eighteen months.

Four years, however, pass, and on July 6th, 1582, James VI as 'over-man,' after hearing both sides, gives the final decree, with advice of the Council :—(1) That John, Master of Forbes, shall pay £4,000 Scots to the wife and family of Gordon of Gight, who had been killed along with his servant by the Forbeses ; (2) that Lord Forbes and those of his kin who had actual rights from the two former Earls of Huntly to parts of

[1] Dict. of Nat. Biogr. xxii. p. 185.

the lands of Keig and Monymusk, shall hold these parts peaceably in accordance with their infeftments [this would secure their possessions in Monymusk to the Forbeses]; but (3) that they shall remove from the whole remainder of the lands of Keig and Monymusk and allow the Earl and his kindred to enter thereon as their heritage,—both sides being relieved from all charges against each other and ordained to live in good neighbourhood, as if these deadly feuds had never occurred.

      James Rex. James Lord of Doun.
      Arrane.   Gowrie.
      Montros.

Few probably even of those well acquainted with the history of our district, are aware of the place that Monymusk has occupied in Roman Catholic literature since the middle of the seventeenth century. Monymusk House has in fact been made famous throughout Europe in history, in biography, and even in drama, as the scene of the marvellous exploits of a Popish missionary, commonly known as "Father Archangel, the Scottish Capuchin." The story of his life was first printed in Italian in 1644, and afterwards amplified in a number of French, Portuguese, German, Dutch or Flemish, Latin, and English editions—eighteen editions being issued in Italy alone from no fewer than nine famous cities. It is one of the strangest fictions in modern hagiology, and having gained such wide-spread notoriety, we can hardly avoid telling the story of the deception as far as it relates to Monymusk. The following account is taken from two articles—"The Legend of Archangel Leslie" in the 'Scottish Review' of July, 1891, and "Archangel Leslie of Scotland: a Sequel" in the 'Nineteenth Century' of
Q

November, 1893, both written by Mr. T. G. Law of the Signet Library, Edinburgh, the learned editor of "Archbishop Hamilton's Catechism" (1552), to which edition (1884) Mr. Gladstone wrote a preface. Mr. Law also, in a paper printed in 1890-91 by the Edinburgh Bibliographical Society, gives a list of about forty-five editions of the Life of Leslie, while Mr. R. B. Cunninghame Graham in the 'Nineteenth Century' for September, 1893, also tells the story in his own way, of course thinking it substantially true, from a copy that he picked up in Spain.

The hero of this wide-spread legend is George Leslie, a son of James Leslie of Peterstone and his wife, Jane Wood. He was born in or near Aberdeen, and went as a youth to the Scots College at Rome in 1608, and then joined the Capuchin friars, a branch of the Franciscan order. About 1623 he was sent on the "mission" to Scotland, and made several converts among the gentry in Aberdeenshire. About six years after he returned to Italy and became acquainted with John Baptist Rinuccini, Archbishop of Fermo, who was afterwards Papal Nuncio to Ireland in the troublous times of 1645-50. He had plausible manners, a facile tongue, inordinate vanity, and a lively imagination. He falsely gave himself out as the son of wealthy and high-born parents who owned Monymusk House, and who had disinherited him on account of his religion, and he fascinated the Archbishop with the tale of his sufferings and adventures, and of his successes as a court preacher to the Queen Regent of France, &c. He told Rinuccini that on arriving in Scotland his first object had been the conversion of his mother. At Aberdeen, so his story ran, he wrote her a letter in his own name, dated from Italy, recommending its bearer to her as his intimate friend. Dressing as a cavalier, he went to Monymusk House and said to her, "Madam, I have come from

Italy, and bring you a letter from your son." Taking it, she exclaimed that he was the most ungrateful son that ever lived. But she made the stranger welcome, and the disguised friar, soon won the favour of the family, although he was horrified at having to sit at table with the heretic minister who acted as chaplain. Five days after, an incautious question addressed too loudly to a deaf servant about a pigeon-house that—as he said—he remembered to have been in the house when he was a boy, was overheard by the astonished mother, and his identity was discovered. The house now became a theatre of joy. The news spread through the town of Monymusk, and the old lady received a thousand visits of congratulation. Fireworks were let off, and cannons fired from the Castle to welcome the return of the banished son. The minister alone was in despair. The mother at first imposed silence on both, but this was unendurable to the zealous friar, who stole out from the Castle under pretence of hunting, and preached to the people in the mountains and forests. In eight months he made three thousand converts (later editions say four thousand). Then a conference was arranged with the minister, who, being defeated in argument, was expelled the house. The mother now submitted to the Roman faith. A large hall at the top of the house was made into a chapel; the ladies offered their jewels, robes, and embroideries, the altar was decked with diamonds, and Archangel, who now resumed his friar's dress, had a massive chalice made out of his mother's rings. Two years after, all priests were commanded to leave the country, and he had to quit Monymusk. In writing to console him, his mother assured him that she now restored to him his inheritance, but she herself—so the story continued—soon became the victim of persecution. She was excommunicated by the presbytery and condemned to the loss of all her goods.

Reduced to distress, she took up her abode in a little cottage, where she earned a miserable pittance by needlework. Archangel was then in Paris, and by his influence with the French Court, obtained letters to the King of England, through which the mansion house and lands were finally restored to her. But before this could be effected, he so longed to console her that he ventured back in disguise as a peasant. As he came near Monymusk he gathered some herbs, and pretending to be a gardener, he went about the streets crying, " Buy my greens ! " The guards stopped him at the gates, for the town was walled, and as he dared not ask where his mother lived, he walked three times through the town. At last she appeared and called, " Here, gardener." He was much affected at seeing her dressed like a servant, and having to buy her vegetables, and while she was bargaining about the purchase, he looked her full in the face, and said, " Madam, this gardener does not sell, but gives to his mother." She uttered a cry that might have been fatal to them. The interview was but short, for the commissaries of the King in matters of religion were at hand, and broke into the cottage, and it was with difficulty that he escaped.

Such is the story that George Leslie told Archbishop Rinuccini and his friend, Father Pica, an Oratorian, in the garden of the Capuchin convent at Ripa Transone in 1631. The Archbishop resolved to put it in print, convinced that it would take wings and fly into every corner of Europe, making thousands of converts. Meanwhile, Leslie once more left Italy for Scotland, and all that is known of this second mission is that he died about two years after, according to a contemporary, "in his mother's poor house just over the river Dee, against the mill of Aboyne."

Rinuccini's biography appeared in 1664, and for the wonders

related in it Leslie alone is responsible. But the fiction did not stop here. In some French editions a supplement was added containing a marvellous story of his shipwreck off the Isle of Wight, and of his making himself known to Charles I, who welcomed him to his palace at Newport (although in truth, Charles never kept court there at that time). The grateful monarch sent him by sea to Aberdeen, and granted the Leslies of Monymusk, as special privileges, the free exercise of their religion and the services of a Roman Catholic chaplain, in return for the benefits rendered by the family to the Crown. The friar henceforth, in several narratives, is styled "Count Leslie," his mother is the "Baroness of Torry," and his younger brothers who have also joined his faith are called "Barons."

The fame of Monymusk House, its counts, and its barons had now, as Rinuccini had prophesied, spread throughout Europe. The noble Capuchin appeared, as one of his biographers declared, "the most illustrious personage Scotland had produced"; "a spectacle to all Europe," said another. A Roman friar celebrated the story of Monymusk and the conversion of its owner, in a drama entitled "Il Cappuccino Scozzese in scena" (1673), of which the first scene is laid in "Monumusco Villa," and the poor presbyterian minister is given the somewhat uncommon name of Lurcanio! But this is not all. In quite recent times some sceptical writers, even among Roman Catholics, suggested doubts about the story, and some of their learned historians were thus led to make, or to pretend to make investigations as to the facts. Bishop Raess of Strassburg in his work in thirteen volumes on famous converts to the Church of Rome, fully confirms the story. The Capuchin historian, Rocco da Cesinale, a theologian of high repute, who attended the Vatican Council, and has written a history of the missionaries of his order, says that he took pains to get at the truth. He came to London in 1867, and learned from a member of the Leslie family that Rinuccini had "accurately described the House of Monymusk," and that "the library was turned into a chapel by Father Archangel and *many traces of that use still remain.*" Lastly, Père Richard, who professes to have made independent researches in preparation for a sumptuous edition of the story in French, entitled " Le Comte Georges Leslie, ou une Mission dans la Grande Bretagne au premier siècle de la Réforme," has learned some points in our local history, and has put them together in a way that has the merit of having been quite unknown to any of ourselves. He is very precise in his topography. "In the North of Scotland," he writes, "not far from the city of Aberdeen there is a rather large burgh ('un bourg assez considerable') called Monymusk. This burgh owed its existence and its name to a strong Castle built at the end of the eleventh century by King Malcolm III, who made it a gift to one of his most faithful subjects, of whom we shall speak presently. The Manor which rose up proudly and majestically in an enchanting situation, was girt on one side by enormous masses of rock, out of which it seemed to be hewn, and on the other by an admirable park, which following the capricious meanderings of the Dee, stretched almost as far as the gates of Aberdeen. Toward the end of the sixteenth century, this princely residence was inhabited by James, Count of Leslie, and Jane Sylvie Wood his spouse. The Count of Leslie was descended from an illustrious house of Hungary which came into Scotland in the eleventh century," and so on.

Well—if we are to believe this Père Richard—on the death of Archangel, the King of England sent to the brothers Leslie, a special messenger to express his regret at the loss of so distinguished a subject. The Barons of Torry who inherited their half-brother's property, now agreed to consecrate the Manor of Monymusk as a centre of the Roman Catholic mission. As long as Charles I. lived, it is told us, the Barons were not molested, but Cromwell put the mansion to the flames, the brothers were driven to the mountains, and when they died without issue, the House of Torry became extinct.

What a strange fiction! How singular that the transparent imposture should have gained such wide-spread currency, which it will doubtless continue to retain in some quarters, for a fresh account of it was published a few years ago in Philadelphia, and even in our own country Mr. Hunter Blair in his translation of Bellesheim's History devotes several pages to the 'fruitful labours' and 'almost unlimited influence' of the distinguished missionary! Mr. Law says, "If we are to believe Archangel, Monymusk House was the home of his boyhood, the property of his mother, the scene of his visit in the guise of a cavalier, the centre of his missionary triumphs, and his own prospective inheritance. Remove Monymusk from the story, and the whole falls as a house of cards, and with it goes Archangel's reputation as a simple-minded Capuchin and an honest man."

We need hardly say that this whole foundation is absolutely false. Monymusk was never in the possession of the Leslie family or any one connected with them. Nor was there any Count Leslie till after the Capuchin's death, Walter Leslie of the Balquhain family being created such in 1637. At the date of the story, Monymusk House was occupied by Sir William Forbes, who, we need not say, was never a Roman Catholic. The lands of Torry, on the other side of the Dee from Aberdeen, also belonged to him, and were sold afterwards by his family to the City of Aberdeen in 1705. Instead of the "impious" minister's being expelled the House, he married

Sir William's eldest daughter in 1632. The Library is indeed at the top of the House, and is a fine room, but it were strange if it still bore " many traces" of having been turned into a chapel, for the room was not then in existence, this part being built years after by the Grant family. The House was never burned by Cromwell or any one else, and our little village with its thirty houses all told, mostly cottages, is doubtless as large now as it ever was, and can hardly boast of streets, much less of having been a walled town with gates. There is not even a substratum of truth in the fiction. George Leslie's parents were in comparatively poor circumstances, and he himself had not much of the hero in him or any great regard for truth—a contemporary, who was of his own faith, being witness. His mother, after the death of her first husband, George's father, married another Leslie, who was "laird of Belcairn," in Meldrum, about fifteen miles from this. As an Aberdeenshire boy, George knew something of Monymusk, and may have been connected through his mother with some persons living in it,—for on the stone inside the Church, which we mentioned (p. 184), John Lesly, Balcarne, is seen to have died in 1601. His first wife was the daughter of John Forbes in Abersnithack, and died in 1583. His second wife and their son were also buried here, and then he himself. So that even if he did not live here, there had been repeated funerals from Balcairn to our churchyard, and through his mother's second marriage there may have been other things making George Leslie familiar in thought with our parish. Of course he could not see the consequences of the deception that his vanity prompted him to play off upon the too credulous Archbishop, and if we look at it as a mere story we in Monymusk may learn how the name of our parish has been celebrated in various languages of Europe, and we also find that we are indebted to him and his many biographers for an object lesson in historical criticism as entertaining as it is instructive. While, if we think of it more seriously, every one sees that the purpose of the narrative as a whole is simply to glorify a popish missionary and the Roman Church and those yielding to it, and to bring others into contempt; but surely no one is justified in continuing to spread such a legend even as a romance, for in no romance, especially when anything sacred is involved in it, is it permissible to use names of persons and families, and connect them and their homes with what is absolutely false and deceptive, under colour of truth and fact.

Since this account was put into the printers' hands, we have had the opportunity of reading again Dr. Joseph Robertson's little narrative of 'The History of the Reformation in Aberdeen,' which we had not seen for some years. It consists of four papers that appeared in 1837, and were collected and reprinted in 1887. The closing paper gives an outline of Rinuccini's work. Dr. Robertson speaks of it in very strong language. He evidently appears to think that the story was a deliberate invention of Rinuccini's. This was not the case. Rinuccini shows not a trace of dishonesty. It was Leslie who deceived the Archbishop, and there is no reason to suppose that he was ever undeceived. But if Leslie's deception was dictated simply by vanity and brag, the guilt of his continuators is of a graver character. We cannot think that writers like Père Richard are justified in propagating the story without more real investigation. His researches were evidently a pretence, and his credulity culpable, and those of his faith ought to learn caution in trusting such legends, which are handed down without historical evidence. When Dr. Robertson quotes the Archbishop's words regarding those who 'will be reduced to dispute the truth of the narrative and give the lie to his work,' he naively remarks, "In this quarter at least such a labour would be superfluous; if the book does not give the lie to itself it may still command implicit credit in the 'large town of Monymusk,' and its 'fame reach *even* to Aberdeen.' We heartily join," he adds, "in the Archbishop's prayer for 'wings to his little book,' that the eyes of the country may be opened to the nature of such " legends.

CHAPTER X.

MINISTERS SINCE THE REFORMATION.
SIR WILLIAM FORBES AND THE COVENANT.
THE FAMILY OF URRY OF PITFICHIE.
THE LAST RECORD OF THE PRIORY.
THE POLL-BOOK OF 1696.
THE FORBES FAMILY.
THE GRANT FAMILY.

IN 1567 James Murray was minister of the parish. At the end of this year the Protestant faith was finally established throughout the country and received the royal sanction. Murray had also Kinernie in charge, a parish half of which about 1743 was joined to Cluny and half to Midmar. He had 100 merks as stipend, and was presented to the parsonage and vicarage in 1573 by James VI, but he does not seem to have got possession. He continued as 'reader' till 1589.[1] "The duty of the 'reader' was confined to reading the Scriptures to the people, without making any remark to them on what he read. From the 'Register of Benefices' compiled about 1570, we learn that the total number of 'ministers' in Aberdeenshire did not exceed thirty; the number of 'exhorters' did not reach half that number; and the chief provision made for the spiritual wants of the people, was in the 'readers,' persons employed simply to read the Scriptures at a miserable pittance of £16 or £20 a year, [as we saw before on page 205.] With three or four exceptions there was not within the county a minister who had not two, three, four, or five parishes under his charge."[2]

[1] Collns. A. and B. p. 227; Fasti.
[2] Dr. Joseph Robertson, The Reformation in Aberdeen, pp. 58, 68, 69.

Regarding this, Dr Chalmers said in a speech in 1835, "Whole tracts of country were rifled by the hand of violence of their ecclesiastical patrimony, and no means were left for the Christian education of the people, who would have sunk into a state of moral barbarism but for the efforts of so many patriots as courageous and enlightened as the world ever saw—the fathers and founders of the Church of Scotland."

In 1572 John Forbes, son of Duncan Forbes of Monymusk, was presented by James VI, but he was not admitted. This year was the beginning of the struggle between Episcopacy and Presbytery, which continued with varying fortunes during 118 years till 1690, after the Stuarts were driven from the throne of England. The periods of Episcopacy as imposed by the Sovereign and resisted on that account were—

from February, 1572, to June, 1592, twenty years,
from October, 1610, to June, 1638, twenty-eight years, and
from May, 1661, to June, 1690, twenty-six years,—in all seventy-four years.

This John Forbes became Forbes of Camphill.[1] In 1599 and 1665 John Forbes of Camphill is mentioned in 'Skene of Skene' and again in 1688 a John Forbes of Camphill is spoken of as 'brother of William Forbes in the manor place of Monymusk.'[2]

In 1574 James Johnnestoune, previously referred to, was presented by James VI to this parish, having Cluny also in charge, John Strachan being 'reader' there.[3] He was a cadet of Caskieben, and in 1607 he executed there a charter to his second son James of a 'solar' third part of Aquhorthies. He was the first 'settled' minister here after the Reformation, and had to pay his own reader. In 1578 or 1585 Bourtie was included under his charge, but in 1593 Fetternear, an original

---

1 Dr. Davidson, Inverurie, p. 236. 2 pp. 50, 32, 28. 3 Collns. A. and B. p. 228.

parish now in Chapel of Garioch, (in Blairdaff, *quoad sacra*) was given instead. He died 19th March, 1615, aged 76. In the 'Fasti' it is said that he seems to have gone to Tough in 1608, but in the record of his death he is called 'parson of Monymusk' leaving his son James his executor, with the by-rents of Isaacston.[1]

In 1587 Parliament passed an Act annexing the temporalities of the various bishoprics to the Crown. 'Every acre of ecclesiastical patrimony now passed into laymen's hands, the Church henceforth receiving a small dole grudgingly of what had once been her own. Nor was the Crown much enriched by this spoliation. James VI soon squandered the plunder among his greedy favourites who grew great upon the spoils of the bishops, and he had nothing left to himself but regret at his double folly.'[2]

William Urry of Pitfichie was about this time married to Agnes, daughter of Alexander Leslie, third baron of Wardes near Inverurie. She married secondly Laurence Leith in Rayne in 1580.

Two interesting notices are given in the 'Burgh Records of Aberdeen,' (Spalding Club) :—" Maister Duncan Forbes of Monewisk and bailye of Aberdeen departtit the xxi day Februar 1584 years." "Annes Gray, the spouse of Maister Duncan Forbes of Monimwsk and bailye of Aberdeen departtit the twenty day of October 1584 yeris and was buried in the pariss of Aberdeen with hir forbearis." As Dr. J. Robertson points out in his 'Reformation in Aberdeen' it is deserving of notice that at this era 'the population of Aberdeen did not exceed 4000.'

In 1588-89 William Forbes of Monymusk received a charter from James VI, dated 20th January, erecting the town into a

---

[1] Dr. Davidson, Inverurie, pp. 155, 236, 209.
[2] Mr. Lippe, Wodrow, p. xxx.

burgh of barony with two free fairs on the muir of Monymusk, (1) on the first feast of St. Mary in autumn and (2) on the last feast of St. Mary. One of these markets dropped off some time ago, but the other was kept up till about 25 years ago, when, one cow only appearing on the muir, it also was allowed to die away.

In 160-- James Irving, minister of Tough, was presented to this parish by James VI. He had a very hard life of it. The Crowns of England and Scotland were united in 1603 and James VI 'suddenly found himself the absolute monarch of a great Kingdom.' He was anxious to bring about a civil union also and promote uniformity in the English and Scottish Churches—"a natural ambition if he had gone about the matter in a kindly and constitutional way. But this was not his way, especially now. He dissolved Assemblies of the Church which he thought would be unruly, and cast the ministers who met in spite of him, into jail. He called other Assemblies when and where he pleased by his own kingly prerogative and filled them with those who, he knew, would do his bidding. In this way the work was easily and effectually done. In an Assembly which met at Glasgow in 1610, the Presbyterian polity was pulled down stone by stone by the hands of Presbyterian ministers and the Episcopal polity set up in its room."[1]

The Church had possessed the right to hold Assemblies yearly, but one meeting that had been appointed for July 1605 at Aberdeen, James put off, as he feared opposition to his measures from the Church. 'It was the last Assembly for many years that was deemed valid in after times.' Only nineteen members attended, and the Assembly was constituted notwithstanding the royal prohibition. The Moderator chosen was

[1] Dr. Cunningham, St. Giles, p. 172.

"an eminent man," Mr. John Forbes, minister of Alford. He was a son of William Forbes of Corse and his wife Elizabeth Strachan of the Thornton family in Kincardineshire. His brother Patrick was Bishop of Aberdeen from May 1618, to March 1635, whose son John, Professor of Divinity in King's College, was "one of the greatest and holiest divines that Scotland has ever produced."[1] Lord Sempill (Sir William Forbes of Craigievar and Fintray, Bart.), is descended from his brother William. Mr. James Ross or Rose, Aberdeen, father of the minister of Birse, of whom we shall speak afterwards, preached the opening sermon before the Assembly. They did not transact any business, but simply met and then adjourned, their sole object being to preserve the rights of the Church. The King, however, declared their conduct, and then their defence rebellious, and they were subjected to the severest penalties. John Forbes and five others were imprisoned in Blackness and tried for high treason, found guilty by a packed jury and banished for life to the Continent. Forbes became a minister at Middleburgh, and then at Delft, and died in exile about 1634. Dr. Sprott of North Berwick writes an account of him in the Dictionary of National Biography, vol. xix. His daughter was married to Andrew Skene, who, in 1633, was infeft in the lands of Overtoun of Dyce.[2] Eight others, making fourteen of the nineteen, were imprisoned in Stirling Castle, among them our Mr. Irving, and the minister of Towie. All were made to feel the heaviest weight of the King's displeasure for refusing to acknowledge his spiritual supremacy and support his episcopal changes. Next year Mr. Irving's confinement was changed, by the King's letter, to the Orkney Islands, and when he refused to obey owing to the distance, it was changed in 1607, to his own parish where he was allowed

[1] Dr. Sprott, Liturgies of James VI. pp. x, xi. [2] Skene of Skene, p. 30.

Ministers since the Reformation. 239

to perform his duties, but was prohibited from attending meetings of Synod or Presbytery. Three years afterwards James induced the General Assembly to assent to the establishment of Episcopacy, and it continued for twenty-eight years, when it was abolished, and Presbyterianism established. "But," as Dr. Sprott says in the 'Conference of the Church Society,' "there was no formation of a separate Episcopal Church, although three-fourths of the clergy were in Episcopal orders, and such were in a majority in every presbytery." Mr. Irving was admitted to this parish before April, 1613. He was deprived before October 27th, 1615, but returned to Tough, and was translated to Arbirlot, near Arbroath, in 1617, and died in 1625. This was the year of James VI's death. Charles I. continued his father's policy, but knowing less of the country he 'adopted even more unworkable plans' for effecting his wishes. 'He alienated the landowners by proposing to take back the tithes and benefices that his father had granted to his favourites, and he irritated the people by trying to impose on them a service-book that was not in accordance with their national feelings.'

In 1615 William Forbes became minister here, the most eminent minister our parish has ever had. He was descended from Forbes of Corsindae, and was thus a relative of Forbes of Monymusk. He was born in Aberdeen in 1585. His father was Thomas Forbes a burgess, and his mother Janet, sister of Dr. James Cargill, a distinguished physician, and the earliest of Aberdeen botanists—the founder, too, of four bursaries in Marischal College, which had been recently founded. When twelve William Forbes entered that College, and graduated when sixteen. Principal Gilbert Gray had such regard for his learning and modesty that he was very soon appointed Professor of Logic, but after four years he resigned his chair, and travelled through Poland, Germany, and Holland, studying at German universities for four or five years, and acquiring a wide knowledge of patristic literature, and a close acquaintance with Hebrew. He was offered the Professorship of Hebrew at Oxford, but declined it owing to the state of his health, and returned to Aberdeen, being then about twenty-five years old. He was ordained minister of Alford about 1614, and was presented to this parish by James VI on the 27th Oct., 1615. He attested a confirmation-charter in 1615 as 'rector of Monymusk.'[1] In August of the next year he preached before the General Assembly in Aberdeen, and in November was translated from Monymusk to one of the city churches in Aberdeen 'with full and uniform consent and applause of the whole congregation.'[2] In 1618 he was a member of the General Assembly at Perth and was selected to defend one of "the Five Articles" that were drawn up by James VI, and which he forced on the Assembly so that it enacted them. Next year he was appointed a Visitor of King's College, and in 1620, at the request of the Town Council and of Earl Marischal, he became fourth Principal of Marischal College, succeeding Principal Gray, but was asked to continue his ministerial services. He also taught Divinity and Hebrew. In the end of 1621, he was translated to one of the churches of Edinburgh, but not finding comfort there owing to the power of the Presbyterian party, he returned to Aberdeen, the stronghold of the Episcopalians, and resumed his former charge.

Charles I. came to Edinburgh in 1633 for his coronation. Laud was with him, being then Bishop of London and Dean of the Chapel Royal, but in that year he was made Archbishop of Canterbury. Charles brought him with him that the Scottish bishops might be instructed to draw up another liturgy, after

[1] Dr. Davidson, Inverurie, p. 233. [2] Records of Kirk Session, Spalding Club, p. 85.

the model of the Anglican one, different from that in use everywhere since the Reformation, and might then forward it to London for revisal, which they did with such disastrous results. William Forbes was one of those who then preached before Charles I., and the King was so pleased with his eloquence, and with the doctrine of his sermon, a report of which is preserved, as in Dr. Grub's History,[1] that he said he had "*found out a preacher who deserved to have a see created for him.*" So he erected Edinburgh into a bishopric, 29th Sept., 1633, and made Forbes its first bishop in February of the next year. But he died on the 12th April, within three months, 'hardly a hundred days,' of his being appointed, in his forty-ninth year, and was buried in St. Giles' Cathedral. His portrait hangs in the hall of Marischal College, painted by Jameson, who was at the height of his fame about 1635, and a print of it is given by the New Spalding Club in Mr. Lippe's 'Wodrow.' A letter in Mr. Cosmo Innes' Sketches[2] shows that Jameson charged for his portraits twenty merks, he furnishing cloth and colours. He was a pupil of Van Dyck. One of Forbes' younger sons, Arthur, became Professor of Humanity at St. Jean d'Angel, near La Rochelle.

Dr. Sprott says that Bishop Forbes was 'a man of immense learning, and of the highest character.' Dr. Joseph Robertson says of him[3]—' In 1635 St. Giles at Edinburgh became the Cathedral of a new diocese erected by King Charles for the greatest of the Scottish divines of the great Caroline School, the learned and pious William Forbes." Dr. Garden in his life of 'John Forbes of Corse,' said of him long ago, ' He was a person who might be numbered with the best primitive fathers for the sanctity of his life, humility of mind, gravity, modesty,

---

[1] Dr. Grub's History, vol. II. pp. 348, 349.
[2] Mr. Cosmo Innes, Sketches, p. 521.
[3] Dr. Joseph Robertson, Abbeys, p. 79.

temperance, frequent prayer and fasting, the practice of good works, care of the poor, frequent visiting of the sick and comforting them, and all Christian virtues.' Mr. Lippe says that 'in his Collections Wodrow does not take sufficient account of the learning and saintly and consistent life for which he was so distinguished.' Spottiswood said of him, ' His works show him to have been a man of vast learning and sound judgment.' Dr. Milroy, in his 'Lee Lecture' for 1891 on this Episcopal period, says of him, " He was the champion of what may be described as the liberal, pacific, and conciliatory tendency in the Scottish Church, having expressed his views when in Aberdeen, in a work published twenty-four years after his death, entitled 'Pacific and Moderate Considerations.'" Of this work Dr. Cooper of St. Nicholas Parish, Aberdeen, in an account of Forbes in the 'Dictionary of National Biography,' vol. xix., says, "Though lacking the author's final touches, and in parts a mere fragment, it is a work of great depth and learning ; it deals with what may be called the imperial questions of the Christian Church, and from its combined seriousness and moderation, it has powerfully affected many who have had at heart, like Forbes, reunion of the Church on a Catholic scale."

In 1636 Laud issued his book of Canons and new Liturgy, the reading of which in St. Giles' Cathedral on Sunday, 23rd July, of the next year, led to the outbreak. It was the spark that set the whole country in a blaze, and indeed kindled the civil war in England, as well as Scotland.[1] The National Covenant was signed March 1st, 1638, at Greyfriars Church, Edinburgh, and the General Assembly, consisting of 140 ministers, and 98 nobles and other laymen, 'fully representing the national feeling,' was held at Glasgow, November 21st, over-

[1] Dr. Cunningham, St. Giles, p. 179

Ministers since the Reformation. 243

throwing the Episcopacy of this period. Its next period of twenty-six years from 1661 was one of the most regrettable periods in the history of our Church.

In 1617, August 12th, Thomas Forbes was presented by James VI, but was translated to Leochel in 1622, where his house "was spolzeit by John Dugar and his companions on the 8th August, 1638."[1]

In 1622 Adam Barclay was translated from Leochel, being presented by James VI on 5th March. He was translated to Alford in 1625, and was elected Professor of Divinity in King's College in 1642. He declined, however, to accept the chair; but, singularly enough, it is in his name that the charter of Charles I. is made out, dated 12th March, 1642, in connection with the professorship, detailing the mode of election that is still followed, the payment of the salary from the rents of Cairntradlyn in Kinellar, and the occupation of the house in the Chaplainry (now sold) that was given by John Forbes of Corse. As minister of Alford he was Moderator of the Aberdeen Synod in October, 1652. His son Adam became minister of Towie, and then of Keig in 1666; and a daughter, Barbara, married Arthur Rose (or Ross) who became the last Archbishop of St. Andrews, of whom we shall afterwards speak, and of whose daughter we shall also hear.[2]

In 1617, the Priory of Monymusk, along with the Abbey of Crossraguel in Ayrshire was annexed to the Bishopric of Dunblane when its bishop, Adam Bannantyne, was appointed Dean of the Chapel Royal of SS. Mary and Michael in the Castle of Stirling, founded by James IV. This arrangement was ratified by Parliament, 4th August, 1621, the see of Dunblane being the poorest in Scotland, its revenue being spoken

[1] Spalding's Memorials, I. p. 94.
[2] Records of Synod, Spalding Club, p. 221; Fasti under Alford.

of as only £120. This seems the only way of explaining what the writer of these notes has seen stated, although unfortunately he is not now able to find the authority for the statement, that the saintly Archbishop Leighton of Glasgow, who had been Bishop of Dunblane in 1662, was at one time, 'Vicar of Monymusk.' "Next in dignity to the Cathedrals were the Collegiate Churches, whose Heads were called Provosts or sometimes Deans. There were at one time thirty-three such churches in this country, the most opulent being the Chapel Royal of Stirling."[1]

In 1625 Alexander Lunan, from being a University teacher, a regent in King's College, was presented by Charles I. In 1628 he was translated to the parish of Kintore, and in 1632 married Jean, eldest daughter of Sir William Forbes, who had been created by Charles I. in 1626 the first Baronet of Monymusk. Their eldest son William was born the next year at Kintore. He was served heir to his father, 2nd June, 1665. He married Barbara Gordon, whose name is entered in the Poll-book of 1696, as then at Ramstone, "the relict of a gentleman, and thus liable in payment of a third part of his poll." They had a son William, born at Delab in 1664, who became a merchant in Aberdeen, and then came to live in the village of Monymusk, his name being also entered in the Poll-book. He married Isobel, daughter of William Thain of Blackhall, near Inverurie, in 1691. She died at Blairdaff in 1739.[2]

Before his death, William Lunan, with his wife, Barbara Gordon, had been in Abersnithack (Braehead). They had a daughter, Anna, who, after her father's death, married in Oct., 1685, John Forbes, Tombeg, who was a son of William Forbes, the brother of Pitnacadle, who were the sons of

[1] Mr. Lippe, Wodrow, pp. xix, xx, lx, lxi, ; Mr. Walcott, Ancient Church, p. 203.
[2] Dr. Davidson, Inverurie, pp. 540, 386.

William Forbes, the seventh laird of Tolquhon, in Tarves. John Forbes, Tombeg, and his wife, Anna Lunan, are also recorded in the Poll-book, the value of the stock on Tombeg "exceeding ten thousand merks." Four children are recorded along with them, and they had afterwards other seven. Their son William, who was born in 1687, died in 1740 at Badifurrow, now Manar.[1]

It anticipates dates very much, but it may be convenient to finish this account here. William Lunan and his wife Isobel Thain, had a son Alexander, who became Episcopal minister at Blairdaff, November, 1729. He was thus the great-grandson of the minister of Monymusk and Kintore. He continued at Blairdaff until April, 1744, when he removed to Inglismaldie, in Kincardineshire, where he died in 1769, aged sixty-six. Blairdaff property then belonged to 'an ardently Jacobite family' named Smith, and Mr. Lunan, according to his diary, which is still extant, dispensed the Communion there to two hundred and seventy or three hundred persons annually. His successor, however, Mr. Morrice, could get only about fifty members of the congregation to bind themselves to give him a house and a stipend of a few pounds.[2]

A most kindly feeling existed here at this time, Mr. Simpson being the parish minister. In 1742, when Lady Grant, her mother Mrs. Potts, and her infant daughter, were all three buried in the churchyard within sixteen days of each other, Mr. Lunan, though an Episcopalian, read the burial service in our church, and preached in it at Lady Grant's funeral, 4th May, his text being Job xiv. 1.—" Man that is born of a woman is of few days, and full of trouble. He cometh up like a flower, and is cut down : he fleeth also as a shadow, and continueth not."[3]

[1] Dr. Davidson, Inverurie, pp. 597, 406, 407, 409, 597.
[2] Dr. Walker, Dean Skinner, p. 14 ; Dr. Davidson, Inverurie, p. 386.
[3] Dr. Walker, Dean Skinner, pp. 114, 115.

Mr. Lunan was a near relative of Alexander Lunan, minister of Daviot, who was deposed in 1716 for the part he took in the Rebellion of 1715. Various descendants of the Lunan family can still be traced, among them Mr. J. Forbes Robertson, London,[1] and the Rev. James Donald, minister of Keithhall, whose father, Rev. William Donald, was minister of Peterhead (dying in 1844), his father, James, being in Mill of Keithhall, whose wife was Ann Forbes (dying in 1828) daughter of James Forbes, a son of John Forbes in Tombeg, and Anna Lunan.

The Episcopal congregation moved from Blairdaff in 1801 to the present Church in Monymusk village.[2]

In 1629 John Gellie, who was a Covenanter, was translated to this parish from Premnay, being presented by Charles I. on 4th September. In 1652 his name is entered in the Roll of Synod, as shown in the Spalding Club 'Records of Synod,' as Mr. John Gellie 'elder' at Monymusk, the 'younger' being at Kinkell, an inscription on the south gable of the old church there, stating that he died 4th August, 1683. Our Mr. Gellie petitioned Parliament, 26th March, 1647, on account of his losses and sufferings, which were certified by Major-General Middleton, on which five hundred merks were ordered to be paid him for his present subsistence. But notwithstanding this, it is recorded in our Session minute book, November 5th, 1682, that there being "need and desire for building a bridge over the burn of Tone, the Session resolved to give a hundred merks out of the box, which Mr. John Gellie, late minister, had bequeathed, as was said, to that effect." He died in 1652 or 1653, leaving two sons and two daughters, and his descendants still remain among us—Mr. Gellie, district-surveyor, Alford, being one of them.

[1] Dr. Davidson, Inverurie, p. 407.   [2] Dr. Walker, Dean Skinner, p. 14.

As we have mentioned, the Solemn League and Covenant was signed on the 1st March, 1638. Dr. Davidson in his work on 'Inverurie and the Earldom of the Garioch' gives a general historical account of the period as regards Aberdeenshire, but our purpose is a much humbler one, for we must simply try to extract from Spalding's 'Memorials of the Troubles,' the notices connected with our own parish. The following year, 1639, was one of constant disorder in Aberdeenshire. Sir William Forbes was an active Covenanter, and 'upon the 14th January, 1639, the name of Forbes had a great meeting at Monymusk for their own business.' The Marquis of Huntly, who had raised an army against the Covenanters, 'hearing of this meeting, convened his friends, about three hundred men, at Kintore, on the 18th. It is said that he wrote for Monymusk and others, his vassals [as we saw in the 'bands' for Inver and Delab], but none came to him, except the laird of Brux.' In February there was a meeting of the Forbeses and Frasers at Monymusk, and on Monday, 22nd April, another meeting which must have been a notable gathering in our little place, 'was held at Monymusk by the Earl Marischal, the Earl of Seaforth, the Lord Fraser, the Master of Forbes, with sundry other barons and burgesses of Aberdeen of the Covenant, who, hearing of Lord Aboyne's [Lord Huntly's] rising, resolved to continue this committee at Turriff from the 24th to the 26th current, in hopes that there should come by that time sundry gentlemen out of Caithness, Sutherland, Ross, Moray, and other parts."[1] The skirmish that came to be known as 'The Trot of Turriff' took place on Monday, the 13th May, and with it the civil war may be said to have opened. The Don-side Forbeses do not seem to have been there, but Major-General Urry, of whom we shall speak immediately, was present

[1] Spalding's Memorials, I. pp. 131, 141, 173, 174.

at it. After this success the Royalists went to 'plunder Echt, Skene, Monymusk, and other houses pertaining to the name of Forbes,' all leading Covenanters. On the 25th, there was an assembly at Aberdeen of an army of men, the lairds of Monymusk, Leslie, Echt, Craigievar, &c., having, it was estimated, one thousand men.¹ Next year, 1640, Sir William Forbes was one of the local committee, under Earl Marischal, as General of the North, for guiding and ruling the town and county, and for levying the tax in support of the cause. In May of that year, as Spalding is careful to record, the laird of Drum, returning from a meeting of the Gordons in Strathbogie, happened to come past where the laird of Monymusk was, 'in a moss, causing cast peats, who sent out William Forbes, brother to Petnacaddell, upon his best horse to ask who Drum was, there being about 24 horse, but through this gentleman's own miscarriage, he was dismounted, and his master's horse taken from him, and he sent on foot to tell the laird tidings, whereat he was mightily offended.'² Three years after, Sir William Forbes and other leaders in the district had to prepare to defend their houses, and the year following, 1644, the Marquis of Montrose, who, when the Covenant was first signed, was in the forefront of the agitation for its defence, but had become Royalist leader, now 'sweeping over the country like a fiery meteor,' having defeated the Covenanters on the 13th September at Aberdeen, burned Pittodrie and Dorlethen on Friday, October 18th, and also 'the rich corn-yard' of Castle Fraser, then called Muchell, the bridge on the main road beside the approach to it being still called 'the Bridge of Muchell." The next day, Saturday, October 19th, Sir William Forbes being, no doubt very wisely, absent, Montrose dined at Monymusk with Lady Forbes, who was a daughter of Sir Thomas Burnett

1 Spalding's Memorials, I. pp. 188, 193.   2 Ibid. pp. 267, 331, 349, 269, 270.

of Crathes, when she managed to get the place exempted from pillage. 'Upon fair conditions he spared him this time,' and on a second occasion, he spared the lands of Monymusk 'unplundered upon some private conditions,' but in 1645, Leith of Harthill, in Oyne, burned the town and lands of Tombeg occupied by William Forbes, but pertaining in heritage to the laird of Monymusk, owing to William Forbes' having plundered from his servant some 'moneys,' with his baggage-horse. Harthill manned and fortified his house which was a stronghold, for his own defence, and the Forbeses and the Frasers gathered against him, but did him no hurt. In January of the previous year, 1644, the lairds of Pittodrie, Monymusk, Echt, Udny, Skene, &c., had to meet the laird of Drum as Sheriff-principal of Aberdeenshire at the Green at Udny.[1] In April, when the Marquis of Argyll came to Dunnottar Castle, Sir William Forbes and others, chiefly Forbeses and Frasers, 'took to themselves strength and came to the fields,' and on September 6th the committee ordered an assembly of all their supporters in Aberdeen, and among the principal men of the shire came Sir William Forbes of Monymusk and John Forbes of Corsindae.[2] This seems to close Spalding's account of Sir William's connection with these Troubles. He died in 1653.

We have, however, strange to say, to think of this era in our nation's history, in connection with the representative of another family that had owned a part of our parish, that of

URRY OF PITFICHIE.

It was in 1642 that the great Civil War broke out in England, the Royal standard being raised at Nottingham in August of that year. On 30th January, 1649, Charles I. was beheaded at Whitehall. During this period mention is made of

[1] Spalding's Memorials, II. pp. 423, 458, 475, 477, 304.   [2] Ibid. II. pp. 349, 401, 402.

Major-General Urry (Urrie or Hurry) the representative of the long line of the Urries of Pitfichie, one of whom we spoke of in connection with the lands of Forglen and the Brecbannoch, and another as a witness to various deeds in connection with our Priory before the Reformation, as on 6th February, 1534. General Urry did not himself possess Pitfichie, although he was probably born there, for his father had sold the property in 1597 to John Cheyne of Fortrie. His mother was Marjory, only child of Alexander Chalmers of Cults, near Aberdeen, another long line, as we shall see. He became a noted cavalry officer, and had served on the Continent, where he had married. He was at first a leader of the Covenanters, and in 1643, commanded a body of dragoons under the Earl of Balcarres, and was on the 24th April in the neighbourhood of his old home, for we have a record of the taxation put upon the ratepayers of Inverurie, with their names, and the sums they each had to pay, amounting to "twentie pounds for Dragonnis to Urrie."[1] But serving under Henry and Baillie, he was involved in two of the defeats that the Covenanters suffered from the Royalist leader, the Marquis of Montrose, one of them the next month, on May 9th, at Auldearn, near Nairn, with great slaughter, and the other two months after, on July 2nd, at Alford, where Montrose had chosen 'a splendid defensible position.' Next year another taxation followed, which extended over the properties in the district, and in it we have mention of the family to whom Urry's father had sold Pitfichie, for on July 10th, 1646, Alexander Cheyne of Pitfichie gives a receipt to Thomas Ronald, burgess of Inverurie, for 26 Libs, "for outputting of an horse and man to the Maister of Fraser."[2] Soon after, Urry became himself a Royalist, and Montrose and he were joined in friendship. He was knighted by Charles I. Claren-

[1] Dr. Davidson, Inverurie, p. 292.   [2] Ibid. p. 293.

don speaks of him in his 'History of the Rebellion,' and Spalding in his 'Memorials' calls him 'a soldier of fortune,' and shows how very changeable he was. Professor Aytoun in his 'Lays,' speaks of this as 'the wildest and most stormy period of our history.' Urry was with Montrose when he landed in Orkney, and raised the standard of Charles II. in 1650, and he was made prisoner along with him after his scanty force was overwhelmed on the 27th April, by General Leslie, at Invercharron, in Ross-shire, and they were both executed together at Edinburgh one month after, on the 27th May, Montrose being dressed 'in his red scarlet cassock.'

When we spoke of the Brecbannoch, we found that in 1387 Gilbert Urry was the husband of Joanna Fraser, daughter of John Fraser and Marjory, the daughter and heiress of Sir John of Monymusk, and that Pitfichie probably came to Gilbert Urry by this marriage. Major-General Urry left three daughters, one of whom applied for a 'family-diploma,' which was granted her under the great seal of Charles II in 1669. It shows how far back the family could be traced in unbroken succession, and as it is a family that has not left a single mark of its existence among us, it may be of interest to recall their lineage, for few know that they ever lived in the parish. The earliest person named in it is also a Gilbert Urry, but from the absence of dates, we cannot say in what relation he stood to the Gilbert mentioned in 1387.

It would almost appear as if we could tell the extent of this ancient property with certainty, for there is no reason to doubt that it was composed of the portions of the parish mentioned in the charter granted by Charles II in favour of Sir John Forbes in 1661, after being only a short time in the hands of the Cheynes :—" Pitfichie with the castle-fort, manor-place, mill,

mill-lands, and salmon-fishing, Ordwood, Ordhaugh, Sandiehillock, Picktillum, [these are all now included in Pitfichie farm and Blackhillock croft, the trees still showing where Picktillum stood] Ordmill, Mildourie, Over and Nether Balforsk [Overton and Netherton,] Rowrandle, with parts, pendicles, multures, all lying in the regality of St. Andrews." This last clause shows that the Pitfichie property originally belonged to the bishops of St. Andrews, being part of Malcolm III's gift to the Church. It doubtless embraced the whole portion of the parish from the west approach to Netherton, except Cornabo, which was held separately, as we saw, under the bishops of St. Andrews, the charter in favour of John Davidson and his family having been already translated.

The writer of the remarks on the Ragman Rolls suggests that Urry of Pitfichie was descended from Hugo de Urre, who, in 1296, swore fealty to Edward I., and who took his surname from Urr, in Galloway, and appears on an assize in 1289 as to the marches there. His son Thomas witnessed a charter of Michael, son of Durand. 'Maucolum de Oueree' subscribed the Ragman Roll in 1296, and in the same year Duncan Urrie, a Scot, was a prisoner in Gloucester Castle. A coat-of-arms was registered in 1672 by Colonel William Urrie, Major of the King's Regiment of guards, the crest being a lion's paw, and the motto *sans tache*, taken from the seal of John Urrie of Pitfichie in 1597.

The following is the substance of the 'family-diploma '—

THE FAMILY OF URRY OF PITFICHIE.

Gilbert U. of P. married(=)Elizabeth Lawder, daughter of the laird of 'Basse.'

Their son, William U. of P. = Barbara Creighton, daughter of the laird, now (1669) the Viscount of Frendraught.

Family of Urry of Pitfichie.

Their son, David U. of P. = Joanna, daughter of Leslie of Balquhain.

Their son, George U. of P. = Elizabeth, daughter of Fraser of Mouchell [Castle Fraser] now (1669) Earl Fraser. [This family came to Castle Fraser about 1450, and the peerage was created in 1633].

Their son, William U. of P.=Agnes, daughter of Leslie [third laird] of Wairdes [near Inverurie; she=(2) Laurence Leith in Rayne in 1580]. (Mentioned in 1535 and 1546. See pp. 185, 236.)

Their son, William U. of P.=Elizabeth, daughter of Erskine of Dun.

Their son, John U. of P.=Marjory, daughter of Alexander Chalmers of Cults, near Aberdeen. (He sold Pitfichie in 1597.)

Their son was Major-General Sir John Urry—beheaded in 1650.

The 'family-diploma' also gives his mother's family-descent, showing that the Chalmerses of Cults were connected by successive marriages with the families of Irvine of Drum, Fraser of Durris, Rait of Hagreine (? Hall-green), Menzies of Pitfoddles, Douglass of Glenbervie, Leslie, and the Earl of Errol.[1]

Major-General Urry himself, when serving on the Continent, married Maria Magdalene, daughter of Christopher Sebastian van Yaxheim of Erlabrun, and had three daughters—Elisabeth (who was married to Bishop John Hamilton of Dunkeld, and died about 1694); Joanna (who died, unmarried, before 1715); and Maria Margaret (who, after her father's death, lived abroad with her mother's relatives). She married Archibald Lamont of Lamont, and was alive in 1715, when she was served heir

[1] Ant. A. and B. III. pp. 500-502.

to her cousin, John Urrie, fellow of Oxford. In 1669 the diploma shows she was living 'in urbe Lytheonacii,' when she applied for this pedigree, which remains as an authentic memorial of a family so ancient, so notable in its connections, and living so long in our parish, but whose name has been heard of by few within it for many years. Some of us, as we look at the picturesque ruin of their Castle, may now recall their name, and think of Sir John's execution along with the great Montrose, which every one now must sadly lament.

In 1653 Alexander Ross, spelled also Rose, who had been licensed by the Presbytery of Elgin in July, 1642, and appointed minister of Kinernie before 3rd May, 1649, was translated from that parish, and instituted here on 9th October. He subscribed toward the new buildings at King's College in 1658, and was appointed by Parliament one of its Visitors. He died after March, 1678. There was daily service, morning and evening prayer, in our Church at this time, as enacted by the Episcopal Synod, October 21st, 1662. The other places specially named were Old and New Aberdeen, Banff, Old Deer, Peterhead, Fraserburgh, Kintore, Inverurie, Kincardine O'Neil, Turriff, Cullen, Ellon, Tarves, Fordyce, and Upper Banchory.[1] For a long time Easter continued to be the Communion Sunday here, and Good Friday the day of preparation, but one year there was such a storm that no one was able to come to Church, and unfortunately the day was changed to midsummer. The elders used to be asked before the Communion if they knew of any in their districts who were not living at peace with each other.

Mr. Rose was descended from the Roses of Kilravock who have owned Kilravock Castle, near Nairn, uninterruptedly for

---

[1] Registers of the Synod, Spalding Club, p. 263.

Ministers of the Parish. 255

six hundred years, since 1290. His father was minister first of Cluny and then of Birse, and his grandfather, of whom we spoke before, was one of the ministers of Aberdeen. He himself owned the lands of Insch, including Flinders, Christ's Kirk, and Temple Croft,[1] and was married to Anna, second daughter of John Forbes of Corsindae by Elizabeth Forbes, his second wife.[2] Dr. Davidson[3] says John Forbes was of Balfluig in Alford, while the 'Fasti' combine the two, 'Balfluig Corsindae.' A sister of hers, Jean, married Robert Forbes of Barnes, 'Tutor of Monymusk,' who, as an elder of the parish, was in March, 1653, chosen to attend the next synod and presbytery meetings. His name is entered on the roll of synod, April, 1652.[4] John Forbes of Barnes appears in the list of names for the tax in Queen Mary's time in 1549, and in a second record as "Mr. John Forbes, portioner of Barnes for his part thereof 9 Libs."[5]

Mr. Rose's brother, Arthur, also became minister of Kinernie, and perhaps, owing to the severity with which his father, the minister of Birse, had been treated, as mentioned in Spalding's 'Memorials,' he was appointed Bishop of Argyll and Galloway. He then became Archbishop of Glasgow, and by and by the last Archbishop of St. Andrews, but he was not popular among the clergy. Mr. Jervise[6] and the 'Fasti' record the well-known story about him:—"When one of his successors at Kinernie waited on him with a view of getting an increase to his small stipend, he replied, 'You country clergymen should learn to moderate your desires. I know what it is to live in the country. When I was minister of your parish, I could afford a bottle of good malt liquor and a roasted fowl for my Sunday's dinner, and I see not to what further you are

1 Ant. A. and B. III. pp. 405, 406.
2 Dr. Temple, Fermartyn, p. 558.
3 Dr. Davidson, Inverurie, p. 240.
4 Records of Synod, p. 214.
5 Colln. A. and B. pp. 115, 116.
6 Epitaphs II. p. 86.

entitled.' On this the poor incumbent is said to have withdrawn from his presence muttering, 'It would have been no great loss to the Church of Scotland though your Grace had still been eating roasted hens at Kinernie.'" His wife, as was mentioned before, was a daughter of Adam Barclay, who became minister here in 1622, and was translated to Alford. Their daughter Anna married the fourth Lord Balmerino in 1687, and was the mother of Arthur, the sixth and last Lord Balmerino, who joined the Pretender in 1745, and of whose execution on Tower-Hill on 18th August, 1746, in the fifty-eighth year of his age, there remains a full record.[1] She died in 1712.

Alexander Rose, son of the minister of Monymusk, became Bishop of Moray and then Bishop of Edinburgh. As such he acted as the representative of the Episcopalians at the time of the Revolution, and it was he who virtually sealed the fate of the Scotch Episcopal Church as the Established Church. Episcopacy in this country was then mostly Jacobite, and this William of Orange knew, but he let Bishop Rose understand through the Bishop of London that if the Scotch Bishops and clergy would give him their support, he would give them his. When Bishop Rose was admitted to an interview, the Prince said to him, "Are you going for Scotland?" to which he answered, "Yes, Sir, if you have any commands for me." William replied, "I hope you will be kind to me, and follow the example of England." The Bishop's strange answer was, "Sir, I will serve you as far as law, reason, or conscience shall allow me," on which William turned on his heel without a word. Bishop Rose died 20th March, 1720.

Another son of the minister of Monymusk was John Rose, D.D., minister of Foveran. He married Isobel, daughter

[1] Dr. Campbell's Balmerino, pp. 294-299.

Ministers of the Parish. 257

of Udny of Udny, and had two sons, Alexander and John. He was served heir to his father in 1680.

A grant was made by the Privy Council from vacant stipends in April, 1683, to aid the daughters of Mr. Rose of Monymusk. Some recent connections of the Rose family are mentioned by Dr. Walker in his Life of Bishop Skinner,[1] and also by Dr. Temple[2] in his account of Mr. John Rose, the great-grandson of the minister of Foveran. He became minister of Udny in 1768, and one of his sons who was surgeon in the 1st Battalion Coldstream Guards, died from wounds received while landing at Aboukir. This family is still represented in several branches ; for instance, James Rose Macpherson, minister of Kinnaird, near Perth, is named after the youngest son James, owing to his mother's relationship, who was the eldest daughter of Professor Duncan Mearns, D.D., of King's College, Aberdeen.

In 1678, John Burnett, who had been ordained at Culross in 1660, the year of the Restoration, was translated to this parish, 18th August, and was presented by Charles II, March, 1680. Our parish session-records begin in 1678. A minute states—" 1679, August 10th. The minister and elders, considering that there is no Church-Bible, and having gotten intelligence that Alexander Orem, merchant in Aberdeen, hes some besyde him, it was ordered that the thesaurer should buy one from him," the price being 15 Libs. 6s. 8d. scots money. This Bible is still preserved. It has lost the date on the title-pages, but the Royal arms bear "C R" (Charles Rex) upon them. In 1685 it is recorded that the Church was re-seated, and a roll of seat-holders is entered, which is given in full by Dr. Davidson,[3] some of them—Shewan, Donald, Adam, and Thomson—being still represented in the parish, and it is

[1] pp. 283-285.
[2] Fermartyn, pp. 417, 420.
[3] Inverurie, p. 348.

S

interesting to compare this list with the names in the Poll-book eleven years later.

Charles II died 6th February, 1685. During the four years of his brother James' reign, the persecutions continued under Claverhouse, &c. In July after Charles' death the minute book records that a proclamation was read from the pulpit prohibiting all persons taking part in regard to Archibald Campbell, late Earl of Argyll, his son Sir Charles Campbell, Sir John Cochran, Balfour (of Burley), and others, this having reference to the Duke of Monmouth's rebellion. The minutes detail the purchase of the six silver Communion Cups that are still used—the four smaller ones being bought in 1691, the two larger in 1712, Mr. William Forbes younger of Monymusk arranging the purchase. The property passed from the Forbes family just after the last two were bought. The engraving on the four smaller cups is very effective, the vine and its fruit being figured differently on the two pairs. A picture of one of them is given in the Rev. Thomas Burns' work on the old Communion Plate of the Church. Their marks are G. W. the maker, ABD the town mark, and an old English D, possibly the deacon's mark or the date. On the large ones the marks are S. R. the maker, AB the town, an old English Q for the deacon or the date, and three Fleurs de lis crowned. Other vessels were also bought in 1691.

In 1697 a large bell was got from Edinburgh, and then a clock for the Church tower. The cost of all these purchases is entered in the minutes. Reference is also made in them to the Rebellion of 1715, and also to the observance of Christmas.

Mr. Burnett and his wife with two sons and three daughters are mentioned in the Poll-book. His youngest daughter married Alexander Schank of Castlerig. He died 22nd May, 1728, aged about eighty-three years.

Tillyfour, in the parish of Oyne, on the north side of the Don, opposite a part of this parish, and separated from Oyne Church by Benachie, was for a time under the charge of the minister of Monymusk, but the minister of Oyne objected to continue the allowance for this duty, and the connection ceased. This is also shown in the Poll-book of 1696, which at the end of the account of our own parish goes on at once to give the "list of pollable persons within the lands of Tillifower, *in the Paroch of Monymusk by annexation.*"

Mr. Burnett must have been one of the very last surviving "Episcopalian Parish Ministers" in Scotland, being nearly sixty-eight years a minister. Presbytery was finally established in 1691, the year the four cups were bought, but Mr. Burnett was one of the many Episcopal ministers who continued undisturbed in their parishes till their death, if they took the oath of allegiance to William and Mary, and gave a general adherence to the new arrangements, which differed little from the former state in regard to the Church courts. 'At the union of the Parliaments in 1707 so tolerant had the spirit of the Church been ever since the Revolution of 1688, that there were 165 Episcopal ministers still within the pale of the Established Church, living in the manses, preaching in the pulpits, and drawing the stipends.' In Aberdeenshire Episcopacy possessed many entire parishes, and in it and also in Banffshire "the mass of the Episcopalian ministers accepted the indulgence, and continued to be parish ministers till their death."[1] Only "they were not allowed to act as members of the Church courts, so that in the North where Episcopacy was strong, the presbyteries were mere skeletons. The whole Synod of Aberdeen, comprising eight presbyteries, had to concentrate itself into one, and even after the lapse of seven years could muster only sixteen clerical

[1] Dr. Davidson, Inverurie, p. 425.

members. At Insch, when the parish became vacant, the parishioners called an Episcopalian curate who did not even take the oaths to Government, but who remained in possession of the living for many years. Of the two colleagues in the ministry of the Tron Church, Edinburgh, in 1692, one was Episcopalian and the other Presbyterian. There were separate Kirk Sessions too, and the services were conducted at different times according to different forms. In matters of creed, worship, and discipline, there was little difference between the two systems, as there were always Presbyteries and Kirk Sessions."[1]

Mr. Burnett's case was an instance of this tolerant spirit, for he was parish minister here for thirty-seven years after the change to Presbyterianism, continuing even after the Rebellion in 1715, being altogether fifty years minister here. He was buried within the Church. One of his sons, Alexander, became regent of philosophy in King's College.

We stated at the close of Chapter VIII that the small sum that now represents the feu-duties which the Forbes family became bound to pay yearly in connection with the Priory and its lands is attached to the funds of the Deans of the Chapel Royal. This sum, along with the part that was redeemed in 1878, was formerly payable to the Crown, and though it is a small sum, there is at this point an interesting history connected with it. This sum, along with the rents of Auchlossan and the money drawn in connection with the ancient Abbey of Crossraguel, which gave its Abbot a seat in Parliament, was in 1695, exactly two hundred years ago, granted by order of William III to his chaplain and chief adviser in all matters that related to Scotland, the celebrated Principal Carstairs. It was he who was

[1] Dr. Story, St. Giles, pp. 244, &c.

able to guide the policy that brought about the Revolution in 1688, and the Union of the Parliaments in 1707.

He had borne the torture of the thumb-screws, had been imprisoned, and in exile. He had been by the side of William of Orange in Holland during all the negotiations that preceded his coming to England for the Throne. He had crossed in the same ship with him, and it was he who conducted the Divine service immediately on his landing on the shore at Torbay, when the troops all along the beach at his instance joined in singing the 118th Psalm. From that time he was William's companion in every field of battle, and his most trusty adviser in every thing that related to Scotland. It is well known what he did in regard to " the Oath of Assurance." Instigated by some of the same advisers who contrived the Massacre of Glencoe, William had consented to send a despatch declaring that no one was to sit in the General Assembly unless he at once took an oath expressing allegiance to him as King ' by right' as well as 'in fact,' 'de facto et de jure.' This would have pressed unduly on such Episcopal clergymen as still retained their parishes, while by the Presbyterian clergy it could not be otherwise regarded than as an insult. Carstairs found William in bed fast asleep, and woke him, saying on his knees 'I am come to ask my life,' and telling him that he had stopped his courier. William saw the wisdom of his advice, bade him write a new despatch, and forwarded it instantly, the intimation being sent to the Assembly that the King would dispense with putting the oaths on the ministers. It was in March 1694, that this midnight scene occurred. Next year Carstairs received the grant of the dues from this Priory, which the King was doubtless free to make, as the money would be no longer required for Dunblane Cathedral. So lenient became the Church policy that, Presbyterian as the Church courts were, "the Sacrament of the Lord's Supper was not celebrated in Aberdeen, for instance, according to the Presbyterian form until 1704, and even as late as 1710 there were 113 Episcopal ministers, of whom nine had not even taken the prescribed oaths to Government, still ministers of parishes."[1]

After the death of William III, Carstairs came to Scotland to be Principal of the University of Edinburgh, and Minister of St. Giles'. He was chosen as the first Moderator of the General Assembly after the Union of the Parliaments in 1707, from which date Scotland ceased to have a separate political history. "There is no name," says Dean Stanley, "which I commend more warmly to the grateful memory of the Scottish people."[2]

*In Principal Carstairs closes the
History of our Priory.*

William III, by Act of Parliament dated June 1695, in order to provide for the national defence by the Army and Navy, ordained 'that all persons of whatsoever age, sex, or quality, should be subject and liable to a pole of six shillings, except poor persons who lived upon charity, and children under sixteen years of age and 'in familia' of all these persons, whose pole did not exceed one pound ten shillings scots.' It is very important to observe that owing to this exception the records of this tax do not give us the means of learning the number of children in a parish under 16 years and living at home with such parents as paid less than thirty shillings of tax. A complete record of this assessment has been preserved in the "Poll-book of Aberdeenshire for 1696"—exactly 200 years ago.[3] It is a mine of authentic information regarding the inhabitants of all our parishes and their employments, capital, or wages. It

[1] Dr. Story, St. Giles, p. 249.
[2] Lectures, pp. 116-122.
[3] I. pp. 573-386.

preserves the value of the different estates, the rents of the farms, the name of every individual that was taxed, and the number of the inhabitants on every farm or hamlet, but unfortunately always omitting the number of the children of peasants under 16. We shall give an analysis of what is said about our own parish. The number taxed will be shown immediately after the name of each possession, but it is to be carefully remembered that with only a few exceptions, these numbers never include the children under 16. It would be quite useless for our purpose to mention the money values;—they are of importance in enabling us to compare the rental of one farm with another at the time, but if one does this now, the change in the boundaries of farms &c., must be considered. ' m-svt.', 'f-svt.', in this analysis stand for men-servants, female servants, 'children' for those at home above 16, 'others' mean those whose occupations are not mentioned, 'cottars' are spoken of as simply cottars, without being tradesmen or weavers, and 'grass-woman' means one who has a house but no land.

THE PARISH OF MONYMUSK IN 1696.

Manor House of Monymusk.—(27) Sir John Forbes (died 1702), Lady Forbes, (daughter of Sir John Dalmahoy), Robert above 21, John, Charles, Agnes, Catherine, and Barbara below 16, 12 m-svts., 6 f-svts., 1 stocking-weaver (John Couts.)

Manor House of Pitfichie.—(24) William Forbes, younger of Monymusk, (sold Monymusk in 1713), who is taxed for property in Kincardineshire, his wife, (Lady Jean Keith), John under 16, Catherine, Barbara, Jean, under 8, 7 m-svts., 6 f-svts., 5 others.

Mains of Monymusk.—(35) 2 tenants and their wives, 7 children, 8 m-svts., 4 f-svts., 5 cottars and their wives (one cottar a weaver, one a smith), 1 tailor and wife.

Inver.—(54) 6 tenants and their wives, 5 children, 11

m-svts., 3 f-svts., 2 shoemakers and wives, 3 others, 5 cottars (4 with wives), 2 weavers and wives, 1 tailor and wife, 1 grass-woman.

Balvack.—(35)   2 tenants and their wives and 1 f-tenant, 1 child, 7 m-svts., 3 f-svts., 3 others, 5 cottars and their wives, 2 weavers, (1 married), 1 wright and his wife, 1 grass-woman.

Rowrandle.—(5)   2 tenants and their wives, and sister of one tenant.

Cornabo.—(9)   2 tenants (1 married, other a widower), 4 children, 1 m-svt., 1 f-svt.

Overton.—(8)   1 tenant and wife, 2 m-svts., 1 f-svt., 1 other, 1 weaver and wife.

Netherton.—(12)   1 tenant and wife, 1 child, 1 m-svt., 1 f-svt., 1 other, 1 cottar and wife, 1 shoemaker and wife, 1 weaver and wife.

Mildourie.—(23)   1 tenant and wife, 5 children, 2 m-svts., 1 f-svt., 1 shoemaker and wife, 1 weaver and wife, 1 tailor and wife, 3 cottars and wives, 1 grass-woman.

Ordmill.—(13)   1 miller and wife, 1 weaver and wife, 1 tailor and wife, 1 child, 6 others.

Blackhillock.—(7)   1 tenant, 2 cottars (1 married), 3 m-svts.

Mains of Pitfichie.—(15)   1 tenant and wife, 5 m-svts., 2 f-svts., 2 cottars (1 married), 1 gardener and wife, 1 grass-woman

Picktillum.—(7)   1 tenant and wife, 1 wright and wife, 1 tailor and wife, 1 m-svt.

Ramstone.—(7)   Barbara Gordon, tenant, "relict of ane gentleman, lyable in payment of a third part of his poll," 2 m-svts., 1 f-svt., 1 miller, wife, and son.

Abersmithack (Braehead).—(20)   1 tenant and wife, 6 children, 1 m-svt., 1 f-svt., 4 others, 3 cottars and wives.

Delab.—(31)   2 tenants, (Archibald Thomson being one) and their wives, and 1 female tenant, (Margaret Lessell), 4

The Poll-Book of 1696. 265

m-svts., 1 f-svt., 5 others, 8 cottars (7 married, 2 of them weavers), " 1 sick man stays there."

Enzean.—(22)   2 tenants and wives, 1 child, 6 m-svts., 5 f-svts., 3 others, 1 cottar and wife, 1 grass-woman.

Coullie.—(68)   7 tenants and wives, 3 children, 3 m-svts., 1 f-svt., 15 others, 7 cottars and wives, 2 grass-women, 1 shoemaker and wife, 2 tailors and wives, 3 weavers and wives, 1 smith and wife, 1 mason and wife.

Tillyfourie.—(11)   1 tenant, 2 children, 3 m-svts., 2 f-svts., one weaver and wife, 1 other.

Tombeg.—(28)   John Forbes and his wife Anna Lunan, William, Alexander, Robert, Jean, their children, 6 m-svts., 2 f-svts., 1 other, 2 weavers and wives, 3 cottars and wives, 1 tailor and wife, 1 grass-woman.

Kirktown, (the Village).—(45)   6 tenants and wives, 6 children, 10 m-svts., 6 f-svts., 8 others, 1 shoemaker, 1 weaver and wife. One tenant was William Lunan and his wife Isabel Thain, and they had a boy and a girl under 8.

Cobleseat.—(? a boat-house; the same name is found in Keig and Alford.) (6)   1 tenant and wife, 2 children, 1 m-svt., 1 f-svt.

Mains.—(Probably the West Mains, which used to be in the field opposite the Deane Cottages.) (4)   Gardener at Monymusk and wife, and 2 others.

Glenstoune.—(7)   1 tenant and wife, 1 m-svt., 1 other, 1 grass-woman, 1 miller and wife.

Todlachie.—(40)   John Shewan and Agnes Adam, his wife, 2 sons; William Adam and Jean Shewan, his wife; John Shewan, Junr., 1 other tenant, 7 m-svts., 4 f-svts., 6 others, 5 cottars and wives, 3 weavers (2 married).

Sandihillock.—(11)   One tenant and wife, 3 m-svts., 2 others, 2 cottars and wives.

Pitmunie.—(55) 2 tenants and wives, 2 m-svts., 1 f-svt., 20 others, (among them Elmslies and Shewan), 2 tailors, 6 cottars and wives, 6 weavers and 4 wives, 1 smith and wife, 1 shoemaker and wife.

Brankanenthim.—(6) John Donald and his wife Elspet Forbes, "their weaver" and his wife, 2 others.

Ardniedly.—(18) James Adam and his wife Margaret Thain, Alexander Adam and his wife Agnes Shewan, and 1 other tenant and his wife, 2 m-svts., 7 others, 1 cottar and wife, 1 grass-woman.

The Manse.—(11) Mr. John Burnet and his wife, Robert, Alexander, Jean, Isobell, and Barbara, their children, 1 m-svt., 3 f-svts.

The Schoolhouse.—(4) Mr. Alexr. Hay and his wife, 2 f-svts. John Gellen, Mr. James Gellen.

The names are thus recorded of about 670 persons in the parish who had to pay the tax, and of these only about 64 were pollable sons or daughters, so that we have no means of knowing the population of the parish at this time. Besides the age limit, there are exceptions and qualifications hardly susceptible of being dealt with by arithmetical calculation. We derive, however, some singular information as to the occupations of the people. There are entered 58 tenants, their holdings being of some size, 108 men-servants, 56 female servants, 28 weavers, besides one man who was stocking-weaver to Sir John Forbes, 3 smiths, 10 tailors, 7 shoemakers, 2 wrights, 3 millers, 2 gardeners, only 1 mason, 54 cottars not already included among the tradesmen, and 10 grass-women. One cannot help being struck with the number of weavers and tailors, and it is interesting to observe how they were distributed over the parish, while Sir John's stocking-weaver is a man that stands out by himself, though men-servants used to get a higher fee if they were able to knit stockings. At Insch there were only 15 weavers and 8 tailors, but there were 15 shoemakers to our 7, as shown in the analysis given by Rev. R. S. Kemp in his 'Historical Notes.' There must have been a great many sheep kept here to supply material for so many hand-looms, and the Leochel market was noted of old as a wool-market. The tenants seem to have done nearly all their blacksmith and carpenter work themselves. The ploughs were almost entirely made of wood, and are said to have been put together in a few evenings at home—and as it was oxen that were used in them, these did not require any shoeing. In the names we recognise families that are still with us. The Adams who were in Ardniedly have many descendants. The Shewans are still numerous. The Donalds in Brankenintum have several representatives, and the direct descendant retired some time ago to Aberdeen. It is singular that on so small a farm a married man should be entered as "their weaver." Mr. Donald of Keithhall, as we mentioned, is a descendant of John Forbes and his wife Anna Lunan, in Tombeg. The Thomsons who were in Delab, sent some of their family who lived to a great age, to be tenants of Netherton, and it is only a few years since the last male of the direct line died there, and his nephews are still tenants of Bogs of Coullie. The descendants of the Lessels are still in Echt and Cluny, and two have been lately buried here. Pitfichie Castle was then fully occupied by the Baronet's eldest son and his family, and when they moved to Monymusk House, on the death of Sir John, it was to remain there for only a few years. The view from Pitfichie was then very different from what it is now, as there were hardly any trees in the parish, and Monymusk House, and the ruins of the Priory which were then standing, would be prominent objects as one looked along the stretch of the river. We do not know if any of the Grant family ever occupied Pitfichie. Probably not, for Nether Inver became the eldest son's home. The village was evidently considerably smaller than it is now, but some parts of the parish must have been populous, as if there were hamlets that have now disappeared, and the Hill of Balvack then lay in heather and broom, instead of having the present crofts. The valuation of the parish came to £2476 scots, but it is hardly possible to say what this might represent now, circumstances being so completely changed.

Sir John Forbes, the third Baronet, who was proprietor at the time of the Poll-book, had a charter of the Pitfichie property from Charles II in 1661, and we have seen that his eldest son occupied the Castle with his wife and family. Sir John was twice married, and his third son John, born at Monymusk House, 7th February, 1680, was married at Frendraught in 1704, to Susanna, daughter of George Morrison of Bognie and his wife Christina Urquhart, Viscountess Dowager of Frendraught. In 1711 he acquired Upper Boyndlie in Buchan, but before this he lived at Pitfichie, his brother having moved to Monymusk House after their father died in 1702. He has left an account of a singular custom of those days :—" My daughter Christian was born at Frendraught, 14th April, 1705, and was baptized the next day by Mr. Hugh Chambers, minister of Marnoch." [She married her cousin, Sir William Forbes of Monymusk, fifth Bart., and was the mother of Sir William Forbes of Pitsligo, the banker.] " My son John was born at Pitfichie, 20th May, 1706, and was baptized the same day by Mr. John Burnett, minister of Monymusk, and died 1st July thereafter." [There is no record of any graves of the Forbeses here.] " My second daughter Barbara was born at Pitfichie, 24th June, 1707, and was baptized the afternoon of

The Forbes Family. 269

the same day by the said Mr. John Burnett," and similarly with others. John Forbes espoused the cause of the Pretender in 1715, and had to leave the country in a vessel sailing from Banff for Holland, but perished at sea.[1]

In 1704-5, Sir William Forbes, having succeeded his father in 1702, had to sell to the City of Aberdeen his half of the barony of Torry, on the other side of the Dee from Aberdeen. This property included Balnagask, Kincorth, Loirston, &c., and had been conveyed, 4th September, 1551, to Duncan Forbes, who is described as a 'burgess of Aberdeen,' and to his wife Agnes Gray, and had remained in possession of the family.[2] They thus got it at the very time they were in process of getting possession of Monymusk, and just as Torry had to be parted with in 1704-5, so also in 1712-13, in order to appease creditors, Monymusk had to be sold, and 'when the day came for bidding adieu to his paternal inheritance,' the last representative of the family here 'drove away from the old home with a pang of regret.'[3] The advertisement of the sale of Monymusk is preserved, and is of great length, for it tells from what an immense number of persons money had been borrowed, and our Church records also prove what difficulty there was in regard to the funds of the parish which the Forbeses held on loan. Sir William's grandson succeeded him in the Baronetcy. He became an advocate in Edinburgh, and in 1741 was Professor of Civil Law in King's College, Aberdeen, but he died in 1743, when only thirty-six years old. The inscription on his tomb in the old churchyard of Kearn, beside Druminnor, was written by Dr. Beattie, author of The Minstrel, but as we have reached the close of the connection of the Forbeses with Monymusk, we may here insert their family record.

[1] Sir James Ferguson's Account of the Forbeses of Pitsligo; Dr. Temple, pp. 153, 155.
[2] Ant. A. and B. III. p. 249.   [3] Dr. W. Chambers' 'Stories of Old Families,' pp. 150-160.

Monymusk: its Church and Priory.

Pedigree of the Forbes Family as far as it relates to Monymusk.

James, 2nd Baron Forbes=Egidia, younger dr. of Sir W. Keith, 1st Earl Marischal.
|
2nd son, William F. of Corsindae=
|
James F. of Corsindae.   Duncan F. of Monymusk=Agnes, dr. of Wm. Gray,
"Band" of 1544 for   died Feb. 1584.   Aberdeen,
Inver. Robber of the   died Oct. 1584.
Cathedral Vessels.
|
William F. of Monymusk=Margaret, dr. of Sir W. Douglas of Kemnay, 9th
died before 1618.   Earl of Angus in 1588, grandson of Sir W. D.
                       who fell at Flodden, whose father was Archibald
                       "Bell the Cat," 5th Earl, 1482.
|
Wm. F. of Monymusk=Elizabeth Wishart of Pitarrow, near   John F. of
created Bart. by   Fordoun. George W. suffered   Leslie.
Charles I. in 1626.   under Cardinal Beaton in 1546.
|
Sir W. F. 2nd Bart.=Jean, dr. of Sir   Alex. in Aber-   Jean, eldest dr.
Covenanter, died   Thos. Burnett   snithack   =Alex. Lunan in
1653.   of Leys and   =One of the   1632; Minister
                    Crathes.   Pitfichie family. of Monymusk,
                                                          then of Kintore
                                                          in 1628.
|
Sir John F. 3rd Bart.=(1) Lady Margaret,   and =(2) Barbara, dr. of Sir
succeeded as minor,   dr. of 1st Viscount   John Dalmahoy.
died 1702; had   Arbuthnot.   John F. of Boyndlie=Susanna
charter of Pitfichie   in Tyrie.   Morrison
from Charles II   of Bognie
in 1661.   in Forgue.
                                                         Christian F.
Sir W. F. 4th Bart.=Lady Jane Keith, dr. of   (see below).
Sold Monymusk   1st Earl of Kintore.
in 1713.
         John F.   =Hon. Mary F. sister of the last Lord Pitsligo.
    died before his father. | Pitsligo was forfeited in 1745.
|
Sir W. F. 5th Bart.=his cousin *Christian* F. (see above).
Professor; died 1743,   Died Dec. 26th, 1789.
aged 36.

The Forbes Family.

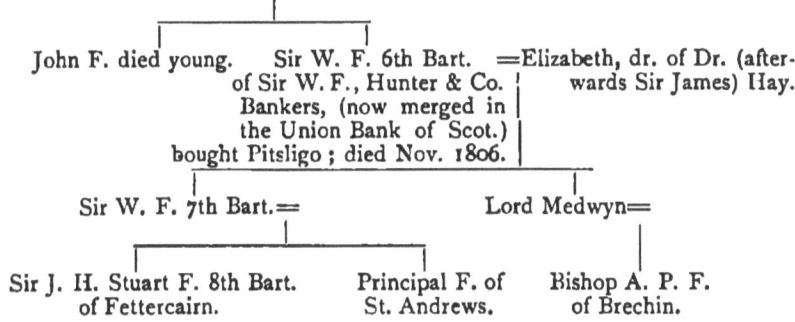

To make our narrative more complete, as the Forbeses have no memorial at all in this parish, we may now give the inscription on the tomb at Kearn :—

> Here are deposited in the firm hope of a blessed resurrection the ashes of Sir William Forbes, Baronet, Advocate, of the family of Monymusk, who left this transitory world on the 12th day of May, 1743, aged 36. Adorned with many virtues, stained with no crimes, with the shattered remains of paternal possessions, once ample and flourishing, he supported through the whole of life, without ostentation, but with dignity and spirit, that rank to which he was by birth entitled. In his death, which he long foresaw, he displayed equal magnanimity, enduring without complaint the attacks of a painful distemper, and calmly resigning his soul to Him who gave it. This marble is erected by his only surviving son, who though deeply affected with his loss, submits to the Divine wisdom that saw proper to deprive him of such a parent before he was able to profit by so bright an example of Christian virtue. Num. xxiii. 10.

His wife was his cousin Christian, daughter of John Forbes of Boyndlie, whom he married in 1730. Bishop A. P. Forbes of Brechin, her great-grandson, edited, after it had lain nearly ninety years in manuscript, 'The Narrative of her Last Sickness and Death,' which was written by her son, Sir William Forbes, the sixth Baronet, who became the head of the Banking House, " Sir William Forbes, Hunter, & Co.," and whose great ambition was to earn means for recovering the estates of Pitsligo or Monymusk. By different purchases he was able to buy Pitsligo, which had been lost to the Pitsligo branch of the family after the Rising in 1715, being forfeited in the person of Alexander Forbes, the fourth and last Lord Pitsligo, of whom Dean Stanley speaks in his Lectures.[1] He also purchased two estates adjoining Pitsligo, and on succeeding to another portion of the Pitsligo estates by inheritance, he founded the village of New Pitsligo, established manufactures in it, erected the Church and endowed the parish *quoad sacra*, and also built an Episcopal Church, as well as schools.

Monymusk was purchased from Sir William Forbes, the fourth Bart., in 1712-13 by Sir Francis Grant, one of the Judges of the Court of Session. He bore the courtesy title of Lord Cullen, taking it from the name of his paternal property of Cullen in the parish of Gamrie, in Banffshire, which had been ratified to him by charter in 1697-98. He has left a brass which is in the library in the House, on which he engraved that he sold his other properties and bought this estate under wrong advice. The description that his eldest son gives of Monymusk three years afterwards, and which is printed in the Miscellany of the Spalding Club,[2] shows it to have been in a very undesirable state. "The House," he says, "was an old castle with battlements, and six different roofs of various heights and directions, confusedly and inconveniently combined, and all rotten, with two wings more modern, of two stories only, the half of the windows of the higher rising above the roofs, with granaries, stables, and houses for all cattle close adjoining. All the farms ill-disposed and mixed, different persons having alternate ridges; not one wheel-carriage on the estate, nor indeed any road that would allow it." Lord Cullen sent some friends to judge of the property before he bought it, who met with a man, William Dickie, who acted in a manner as manager

---

[1] pp. 50, 51; Mr. Jervise, Epitaphs, II. p. 215.   [2] II. pp. 96, 97.

to the Forbeses. He answered their inquiries, and gave them some refreshment. He was the uncle of the grandfather of Alexander Dickie, who is one of the present workmen on the estate. This family has now worked continuously for the Grants of Monymusk for 183 years. A life of Lord Cullen is given in the 'Biographia Britannica' (1757), and there are articles upon him and his second son William, Lord Prestongrange, written by Mr. G. F. Russell Barker, in the 'Dictionary of National Biography,' vol. xxii (1890).

Lord Cullen's father was Archibald Grant of Ballintomb, in Morayshire, a descendant of the Grants of Freuchie. He was born in 1658, and educated at King's College, Aberdeen, and at Leyden, in the Netherlands, under the learned civilian, John Voet. When constitutional questions were being keenly discussed at the time of the Revolution, he wrote a book arguing strongly for the power of the Estates to establish a new succession in the Prince of Orange, and when he passed as an Advocate in 1691, the reputation he had thus gained, quickly brought him a large practice at the bar. He was made a Baronet of Nova Scotia by Queen Anne in 1705, and took a leading part in helping forward the Union of the Parliaments in 1707. He was appointed a Judge in 1709, and in 1720 received under George I. a grant of supporters, two Angels proper, and an addition to his coat of arms, taking as one of his mottoes the words, "Jehovah Jireh," the only instance in Scottish heraldry of a Hebrew motto, there being also an open Bible with the motto "Suum Cuique" above the helmet. He was married three times. He died at Edinburgh on the 23rd March, 1726, and was buried in Greyfriars Churchyard there. A picture in the dining-room of Monymusk House, eleven feet wide by seven feet high, represents him seated in the midst of his family. It was painted by Smybert, a Dutch

T

artist, in 1720, and corresponds strikingly in style with an engraving that is given in Mr. J. H. Green's Illustrated History of England,[1] in which Smybert gives a portrait of himself. As we have said so much about the Forbeses, we may mention that, as an instance of Lord Cullen's generosity of character, it is told us in the 'Biographia Britannica' that when certain circumstances determined him to part with the estate of Cullen which was left him by his father, and being prevailed on to buy this estate from 'an unfortunate family who had a debt on it of more than it was worth, he first put their affairs into order, and by classing the different demands, and compromising a variety of claims, secured some thousand pounds to the heirs without prejudice to any, and of which they had never been possessed but for his interposition and vigilance on their behalf.' 'He was a deeply religious man, a learned lawyer, and a conscientious judge.' He had such a regard for the Church of Scotland that he wrote a pamphlet on Patronage which was reprinted in 1841 during the Secession controversy. Ten other works of his are mentioned in the Dictionary of National Biography. In Chambers' 'Domestic Annals' he is mentioned as joining with Lord Crossrig in a society in Edinburgh that met every Monday afternoon for prayer and conference, a meeting that laid the foundation of much good to the country. He settled two chalders of meal (thirty-two bolls) yearly from the estate for educational purposes, the deed being framed by himself in 1718, and testifying to his large-mindedness in regard to the godly upbringing of the young, and showing his anxiety to give facilities for education in different districts of the parish by means of evening schools, &c. The trust was afterwards arranged by the Court of Session, and an endowed school on the north side of the Don, close to St. Ffinan's, was built out

[1] IV. p. 1612.

of part of the accumulated funds in 1825, which was continued until changes were made in the application of the funds which now amount to about £80 yearly, by the Royal Commissioners in 1888, resulting in Sir Arthur H. Grant, the present proprietor's building a much larger and finer school in a more central position, in 1890, at his own expense.

Lord Cullen's eldest son, Archibald, was born in September, 1696. He passed as an Edinburgh advocate, and was elected Member of Parliament for Aberdeenshire in 1722, and again in 1727, but he was unfortunate in the close of his parliamentary career in 1732. He began during his father's life-time to devote himself to the improvement of the estate, and as early as 1716, when only twenty years of age, he began 'to enclose, and plant, and provide, and prepare nurseries. At that time,' he says in his Description, from which we quoted, 'there was not one acre upon the whole estate enclosed, nor any timber upon it but a few elm, sycamore, and ash about a small kitchen garden adjoining the House, and some straggling trees at some of the farmyards, with a small copse-wood, not enclosed, and dwarfish and browsed by sheep and cattle.' Dr. Stuart in printing the Description in 1842, says in a note, 'The judicious measures adopted by Sir Archibald Grant for the improvement of his estate, are in nothing more observable than the noble masses of plantations which, under his fostering care, arose on hill and dale. The appearance of the country must have been wonderfully changed for the better as these woods advanced. Indeed, it is difficult now to conceive of that bleakness of which he complains; and among the many thousands of acres of wood which were planted by this indefatigable improver, there are trees of a size so gigantic that few, if any, can be found to equal them in Scotland.' He is said to have planted about 48,000,000 trees on the property. One of the original larches of our country was kept by him in a kind of tub in one of the windows of the dining-room as long as its size permitted, and was then planted out to take its chance. It is still among the lime trees in the flower garden, and is seen from the same window. The Norway spruce trees on the river side in 'Paradise' were planted in 1720, and the other large trees there in 1741. One of the spruce there, lately blown down, was 112 feet high, and its solid contents were 420 feet; and a larch, 101 feet high, has 416 feet of solid contents. This spot was laid out by him as a landscape garden, but great injury was done to it by the long-remembered floods of 1829. A parishioner who died twenty-five years ago, aged eighty-one, used to speak of the staff of gardeners that were kept to attend to it, and of the summer house where Lady Grant and her family spent the summer afternoons, and had refreshments. The trees all over the estate took so kindly to the soil that the Rev. Dr. Skene Keith of Keithhall in his work on Agriculture,[1] published in 1811, says that Sir Archibald lived to see some of the trees he planted two feet in diameter, and adds, 'His son and grandson have already sold wood to the amount of much more than the estate cost a century ago.' In former times all over this district in specifications for houses of any importance a clause was often inserted that 'Monymusk wood' was to be used. The soil seems specially suited for the growth of fir trees. John Wesley in his Diary in 1761, writes thus:—'I rode over to Sir Archibald Grant's, near Monymusk, about twenty miles N.W. from Aberdeen. It lies in a fruitful and pleasant valley, much of which is owing to Sir Archibald's improvements, who has ploughed up abundance of waste ground and planted some millions of trees. His stately old house is surrounded by gardens and rows of trees, with a clear

[1] pp. 112, 113.

river on one side, and about a mile [two miles] from his house he has laid out a small valley into walks and gardens, on one side of which the river runs. On each side rises a steep mountain, one rocky and bare, the other covered with trees, row above row, to the very top. About six o'clock we went to Church. It was pretty well filled with such persons as we do not look for so near the Highlands. But if we were surprised at their appearance, we were much more so at their singing. Thirty or forty sang an anthem after the sermon with such voices as well as judgment that I doubt whether they could have been excelled in any Cathedral in England.' In 1764, he again writes, ' I rode over to Sir Archibald Grant's. It is surprising to see how the country between is improved even within these three years. On every side the wild dreary moors are ploughed up and covered with rising corn ; even the ground near Sir Archibald's in particular is as well cultivated as most in England. About seven o'clock I preached. The Church was well filled, though upon short notice.' In a letter dated 5th June, 1770, in the 'Letters of David Hume,' edited by J. Birkbeck Hill, D.C.L., Hume speaks of 'Sir Archibald's extensive and noble plantations,' and Mr. Stuart in his preface to the volume of the Spalding Club Miscellany, says that he 'was the first to engage in those agricultural improvements that may be said to have almost changed the face of the North of Scotland.' Arthur Young in his Tour has left a description of his home farm. He was the first to introduce turnip culture into this district, and there are various accounts of the improvements he made in the system of farming. In 1756 he printed a letter on the subject, and distributed it among the tenants as a New Year's gift. Among other things he seems to have tried some glass manufacturing, for in the fields on Enzean, then a part of his home farm, the plough still turns up occasionally the bottom of a bottle with his initials upon it. He also tried to polish granite, thus anticipating one of the great modern industries of Aberdeen. The building still remains in the village, but much changed, that he used for the lapidaries' workshop. He was married four times, and died at Monymusk in 1778, at the age of eighty-two.

His younger brother, William, also became an Edinburgh advocate, being admitted in February, 1722. In 1731 he was appointed Procurator of the Church of Scotland, and Principal Clerk of the General Assembly. Like his father he wrote a pamphlet on Patronage in the Church, which was also reprinted in 1841. In 1737 he became Solicitor General, and in 1746 Lord Advocate, and next year was elected M.P. for the Elgin burghs, and was returned for the same at the next two general elections. In 1754 he was appointed a Judge, and sat as Lord Prestongrange, a property in East Lothian which he had bought in 1745. Tytler speaks highly of his integrity, candour, and winning gentleness, and says that his conduct in the adjustment of the claims on the forfeited estates merited universal approbation. He died at Bath, May 23rd, 1764, and was buried at Prestonpans. When the Church there was recently being repaired, in the vault where he was interred, many banners with curious figures, &c., were found, Monymusk among them, which were all replaced. His eldest daughter was married to the fourth Earl of Hyndford, and on her death in 1818 Sir James Suttie, the son of his second daughter, succeeded to the Prestongrange estate, and assumed the additional name of Grant, the family being now the Grant-Sutties.

Lord Cullen's third son, Francis, was appointed one of the Surveyors-General for forfeited estates in 1749-50, and died unmarried in 1762.

Sir Archibald's eldest son, the third Baronet, was born in

1731, and entered the H.E.I.C.S. in 1748. He raised a company of a hundred men, and went with them as their Captain to St. David's. His father's third wife was the widow of Dr. Calendar, Jamaica, and he married her daughter, Mary Calendar. In 1756 they had their portraits painted together. He stands in his uniform with a map of Jamaica in his hand, while she is pointing to a place upon it, perhaps where she was born. On his succeeding to the estate in 1778, he did not care to continue the large staff of labourers that his father required, and his disposing of the implements used on the farms enabled persons in the district to get such as were much in advance of those they had before. He had two sons—Archibald, the fourth Baronet, and James Francis, who became Rector of Merston in Sussex, and of Wrabness in Essex, whose second son, Arthur, entered the Royal Navy, and became a Commander. He died in 1850, having been thrown from his horse in the hunting field, and his only son is now the ninth Baronet, having succeeded the last male descendant of the fourth Baronet in 1887.

One of the tablets in the Church is in memory of Mr. Robert Grant of Tillyfour, in Oyne. While serving in the 4th Dragoons he was quartered at Taunton, in Somerset, in 1820, and married Miss Charlotte Yea of Pyrland Hall, Taunton. A tablet to her memory is placed in the Episcopal Church. Her nephew, Colonel Lacy Yea, 7th Royal Fusiliers, fell at the Redan, 18th June, 1855. Mr. Robert Grant was Convener of the County of Aberdeen for 23 years. His son, Sir Francis, died one year after his marriage to Miss Laura Fraser.

We may now give the pedigree of the Grant family as far as it relates to the estate.

The Family of the Grants as far as it relates to Monymusk.

Sir Duncan Grant of Freuchie, Strathspey, died 1485.

John died before his father.

John, 2nd of Freuchie=Margaret, dr. of Sir James
'The Bard,' died 1528 (p. 396) | Ogilvie of Deskford.

James, 3rd of Freuchie=(2) Christian Barclay. John of Corriemony.
'The Bold,' died 1553
(p. 387). Grants of Corriemony & Shenglie

John, 4th of Freuchie. Archibald, died 1619. Charles Grant, Lord
Glenelg, 1778-1866.
John, 5th of Freuchie, Duncan. (p. 380).
died 1622 (p. 396).
got Ballintomb in Knockando Archibald=1653, Christian, dr. of Patrick
in 1656 from G. of Freuchie. Nairne of Cromdale.

FRANCIS, 1658-1726 (p. 385), =(1) 1695, Jean, dr. of Rev. W. Archibald,
made Bart. by Queen Anne, Meldrum, Minister of Meldrum got
7 Dec. 1705; Judge of Session =(2) 1708, Sarah, dr. of Rev. Ballin-
(Lord Cullen) 1709; sold Cullen A. Fordyce, Minister of Ayton tomb
in Gamrie (Banff) and bought (issue 2 daughters.) from his
Monymusk 1713; buried at =(3) 1718, Agnes. dr. of father.
Greyfriars, Edinburgh. H. Hay.

Sir Archibald, 2nd Bart. =(1) 1717, Anne, dr. of Jas. William, Lord
1696-1778; Edinb. Advo- Hamilton, Pencaitland. Prestongrange
cate; infeft in Ballintomb =(2) Anne, dr. of Charles 1754; bought
in 1730 as heir to his uncle; Potts of Castleton, Derby, Prestongrange
M.P. for Aberdeenshire; died here 1742. 1745; died
1749 Keeper of Register of =(3) Elisabeth Clark, 1764, buried at
Hornings for life; planted widow of Dr. Jas. Calendar Prestonpans.
about 48,000,000 trees in Jamaica, died here 1759. (p. 404)
Monymusk. =(4) 1770, Jane, widow of
(p. 386) Andrew Millar, London,
died there 1788; gave
baptismal bowl; left the
Charitable fund.

Sir Archibald, 3rd Bart. 1731-1796=(1) Mary, only child of Dr. Calendar and
entered H.E.I.C.S. in 1748. In 1783 his stepmother; died at Edinburgh
acquired Coullie on resignation of 1787.
the Duke of Gordon. =(2) 1794, Jessie, dr. of Macleod of
Coldbecks.

The Grant Family.

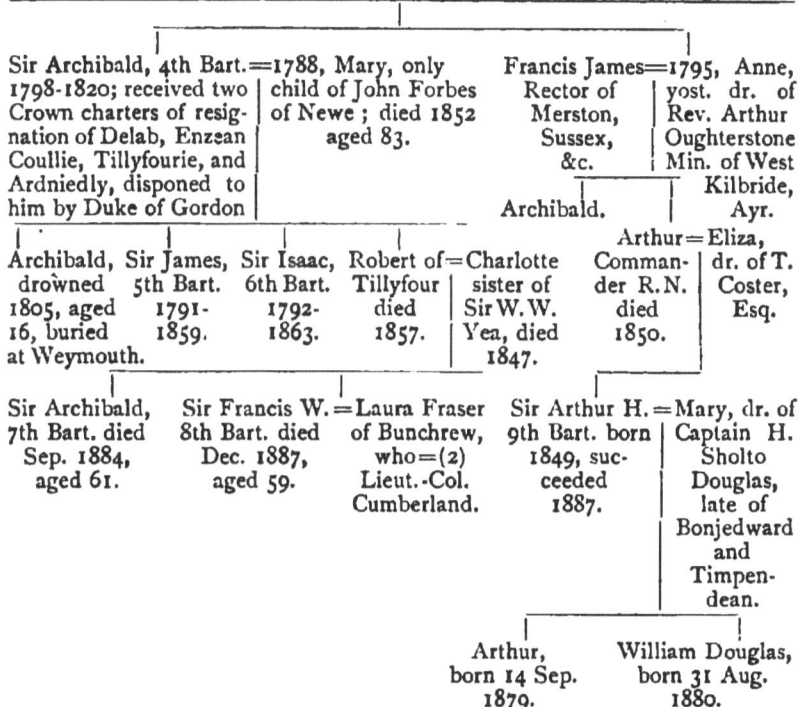

References are to Dictionary of National Biography, Vol. xxii.
Full accounts are given in Sir W. Fraser's 'Chiefs of Grant.'

About 1726, some two years before Mr. Burnett's death, it is said that notwithstanding his remonstrances "the foundations" of the Priory were dug up, but in a lady's diary, the reference to which has gone amissing, she says that on a visit here, she saw some ruined walls at evidently a later date.

In 1729, May 29th, Alexander Simpson who had been ordained at Insch in 1720, was translated to this parish. He died 3rd Jan., 1781 'Father of the Church' in his 83rd year and in the

61st of his ministry. One of his two sons was minister of Kemnay, and was translated to Inverurie in 1757. In the " Fasti " under Forbes parish, it is said that Alexander Orem was translated to Monymusk 20th October, 1756, but there seems some mistake in this. In 1772, December 9th, William Marr, parish schoolmaster, was ordained as Mr. Simpson's assistant and " eventual " successor, without a presentation's being issued, "at £18 sterling," says the minute of Presbytery, "that Mr. Simpson be not too much burdened and yet Mr. Marr be decently maintained," but he was not able to stand it long, for he died only six months after, June 12th, 1773, being about 28 years of age. He had been " received as a member of Presbytery, and his name was added to the roll." He had married Mr. Simpson's daughter on the 14th January.

Mr. Burnett and Mr. Simpson were together ministers of this parish for 120 years, (but at Polwarth in Berwickshire, Robert Home and his son Walter held the living between them for 112 years, from 1769 to 1881.)

About 1739, 1740, John Skinner, author of ' Tullochgorum,' &c., was assistant schoolmaster here. He became Dean of Aberdeen, and died in 1807. The Rev. Dr. Walker has written his Life.

In 1742 there was a sale by auction of the pictures &c., that had belonged to the Bishop of Aberdeen, when the House of Fetternear was his summer residence. The inventory is still preserved, and many of the pictures came to Monymusk House. In the Register of the Bishopric[1] there is preserved the charter of Bishop William Gordon, brother of the Earl of Huntly, handing over his palace of Fetternear &c., to William Leslie, 9th baron of Balquhain, a grant that received Royal confirmation in 1602.[2]

In 1761 and 1764, John Wesley visited Sir Archibald Grant,

---

[1] II. pp. 320-322. [2] Dr. Davidson, Inverurie, p. 145.

as we mentioned before, and preached, remarking upon the singing. It is said that Sir Archibald used to have the practising in the House, accompanied by the organ that was formerly in the library, and superintended it himself, and it is also said that in church he sat beside the choir.

When speaking of the Poll-book of 1696, it was said that one could not venture from its records to reckon the population of the parish. The earliest calculation of the population of Scotland which, from the point of view of a statistical department, can be looked upon as in any degree trustworthy, is that of the well-known Dr. Webster, of St. Giles', completed about 1755, in which he gives the population of Monymusk at 1005. In Sir John Sinclair's Statistical Account, 1790-98, it is given in one place at 1127, and in another at 1130.

In 1765, May 8th, Archibald Robertson, connected with the Robertsons of Struan, was born in the village. He went to King's College, and then studied art in Edinburgh and London, and was so favourite a pupil of Sir Joshua Reynolds that before he was thirty he became known as the 'Reynolds of Scotland.' He used to spend the summer with Sir Archibald Grant, and has left a water-colour picture of the House, and an account of the parish. He went to America in 1791, and became one of the most notable pioneers of American Art.[1] His youngest brother Andrew, born at Aberdeen in 1777, graduated there, and went to Edinburgh where he studied under Alexander Nasmyth and Sir Henry Raeburn. In 1801, he went to London and was appointed miniature painter to H.R.H. the Duke of Sussex. He was the first treasurer of the Royal Caledonian Asylum, Upper Holloway. He died in 1845, and his daughter, who lives at Hampton Wick, has presented to the Asylum a collection of antiquities that he formed.

[1] 'The Century Magazine,' May 1890.

The mother of Dr. Milne, of Bombay, was also born in the village, but we do not know the date. This led him to give our parish school a preferential right to be always on his Bequest, but this has been taken away by the recent Commission.

In 1772, Lady Grant, previously Mrs. Millar, presented a silver Baptismal Bowl to the Church. When closely examined it seems to have had some engraving on the side opposite the inscription; from the outline left there are indications of scroll-work, and it may have been a church emblem or more probably a coat of arms. The hall-marks on the bottom show it to h᷉ ᷉e been made in London, as long before as 1726-1727, L bei᷉.ǵ the date of that period. The same Lady left £765 to the pcor of the parish, the interest of which, £20 or so yearly, has been regularly distributed for 103 years in accordance with the Deed of Chancery.

Sir Archibald died in 1778, and this Lady Grant in It was about this time that the Strathspey "Monymusk᷉ .as composed. The composer Daniel Dow, violinist and mus ᷉an, was born in Perthshire, in 1732, and died at Edinburgh, 20th January, 1783. He was a teacher and concert-giver in Edinburgh from 1763 until his death. He published various collections of Strathspeys &c., in one of which "Monymusk" appeared as "Sir Archibald Grant of Monemusk's Reel," probably some time after 1774. Hume's letter, part of which we quoted and which is dated 'Edinburgh, 5th June, 1770,' the year of Sir Archibald's marriage to this Lady Grant, shows that they were both well-known persons in Edinburgh society at this time, "making everybody in love with the marry'd state," and this may account for the Edinburgh musician's giving his composition its name. Being intended only for playing, not for singing, it is not adapted for the sol-fa notation, but as so many of our young people do not know the ordinary staff notation, the air is

given on the accompanying page in the sol-fa notation. It has many associations connected with it, and persons who may not know where our parish is situated, are often familiar with the name through this Strathspey, for it is played not only in the dancing-room, but also by our military bands, and Horse regiments trot past the saluting post to its music. The writer recollects reading in " The Times " an account of a review in the heights of Afghanistan, after the last dismal act of treachery in which an Aberdeen student, Mr. Jenkins of the Indian Civil Service was one of those who were murdered, when the report mentioned that part of the troops went past the General in Command to the tune of ' Monymusk.'

Alexander Duff, who had been ordained by the Presbytery of Abernethy, became Assistant to Mr. Simpson in 1776. The minutes of Presbytery show that in this year an irregular effort was made to have him settled as successor, but in 1781, May 2nd, a royal presentation was laid before the Presbytery. He died in February, 1814, and was the last minister buried within the Church. It is said that when the Rev. Dr. Skene Keith, Keithhall, heard that this was not to be permitted, he came up and said that rather than that it should not be done, he himself would dig the grave—taking off his coat and beginning to suit the action to the word. He left two sons Alexander, and Lewis who was parish schoolmaster and died in 1840, aged seventy-two. Mrs. Duff and her daughters left the residue of their means—about £120—to the poor of the parish, which sum became available in 1857, and is invested by the Session. Miss Duff died in Kemnay, and the Rev. George Peter was one of the executors. She used to say they were of the old Duff family—"the right Duffs." No descendants of this family remain.

In 1793 Alexander Nicol was born in the village. He was

Dr. Pusey's predecessor as Canon of Christ Church and Professor of Hebrew at Oxford. He was so retiring a man that when he was offered the appointment, he carried Lord Liverpool's letter in his pocket until he casually spoke of it to a friend, who assured him that the signature was not a practical joke. It was said of him that "he could speak his way to the Wall of China."[1] About this time there was a lace industry carried on in a house close to the village.

We mentioned that the Episcopal Congregation moved from Blairdaff to the present Church in the village of Monymusk in 1801, and we would here state the succession of Episcopal ministers in it.

1799-1801. Rev. James Andrew, LL.D., who became Principal of Addiscombe College.[2] He published a Hebrew Grammar in 1823.

1801, 1802. Rev. William Murray.

1802-1807. Rev. Alexander Cay.

1807-1819. Rev. Alexander Walker, who had also the Church in Meldrum in charge for four or five years.

1820-1829. Rev. David Buchan.

1829-1842. Rev. Alexander Allan.

In 1844 the Rev. William Walker, now LL.D., was appointed, who is so highly esteemed among us, and whose jubilee as a clergyman was celebrated a few years ago. His works have done much to elucidate the history of the Episcopal Church in our country during the last two hundred years—his principal writings being 'The Life of Dean Skinner of Aberdeen,' author of 'Tullochgorum,' 'The Life of Bishop Jolly of Moray,' 'The Life of Bishop Gleig of Brechin,' 'The Life of Bishop John Skinner of Aberdeen,' and 'Three Churchmen: Sketches of Bishop Russell of Glasgow, of Bishop Terrot of Edinburgh

[1] Dr. Walker's Life of Dean Skinner, pp. 159, 160. [2] Ibid. pp. 159, 160.

and of Professor Grub, LL.D., advocate, Aberdeen.' His son, Rev. George Barron Walker, M.A., is Episcopal clergyman at Peterhead, in this county.

In 1814, Robert Forbes, M.A., teacher in Aberdeen, being presented by George Prince Regent, was ordained parish minister here in September. He died in February, 1853, aged seventy-five. His wife was Rachel Copland, and they had six sons and two daughters. The eldest son, Alexander, was the first teacher of Lord Cullen's School, and then went to Hamilton, Ontario, Canada. Robert and James went to Ceylon, William and John died in Glasgow. Charles became Vicar of South Banbury, in Oxfordshire, and chaplain to Earl Grey, and died 10th September, 1869, aged fifty-four. He was nearly twenty-five years Vicar there, during which time he raised money to build a beautiful Church, and also schools, and to buy a vicarage. He married Georgiana Jane, third daughter of Major-General Mills of Willington, County Durham. She now resides in York. He left two daughters and two sons, the elder of whom, Robert William, lives at Gate Helmsley, near York, and is a land agent, while the younger, Charles Mansfeldt, is agent for the Dean and Chapter of York, Earl Cathcart, and others, and lives in York.

Mr. Burnett and Mr. Simpson died each 83 years of age.

Mr. Duff and Mr. Forbes died each 75 years of age.

Mr. Burnett came here in 1678, and Mr. Forbes died here in 1853, so that these four ministers served the cure for 175 years among them.

In 1853 Thomas Henry Dawson, M.A., Schoolmaster of the neighbouring parish of Chapel of Garioch, was presented by the Crown. He died in October, 1867, in the forty-third year of his age, and the fifteenth of his ministry. He married Miss Milne of Kinaldie, and had three daughters. She married secondly, Provost Jamieson, Aberdeen.

Dr. Mitchell, who held the farm of Delab and then of Nether Inver, was so much respected that in 1856 he was asked by the Grant family to let them have his portrait painted by Mr. James Cassie, R.S.A., the inscription on it stating that at that time he had practised his profession in the district for upwards of forty years. Dr. John Robert Trail, who lived at Tombeg, was also held in great esteem. He died in 1875, aged fifty-six.

In 1860 the last portion of £100 bequeathed by Lady Grant, who died in 1852, aged eighty-two, became available, amounting to about £65. This sum, along with Miss Duff's legacy and some other money, making in all £250, has been preserved. They bring a small yearly dividend for distribution among the poor. This Lady Grant was Miss Forbes of Newe. It has been said of her that the wool of all the sheep fed in the park was reckoned her pin-money, and was never sold, but made into blankets, &c., for gifts to the poor. Her eldest son was drowned in the Abergavenny at Portland Roads in 1805, aged sixteen. A tablet is placed to his memory in the Church, and his tombstone is in the Weymouth Churchyard, where he was buried. A brother of Wordsworth the poet's was also drowned in the Abergavenny. "John's Grove" was called after him by the poet, of which there is a picture in "Through Wordsworth's Country." One of the Forbeses of Blackford in this county was also drowned at the same time.

In July, 1879, George Watt died here, aged eighty-four. He had been in the Royal Horse Artillery, and was engaged in the Battle of Waterloo, for which he held the medal and received a pension. He was also present at the entry into Paris of the allied forces.

Sir Francis W. Grant, the eighth Baronet, died on 13th December, 1887. He bequeathed £1000, free of legacy duty, for the poor, to be administered by the Trustees of Lady

Grant's charity which we previously mentioned. There are thus altogether £2000 invested in behalf of the poor of the parish.

Information in regard to the early Schoolmasters is almost entirely wanting. Dr. Davidson[1] mentions Rev. W. Gordon in 1658, and Rev. W. Watson in 1678. In 1696, Rev. Alexander Hay and his wife are entered in the Poll-book. In 1739-40, John Skinner, author of 'Tullochgorum' was assistant schoolmaster. He also wrote a poem describing the Christmas amusements, and another on a 'Visit to Paradise' which had been laid out before this time. We spoke of Rev. W. Marr in 1772. A tomb-stone is placed in the Cluny churchyard in memory of 'Alexander Law, M.A., (son of the farmer in Denmill), Schoolmaster of Monymusk, who died in 1821, aged sixty-three.' We do not know whether he continued in office until his death, but the Rev. Lewis A. Duff, son of the minister of the parish, was schoolmaster for a long time, and died in 1840, aged seventy-two. Rev. James Grant Riach, M.A., succeeded him in 1840, and in September, 1843, he became minister of Culter parish, in the Presbytery of Biggar, where he died in September 1862. He was a distinguished scholar, and gained the Dick Bequest prize for passing first in the examination. His brother is minister of Robertson Memorial Parish, Edinburgh. In 1844, Rev. James L. Blake, M.A., was appointed. He became minister of Stobo, in the Presbytery of Peebles, in 1850, and was translated to Langton, near Duns, in October 1867, where he died on May 14th, 1892. In 1846, Rev. John Donald, M.A., was appointed and died in 1849, aged thirty-six. He was of the Brankenintum family of Donalds who have been so very long in the parish. Rev. Duncan Anderson, M.A., succeeded him in

[1] Inverurie, pp. 311, 326.

1849. He left in 1854 for a ministerial charge in Canada ; he has now retired, and lives at Chaudière Basin, County Levis, Quebec. In 1854, Rev. Alexander Ogilvie, M.A., was appointed, one of a family of distinguished teachers. Under him the school stood at the head of all the schools on the Dick Bequest for efficiency. He was appointed Head-master of Gordon's College, Aberdeen in 1872, and is now LL.D. The success of his administration has been so marked that in an article upon Robert Gordon, the founder, in the twenty-second volume of the Dictionary of National Biography, it is said of him :—'Under his charge the college rose rapidly to a high degree of prosperity.' His eldest son, Francis Grant, is Principal of the Heriot-Watt College, Edinburgh, and his second son, James Nicol, is Chaplain of the Church of Scotland, at Bangalore, Madras. Both were born here. In April, 1873, Mr. Robert M'William, M.A., became schoolmaster, and is now Principal of Gill College, Somerset East, South Africa. In December, 1874, Mr. James Spittal, M.A., was appointed. He is now Head-master of the Ellon School. Mr. W. Rollo, M.A., succeeded him in August, 1881. He is now Incumbent of St. James' Episcopal Church, Springburn, Glasgow. In September 1885, Mr. Peter Smith, M.A., was appointed. He is now Head-master of the Public School, Craddock, South Africa. He was succeeded in August, 1889, by the present teacher Mr. Alexander W. Simpson, M.A. The junior department has been under the charge of Miss Margaret Dunbar since August 1874. The fully-appointed teachers of Lord Cullen's school were four in number. Mr. Alexander Forbes, son of the minister, was appointed in 1825, and continued until 1844, when he went to Canada. Rev. John Donald was then appointed, and two years after became parochial teacher. Rev. Gordon Smart, M.A., succeeded him in 1846, and became minister of the parish of

Cabrach in 1849. The Rev. J. M. Laing, M.A., was then appointed, and taught until his death in February, 1886, being also preacher at Blairdaff Church.

The valuation of the parish for this year, 1895, amounts to £6531, and the railway valuation to £1477. The total number of acres is 10,816, there being on this side the river 8660, and on the north side 2156. There are 5431 acres arable, being almost exactly half of the whole, while a large number are under wood. The population in 1891 was 1025, whereas in 1881 it was 1155, the diminution being chiefly owing to the closing of the granite quarry at Tillyfourie, which was leased mostly for paving purposes by Messrs. Mowlem, Burt, & Co., London. In conjunction with Sir Francis W. Grant, and Mr. John Fife of the neighbouring quarry on the Cluny property, they built a recreation hall for the workmen, which is now used as the third public school in the parish, and is under the charge of a mistress. Since it was built it has been used for public worship once a month, greatly to the convenience of the district.

INDEX.

Abbatial system in Celtic Church 24, 40
Aberdeen, population of, at Reformation 236
Abernethy on Tay 1, Culdees 48, Early bishops 48, Lay-abbot 49, Round tower 54, Augustinian canons 65 ... 57
Abersnithack (Braehead) 83, 204, 244
Adamnan 27, Life of Columba 5, 20
Adrian VI 160, 168
Aedan's coronation 6
Aidan, Apostle of England ... 26
Alexander III's death 136
Alford, gift of Church 101, 128, Priory lands in 202, Defeat of Covenanters at 250
Antiqua taxatio 134
Appeal of canons to Pope against Prior 173
Appin 45, 46
Appropriation of Priory lands 193
Archangel Leslie, fiction of ... 225
Arbroath Abbey founded, and gift of Brecbannoch 4, 137
Ardniedly 167, 217
Argyll, Marquis of 249
Auchendryne, gift of land at ... 120
Augustinian canons 59, 95, 113, 128
monasteries ... 114
system 115
Balmerino, Canon John Hay at 189
Lord, executed ... 256
Balvack, oratory at 82, tax on 196
Bands of service... 180, 190, 209
Barclays of Garntuly 141
Barclay, Adam, minister here 243
his daughter .. 243, 256
Beaton, Cardinal, gift of lands to Earl of Huntly 186, 220, his life 189

Benedict and Columba 25
Bernham, Bishop, gifts 125, 126, Churches consecrated by ... 127
Birnie, Church of ... 75, 81
Bishops' dues from Churches ... 135
Blairdaff, Episcopal Church at 245
Boiamund's Roll (Baiamund, Bagimont) 133
Braehead (see Abersnithack)
Brecbannoch ... 3, 107, 136, 251
Brechin, Culdees at 43, Round Tower 43, 54
Buchan, Earls of, gift 91, account of 93
Burial dues, ancient 111
Burnett, John, minister here ... 257
Caithness, Bishop of ... 44, 53
Carstairs, Principal 260
Celtic Church and Queen Margaret 64
Celtic Church, Liturgy and Ritual of 19, 20
Celtic Scotland 60
Chalmers of Cults 253
Chancel of Church 73
Chapel Royal, Deans of 217, of Stirling 243
Charles I. 239
Church-Bible 257
Churches, gift of, to monasteries 106
Cistercian priories 118
Columba, time 3, 6, journeys and death 7, labour 12, devotion 15, own MSS. 19, hymns 21, teaching 22, Chief Abbot 24
Columban Church 7, missionaries 9, wattle-buildings 9, dedications 10, 22, monastic system ... 11, 13, 24, 25

Index. 293

Columban Church, missionary system 11, celibacy 12, foundations 14, dress of clergy 15, fasts, festivals 16, tonsure 16, classes of monks 17, MSS. 18, culture 19, Creed 21-23, independence of Rome 22, 23, form of Episcopacy 24, reckoning of Easter 26, resists Rome 27, its end 28
Communion cups 258
Corsindae (see Forbes of,) feu-duty... 206
Crinan, Lay-abbot of Dunkeld... 42
Cornabo 151
Cross, Monymusk Celtic ... 84
Crossraguel Abbey ... 243, 260
Crusade, taxing for last... .. 132
'Cudri' of cheese 93
Culdees, meaning of word, 30, 31, 33, distinct from Columbans 31, origin of 32, 37, 38, in Ireland 33, 34, in England 34, in Wales 35, in Scotland 35, earliest record of 35, head of 36, homes in Scotland 39, number at St. Andrews and here 38, 40, no zeal 39, doctrine and worship 55, influence 56, marriage among 57, dedication of Churches 57, decay of 58, suppression 59, library at St. Serf's 97, suppression there 48, 96, constitution here in 1211 109, Episcopacy among 49, existing Culdee buildings 54
'Culdees or canons' 101, 103, 117, 119, 124
Cullen, Lord (Sir Francis Grant)
Cullen's, Lord, School .. 274, 289
Daily service in Church ... 254
Date probable of Church ... 77
Dauach of land 104
Dawson, T. H., minister here 287

David I. Reformation of 58, founds bishoprics 81, gives over St. Serf's 96
David II. visits Monymusk ... 141
Decay of old monasticism in England 32, in Scotland... 46
Deer, Abbey of 1, 2, 7, Charter 43, no Culdees at 56
Deer, Book of 19, 20, 56
Delab 209
Discipline of Priory 171
Dolbethoc and Fornathy given 102, taken away 111, restored 126
'Dominus' 137
Donald, Rev. J., Keithhall ... 246
Dornoch, Culdees at 44, buildings 53, 142
Dow, Daniel, composes 'Monymusk' 284
Druidism 10, 13, 14
Duff, Alexander, minister here 285, Mrs. Duff's bequest ... 285
Dull in Athol 86
Dunblane, Culdees at 44, tower 54, 78, bishopric 243
Dunfermline Abbey Church 78, 80
Dunkeld, Columban origin 7, 28 Culdees 42, 'first' bishop 43, buildings 52
Durrow, Book of 18
Durward (Door-ward) gifts by 123
Easter in Celtic Church ... 26
" the Communion Sunday here 254
Echt 163
Edinburgh made a bishopric ... 241
Ednam, earliest parish erected 94, 105
Eglismenythok ... 94, 111, 132, 183
Elgin Cathedral built 142, burned 148
Elphinstone, Bishop ... 155, 157
" John, co-prior ... 186
" character ... 209
Endowments of the Priory 87-130
Episcopacy in England and Scotland 211
" periods of ... 235, 243

Index.

	Page
Episcopacy, tolerance toward	259
Episcopal Clergy in Episcopal Church here	286
'Ferleginn' of Turriff	92
Feu-duties from the estate 215, 243, 260	
Flodden	157, 178
Foedarg and Foleyt, grain and cheese from'	91, 131
Forbeses of Corsindae 164, 167, 182, 190, 192	
Forbes, Lords 164, 182, rent-roll of	201, 205
Forbes, Duncan, secures Monymusk 193, 196, 209, 225, death	236
Forbeses and Gordons, strife between	220
Forbes, Sir William, Covenanter	247
Inscription at Kearn	271
Forbes family pedigree	270
Forbes, ' Bousteous John '	183
Forbes, John, Tombeg, and Anna Lunan	244
,, John, minister of Alford	238
,, Robert, minister here	287
,, Thomas, minister here	243
,, William, minister here 239, first Bishop of Edinburgh	241
Forglen, lands and dedication 4, 10, 137, 138, 144,	146
Fowlis, Easter and Wester 180,	181
Gall, St.	8
Gellie, John, minister here	246
Grant, Sir Francis (Lord Cullen)	272
,, Sir Archibald	275
,, family tree	280
Grant's, Lady, trust	284
,, ,, bequest	288
,, Sir Francis, bequest	288
Harlaw, battle of	148
Hay, Canon John 162, 163, 165, envoy from Queen Mary	189
Hepburn, John, Prior of St. Andrews	178
Hinba, Columban remains at	14
Holyrood Abbey	98
Hostiarius, gifts by	123

	Page
Huntly, Earls of	186, 223
Hurry of Pitfichie (see Urry)	
Hymns in ' Use of Sarum '	82
Innocent III	107, 109
,, IV	128, 132
Installation of Prior	160
Interdict, effects of Papal	102
Iona, Columba reaches 6, influence of 8, 26, Abbot of, supreme 24, Culdees 51, lay-possession 51, buildings at	10, 53, 54, 78
Irvine of Drum and Brecbannoch	5
Irving, James, minister here, imprisoned	238
James I. of Scotland, letter to Priors	148
James VI of Scotland, Church policy	237
Jameson the painter	241
Julius III	199
Keig, gift of Church of	116, 131
,, ,, two acres at	125
,, Priory lands in	203
,, and Monymusk, Malcolm III's gift	87
Keledei (see Culdees)	
Kells, Book of	18
Kennedy, Bishop	151
Kildrummy quarries	72, 80
,, Castle	104
,, minister deposed	122
Kindrocht (Braemar) gift of Church and land	120, 131
Kinernie, Arthur Rose, minister of	255
King's College founded	155
Kinloss	93
Law, Mr. T. G., on Archangel Leslie	225
Laud, Archbishop	240
Lay-abbots at Abernethy 49, Brechin 43, 92, Dunkeld 42, 47, Lismore 45, Monifieth	50
Leochel, gift of Church 100, pasture at 124, lands in 179, 181, 203	

Index. 295

	Page
Leslie, Archangel	225
Library, Culdee at St. Serf's	97
Lightfoot, Bishop, on Celtic Church	26
Lindisfarne	26
Liturgy of Celtic Church 19, its Gallican origin 20, suppressed	27
Lismore, Culdees at 45, buildings	52
Llanffinan in Anglesey	83
Low, Rev. A., of Keig on boundaries of lands	89
Lumphanan, Macbeth killed at 61, meaning of	83
Lunan, Alex., minister here	244
" " Episcopal minister of Blairdaff	245
Macbeth's gift to St. Serf's 36, death	61
Machar St. 7, Cathedral begun	147
'Magister'	137
Malcolm III his gift of lands 60, 87, with Edward the Confessor 61, conquers Macbeth 61, death 62, family	66
Malvoisin, Bishop 112,	117
Mar, Earls of, 99-108, 119-123, 147,	148
Margaret, Queen 60, marriage 62, character and influence, 62, her 'Book of the Gospels' 63, reforms Celtic Church 64, introduces Norman architecture	66
Mary Queen of Scots 189, and Darnley 190, taxing 195	212
Masses endowed for souls of rectors 154, 159,	160
Merk, value of	135
Midmar, dedication of	84
'Miles'	137
Milne, Dr., of Bombay	284
Mitchell, Dr.	288
Monasteries, gift of Churches to	106
Monifieth, Culdees at	49

	Page
Monifieth, lay-abbot 50, buildings 53,	56
Montrose, Marquis of, at Monymusk 248, executed	251
Monymusk reliquary	3
'Monymusk' Strathspey	284
Monymusk, early tradition as to 1, first record of Culdees at 50, 57, Church at 54, Malcolm III's gift 60, 87, under St. Andrews 65, Priory buildings 69, Church and Tower 70, Chancel 73, probable date	77
Monymusk Priory, Endowments 87-130, Earl of Buchan's gift 91, Bishop Robert's 94, Earls of Mar 99-108, 119-123, 'Hostiarius'' gifts 123-125, Bishop Malvoisin's 116, Bishop Bernhame's gift and restoration 125, 126, Pope confirms gifts and recognises Augustinian order 127, burned 208, value at Reformation 212, feu-duties now paid in connection with it	217
Monymusk, Priors of, Bricius 110, Andrew 147, ? Gavin of Douglas 154, Strachan 155, Akenhead 160, Farlie 160, Elphinstone 186, 193, 207, 209, ? John Hay 190, Robert Forbes	211
'Monymusk' Henry de 140, Sir John de 141, Malcolm de 4, 137, Marjory de 144, Michael de 142, Sir Thomas de	139
Monymusk Church in Aberdeen Cathedral body 151, 157, 166, town manse	151
Monymusk, House of, saved from Montrose	248
Monymusk sold by Forbes family	269
Description of	275

Index.

	Page		Page
Monymusk, Episcopal Church at	246	Paul III	176
Monymusk Parson or Rector, Baldwin 127, Symon de Katness 147, John Myrton 153, Richard Strathaquhyn 154, ? John Litster 157, Alex. Symson 157, 165, Patrick Dunbar 166, Henry Forsyth 185, James Johnston	213	Pedigree of Forbes family	270
		,, Grant family	280
		,, Urry family	252
		Pitfichie, tithes of 158, size of property 251, occupation of Castle 267, Urry of	144
		Pitsligo, Lord	272
		Plate, Cathedral, stolen ...	192
Monymusk, Vicars of, Thomas Scherar 157, 165, John Reid 167, 169, 172, 173, 176, ? Archbishop Leighton ...	244	Ploughgate of land	94
		Pluscardine Priory	118
		Poll-book of 1696	262
		Population of parish ...	283, 291
Monymusk ministers since Reformation, James Murray 234, James Johnston 235, James Irving 237, William Forbes (first bishop of Edinburgh) 239, Thomas Forbes 243, Adam Barclay 243, Alex. Lunan 244, John Gellie 246, Alex. Rose or Ross 254, John Burnett 257, Alex. Simpson 281, (Wm. Marr 282), Alex. Duff 285, Robert Forbes 287, T. H. Dawson	287	Prestongrange, Lord	278
		'Procurations,' Bishops' ...	135
		Priors (see Monymusk)	
		,, Installation of	161
		Priory, perhaps built by Earl of Mar 100, 103, burned 208, dues annexed to Dunblane Cathedral 243, given to Principal Carstairs	260
		Quarterly preaching	205
		'Readers'	205, 234
		Reformation in Aberdeenshire, The ... 210, 234 difference in England and Scotland	211
Monymusk proprietors, (see Urry, Forbes, Grant)		Reliquary, The Monymusk ...	3
Moravia, family de	142	Remaining link with Priory ...	215
Mortlach	1, 7, 56	Rent-roll of Priory lands, Lord Forbes'	201
' Multo ' (a sheep)	93		
Muthil, Culdees at 49, Norman tower	54	Return of Churches and lands in 1268	131
Nectan expels Columbans	27, 47		
Nicol, Canon, born in village ...	285	Revolution, Bishop Rose at the	256
Norman arches in church ..	73	Rinuccini's Life of Archangel Leslie	225
Northumbrian Church	26		
Ogilvie, Rev. A., LL.D. ...	290	Robert II's marriage	142
Oran's St., Chapel at Iona	53, 68	Robertson, Archibald and Andrew, artists	283
Orders, Roman, rise of	25, 58		
Orkney, Cormac in	14	Roman orders, rise of... ...25, 58	
Outhirheyclt (Upper Echt) 124,	132	Romanesque architecture ...	77
Papal confirmations 107, 128, protection 118, permission to sell land	199	Roses of Kilravock	254
		Rose or Ross, Alex., minister 254, his son, Bishop of Edinburgh 256, his brother, Archbishop of St. Andrews	255
Parishes, erection of ...	94, 105		
Patrick, St.	12		

	Page
Rosemarky, Culdees at 44, buildings	...52, 56
Rule, Regulus (see St. Rule)	
'Safe-conduct' letter of, to England	143
Sanctuary, right of	85
Sarum, Use of	82
Schoolmasters of the parish	289
Scollatisland here	69
Serfs (slaves), actual names and conveyance of	107
Simpson, Alex., minister here	281
Skinner, Dean	282
Spoliation of lands	190
Strife in Priory	169
Strauchine, Prior's daughter	156, 184
St. Andrews, Culdees at 40, buildings 52, Priory of 41, 65, cells of 68, Register of 90, Cathedral 78, early bishops 118, ancient diocese	68
St. Diaconianus of Keig	116
St. Ffinan's oratory	83
St. Marnan of Leochel	102
St. Rule or Regulus, legend of	122
St. Rule's tower at St. Andrews	41, 78, 79, 80, 95
St. Serf at Dysart 37, at Culross 99, his fair	99
St. Serf's, Lochleven, Culdees of, earliest record 36, 46, buildings 52, MS. Library	97

	Page
St. Serf's, Macbeth's gifts to 36, Queen Margaret's 63, Ethelred's 47, harshness in suppression of	47, 96
Teinds, tithes	104, 202, 203
Tithes, second	147, 160
Tillyfour in Oyne	259
Tombeg burned	249
Trail, Dr.	288
Trees on the estate	275
Turriff, no Culdees at 56, 'Ierleginn' of 92, 93, Trot of	247
Urry (Hurry) of Pitfichie 144, 170, 172, 185, family of 252 ,, Major-General 250, death 251, daughters	253
'Use of Sarum'	82
Valuation, 'old,' of Priory Churches	134
,, of parish	291
Wallakirk in Glass	102
Walker, Rev. Dr.	286
Weavers in parish in 1696	266
Welsh missionaries in this county	83
Wesley's visit	276
Whitby, synod of	26
William the Lion founds Arbroath Abbey	4
William of Orange and Episcopal Church	256
Wishart of Pitarrow	189
Wycliffe	144

www.ingramcontent.com/pod-product-compliance
Lightning Source LLC
Chambersburg PA
CBHW022027240426
43667CB00042B/1221